# CONCISE ANSWERS TO
# FREQUENTLY ASKED
# QUESTIONS

## ABOUT
## ASSESSMENT & GRADING

NICOLE
**DIMICH** | CASSANDRA
**ERKENS** | JADI
**MILLER** | TOM
**SCHIMMER** | KATIE
**WHITE**

Solution Tree | Press  a division of  Solution Tree

the Solution Tree
Assessment Center

555 North Morton Street
Bloomington, IN 47404
800.733.6786 (toll free) / 812.336.7700
FAX: 812.336.7790

email: info@SolutionTree.com
SolutionTree.com

Visit **go.SolutionTree.com/assessment** to download the free reproducibles in this book.

Printed in the United States of America

Library of Congress Cataloging-in-Publication Data

Names: Erkens, Cassandra, author. | Schimmer, Tom, author. | Dimich,
   Nicole, author. | Miller, Jadi K. (Jadi Kai), author. | White, Katie,
   1977- author.
Title: Concise answers to frequently asked questions about assessment and
   grading / Cassandra Erkens, Tom Schimmer, Nicole Dimich, Jadi Miller,
   Katie White.
Description: Bloomington, IN : Solution Tree Press, [2022] | Includes
   bibliographical references and index.
Identifiers: LCCN 2021056271 (print) | LCCN 2021056272 (ebook) | ISBN
   9781954631052 (Paperback) | ISBN 9781954631069 (eBook)
Subjects: LCSH: Educational tests and measurements. | Grading and marking
   (Students) | Academic achievement--Testing. | Educational evaluation. |
   Competency based education.
Classification: LCC LB3051 .E733 2022  (print) | LCC LB3051  (ebook) | DDC
   371.26--dc23/eng/20220222
LC record available at https://lccn.loc.gov/2021056271
LC ebook record available at https://lccn.loc.gov/2021056272

**Solution Tree**
Jeffrey C. Jones, CEO
Edmund M. Ackerman, President

**Solution Tree Press**
*President and Publisher:* Douglas M. Rife
*Associate Publisher:* Sarah Payne-Mills
*Managing Production Editor:* Kendra Slayton
*Editorial Director:* Todd Brakke
*Art Director:* Rian Anderson
*Copy Chief:* Jessi Finn
*Production Editor:* Alissa Voss
*Content Development Specialist:* Amy Rubenstein
*Copy Editor:* Alissa Voss
*Proofreader:* Sarah Ludwig
*Cover and Text Designer:* Abigail Bowen
*Editorial Assistants:* Charlotte Jones, Sarah Ludwig, and Elijah Oates

# ACKNOWLEDGMENTS

We would like to thank the many, many researchers and thought leaders who have informed and inspired us over the years. Check out the lengthy bibliography for a sense of the countless names of assessment leaders who have provided us with powerful insights, answers, and practices that work. We stand on the shoulders of giants whose influence on the field can never be forgotten.

And, we are extremely grateful to the hardworking educators who strive to implement these answers and practices in an effort to relentlessly pursue learning for all students and keep classrooms aligned to effective practices focused on continual improvement. Your ability to bring these answers to fruition in your settings will make all the difference. We dedicate this book to you.

With gratitude,
Nicole, Cassie, Jadi, Tom, and Katie

Solution Tree Press would like to thank the following reviewers:

John D. Ewald
Solution Tree Associate
Former Superintendent, Principal,
    Teacher
Frederick, Maryland

Lorrie Hulbert
Principal
Floyd L. Bell Elementary
Windsor, New York

Rosalind Poon
Vice Principal 8–12
Richmond School District
Richmond, British Columbia

Lana Steiner
Math Coach
Horizon School Division
Humboldt, Saskatchewan

# TABLE OF CONTENTS

*Reproducible pages are in italics.*

# ABOUT THE AUTHORS

**Nicole Dimich** has a passion for education and lifelong learning, which has led her to extensively explore, facilitate, and implement innovative practices in school transformation. She works with elementary and secondary educators in presentations, trainings, and consultations that address today's most critical issues, all in the spirit of facilitating increased student learning and confidence.

Nicole was a school transformation specialist, where she coached individual teachers and teams of teachers in assessment, literacy, and high expectations for all students. Nicole was also a program evaluator and trainer at the Princeton Center for Leadership Training in New Jersey. A former middle and high school English teacher, she is committed to making schools into places where all students and educators feel invested and successful.

A featured presenter at conferences internationally, Nicole empowers educators to build their capacity for and implement engaging assessment design, formative assessment practices, common assessment design and analysis, response to intervention (RTI) systems, data-driven decisions, student work protocols, and motivational strategies.

Nicole earned a master of arts degree in human development from Saint Mary's University and a bachelor of arts degree in English and psychology from Concordia College.

Nicole is the author of *Design in Five: Essential Phases to Create Engaging Assessment Practice* and the coauthor of multiple books including *Motivating Students: 25 Strategies to Light the Fire of Engagement*, *Growing Tomorrow's Citizens in Today's Classroooms: Assessing Seven Critical Competencies*, *Instructional Agility: Responding to Assessment With Real-Time Decisions*, and *Essential Assessment: Six Tenets for Bringing Hope, Efficacy, and Achievement to the Classroom*. She has also contributed to the best-selling *The Teacher as Assessment Leader* and *The Principal as Assessment Leader* series.

To learn more about Nicole's work, visit http://allthingsassessment.info or follow @NicoleDimich on Twitter.

**Cassandra Erkens** is a presenter, facilitator, coach, trainer of trainers, keynote speaker, author, and above all, a teacher. She presents nationally and internationally on assessment, instruction, school improvement, and Professional Learning Communities at Work® (PLC at Work).

Cassandra has served as an adjunct faculty member at Hamline and Cardinal Stritch universities, where she took teachers through graduate education courses. She has authored and coauthored a wide array of published trainings, and she has designed and delivered the training-of-trainers programs for two major education-based companies.

As an educator and recognized leader, Cassandra has served as a senior high school English teacher, director of staff development at the district level, regional school improvement facilitator, and director of staff and organization development in the private sector.

Cassandra is the author of *Collaborative Common Assessments, The Handbook for Collaborative Common Assessments,* and *Making Homework Matter,* and the coauthor of *Leading by Design: An Action Framework for PLC at Work Leaders, Growing Tomorrow's Citizens in Today's Classroooms: Assessing Seven Critical Competencies, Instructional Agility: Responding to Assessment With Real-Time Decisions,* and *Essential Assessment: Six Tenets for Bringing Hope, Efficacy, and Achievement to the Classroom.* She has also contributed to *The Teacher as Assessment Leader* and *The Principal as Assessment Leader* as well as *The Collaborative Teacher* and *The Collaborative Administrator.*

To learn more about Cassandra's work, visit http://allthingsassessment.info or follow @cerkens on Twitter.

**Jadi Miller, EdD,** is director of assessment for Elkhorn Public Schools in Elkhorn, Nebraska. She has experience as a teacher and an administrator at the elementary, secondary, and district levels. Jadi was principal of two elementary schools identified as low performing and led the processes for building teacher capacity and improving student achievement. These efforts resulted in both schools winning awards for school improvement.

Jadi has worked with teachers, schools, and districts to implement standards-based curriculum, instruction, and assessment, as well as effective collaborative practices. She has designed and delivered ongoing, job-embedded professional development that enhances school and district improvement efforts.

Jadi received a bachelor's degree in education from the University of Kansas. She earned a master's degree and a doctoral degree in educational administration from the University of Nebraska–Lincoln.

To learn more about Jadi's work, visit http://allthingsassessment.info or follow @JadiMiller on Twitter.

**Tom Schimmer** is an author and a speaker with expertise in assessment, grading, leadership, and behavioral support. Tom is a former district-level leader, school administrator, and teacher. As a district-level leader, he was a member of the senior management team responsible for overseeing the efforts to support and build the instructional and assessment capacities of teachers and administrators.

Tom is a sought-after speaker who presents internationally for schools and districts. He has worked extensively throughout North America, as well as in Vietnam, Myanmar, China, Thailand, Japan, India, Qatar, Spain, and the United Arab Emirates. He earned a teaching degree from Boise State University and a master's degree in curriculum and instruction from the University of British Columbia.

Tom is the author and coauthor of multiple books, including *Growing Tomorrow's Citizens in Today's Classrooms: Assessing Seven Critical Competencies, Standards-Based Learning in Action: Moving From Theory to Practice, Instructional Agility: Responding to Assessment With Real-Time Decisions, Essential Assessment: Six Tenets for Bringing Hope, Efficacy, and Achievement to the Classroom*, and *Grading From the Inside Out: Bringing Accuracy to Student Assessment Through a Standards-Based Mindset*.

To learn more about Tom's work, visit http://allthingsassessment.info or follow @TomSchimmer on Twitter.

**Katie White** spends her days working to transform the educational experience for teachers and students. She has been an integral part of her own school system's multiyear journey through educational reform and has assisted systems worldwide in their work toward approaches that honor learning relationships.

She has a passion for helping educators develop a personalized understanding of the connections between curriculum, assessment, and instruction and creative approaches for reaching and teaching every single learner in every single classroom.

In living out this passion, she not only works within her system, but serves as an educational consultant and author. Her sense of humor and responsive approach to adult learning makes her a sought-after professional support for systems and schools. In addition, she is a co-moderator of the well-known #ATAssessment Twitter chat and is the president-elect of the Canadian Assessment for Learning Network.

Katie has a bachelor of education and master of education in curriculum studies from the University of Saskatchewan. She has served the role of classroom teacher (K–12), online high school teacher, instructional coach, principal and vice principal, and central office leader.

She has authored *Softening the Edges: Assessment Practices That Honor K–12 Teachers and Learners*; *Unlocked: Assessment as the Key to Everyday Creativity in the Classroom*; and *Student Self-Assessment: Data Notebooks, Portfolios, and Other Tools to Advance Learning*.

To learn more about Katie's work, visit https://www.kwhiteconsulting.com/ or follow @KatieWhite426 on Twitter.

To book Cassandra Erkens, Tom Schimmer, Nicole Dimich, Jadi Miller, or Katie White for professional development, contact pd@SolutionTree.com.

# INTRODUCTION

There can be little doubt that education is in the middle of some monumental changes. School systems, administrators, teachers, and learners are all grappling with ways to increase student achievement in a rapidly changing and chaotic world. The demands to focus on critical competencies, to ensure college and career readiness for all learners, to scrutinize curriculum for biases, and to incorporate in-demand technology in ways that broaden the classroom to a global society have all converged and now require educators, parents, and learners to change practices and address the ever-evolving learning expectations including standards, outcomes, objectives, and competencies.

Classroom assessment sits right at the center of all this change, impacted by each demand. Most educational systems are exploring and refining how students are assessed, under what conditions, and for what purposes. Further, teachers are searching for the best ways to communicate assessment results, interpret data, and report growth and achievement in academic as well as behavioral realms. These decisions are then applied in both online and face-to-face educational landscapes, making this work both essential and challenging.

The authors of this book, in their travels across countries and in their time in educational systems of all sizes, have found that teachers of all age groups and disciplines often have important questions about assessment. In search of answers, educators sometimes come across conflicting messages and uncertain or fragmented approaches. This book, designed with a collective 140 years of experience from five assessment experts, is intended to help readers navigate assessment decisions by doing three things.

1. Offering short answers to important questions, quickly (Please note this book is *not* intended to replace a deeper and more thorough investigation on behalf of educators. Rather, it aims to point the reader in the right direction of current best practices so the reader can continue learning beyond this concise text.)

2. Helping educators identify places of concern and then align all assessment work to promising practices and focused research in the field

3. Assisting educators in finding ways to practically address conflicting messages or misaligned systems so they can begin and then sustain this very important assessment work

Each response to a question this book provides is filtered through the lenses of hope, efficacy, and achievement within an authentic culture of learning. While a critical goal of assessment design is always to support optimal student achievement, this cannot happen in the absence of continuous and sustainable hope and the power to make meaningful decisions by both teachers and learners. The focus of assessment must be to support learning above all else.

# Assessment Tenets and How This Book Is Organized

In the Solution Tree Assessment Center's foundational book *Essential Assessment: Six Tenets for Bringing Hope, Efficacy, and Achievement to the Classroom* (Erkens, Schimmer, & Dimich, 2017), the center's architects Nicole Dimich, Cassandra Erkens, and Tom Schimmer explore assessment as organized around the following six tenets: (1) assessment purpose, (2) assessment architecture, (3) communication, (4) accurate interpretation, (5) instructional agility, and (6) student investment. At the center of all six tenets are hope, efficacy, and achievement, and surrounding every tenet is a culture of learning. Figure I.1 captures this relationship.

Accordingly, this book is also organized around these key features. Understanding the meaning of each tenet will help readers locate questions within this resource. The following definitions briefly capture the meaning of each tenet.

- **Assessment purpose:** Possessing clarity about why teachers are assessing and how they plan to use the information they gather

- **Assessment architecture:** Designing assessment systems in advance of instruction in order to maximize support and learning

- **Communication:** Planning how teachers intend to share and then utilize the results of an assessment experience to impact future learning

- **Accurate interpretation:** Ensuring that teachers and students draw similar inferences from assessment results by making the results accurate, accessible, and reliable

- **Instructional agility:** Making real-time maneuvers in a deliberate, purposeful, and accurate way to propel learning forward

- **Student investment:** Using assessment to build a student's ability to access academic achievement, self-regulation, self-assessment, and optimism

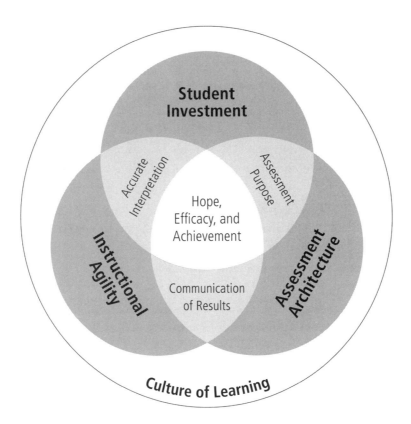

*Source: Erkens et al., 2017, p. 6.*

**Figure I.1:** *The Solution Tree Assessment Center framework.*

The questions posed in this book are organized around these tenets, but it should be noted that the interdependent and necessary relationships between the tenets make this compartmentalization difficult. A single question will likely touch on each tenet in some way. With this in mind, we offer a second organizational structure: by topic (for example, preassessment, reassessment, feedback). There is a topic chart and corresponding page numbers at the front of the book (page vii). In this way, this resource can be read from beginning to end, or it can be used in the moment, when a single answer to a single question is required.

# A Final Word of Clarification

It might be tempting to use this book as a singular resource and the final word on assessment. While it offers important and succinct answers to critical questions, it does not provide processes and approaches with the level of nuance and complexity required to capture all aspects of assessment design and response. It is a resource that can be used in conjunction with other resources that explore topics more fully.

Please see the Solution Tree Assessment Center comprehensive resource list on page 237 for deep explorations of any number of topics related to assessment.

Unfortunately, there are no shortcuts or easy options in designing assessment systems that foster hope, efficacy, and achievement for every learner. Assessment is complex, and doing it well requires clarity and intention. Despite the challenges, assessment holds tremendous potential to inform decision making for both teachers and learners. This resource is intended to provoke thoughtful decision making on behalf of learners and clarify misconceptions and misunderstandings that might be making this essential work challenging. In addition, the responses in this book are intended to generate rich conversations with colleagues to develop clarity in both description and implementation. Context contributes to how educators interpret each of these assessment concepts, and that means it will be the conversations that occur following reading that will lead to deeper clarity and impactful implementation. Educators can use the question responses to propel positive assessment reform forward and contemplate its importance within classrooms and schools.

# CHAPTER 1
# HOPE, EFFICACY, AND ACHIEVEMENT

A healthy assessment system in schools and classrooms begins with a foundation of hope, efficacy, and achievement for each and every learner. Everyday assessment decisions either contribute to or detract from a culture that supports the development of skilled, productive learners. If educators are going to support their learners in becoming independent, optimistic, and proficient, they must use assessment to build both confidence and resilience in the face of inevitable challenge. Educators must nurture learning environments that build trust and rapport, support play and creativity, and reflect reciprocal relationships and humility among all learners, including teachers.

Teachers can sustain hope, efficacy, and achievement, and even improve them, when they intentionally structure assessment systems to support these ends. Many educators ponder how it might be possible to use assessments in that manner. It is completely logical that educators—most of whom have never experienced the use of assessments to increase hope, efficacy, and achievement as learners—would want answers to the very important questions that follow in this chapter.

## Hope, Efficacy, and Achievement in Assessment

### What do we mean by *hope* in the context of assessment?

Hope is a belief—not a wish—that success and opportunity are within view or reach and *can be attained*. It is a firm conviction in the promise of something better to come.

5

Learners who have hope are positive about their future, are goal oriented, and can overcome obstacles in the learning process, enabling them to make decisions that support their growth as learners. Hope, then, is paramount to their ability to self-motivate, to remain engaged, and to persist through difficulties. If learners don't have a sense that success is imminent, then they are likely to provide half-hearted attempts, if they don't shut down completely. Without hope, learners navigate the learning process as if it were a minefield of traps and guaranteed pitfalls. Educators must use assessment processes—from the input to the output—to help keep learners hopeful.

It's important to distinguish hope from naïve optimism. Hope encompasses the big picture, with the full breadth of the positive and the negative at play, while naïve optimism focuses only on the positive—often outside of the context of a broader reality. In a truly hope-filled environment, then, it would be safe for learners to make mistakes because the continued possibility of success mitigates the impact of missteps along the way. In order for that to happen, however, the idea of holding out hope for learners must go beyond nods of encouragement to incorporate hope into the scoring and reporting systems.

> **Connected Tenets:** Student Investment
>
> **Topics:** Growth Mindset, Student Engagement and Motivation

## How can assessment destroy hope? How can I avoid this?

The assessment process is so powerful that a single learning experience can either create or destroy hope (Stiggins, 2007, 2008; Wiliam, 2011, 2013a). The traditional assessment process—assess, evaluate, record, report (but do little to intervene or allow for final grades to reflect the improved scores later)—contains at least five aspects that immediately destroy hope.

1. The assessment pathway contains no practice opportunities in which early results can intentionally *feed forward* into improved summative experiences.

2. Assessment expectations remain hidden so learners are left to guess what teachers will test and how they might test it.

3. Assessment feedback focuses only on what is missing or erroneous; it does not identify strengths.

4. Assessment is employed as an event that results in evaluative marks or scores (for example, 50 percent, D–, or 2/15) without any feedback or opportunities that would allow for a change in the results.

5. Assessment results are limited to evaluation scores that teachers average over time so early failures impede future success.

At *each* juncture of the assessment process, learners—the ultimate decision makers in their personal interventions to change their outcome—make choices that impact their final outcome. But it's critical to avoid blaming or shaming the learners for poor results or lack of hope. Instead, seek to find and repair the systems that kill motivation and encourage learners to give up in hopelessness. Consider the following strategies.

1. Create an assessment plan that incorporates formative assessment opportunities for learners and teachers to gain a better understanding of the learners' progress toward the learning goals, building toward the summative experience.

2. Be clear about learning expectations and goals. Make success criteria transparent to students.

3. Be intentional with feedback to include both strengths and areas of growth. Help students see how these interrelate and ultimately connect to the learning goals.

4. Scores or grades only tell part of the story. Make sure that the feedback makes the next steps more clear.

5. Establish grading practices that recognize student learning progressions and do not penalize errors in the early stages of learning.

**Connected Tenets:** Student Investment

**Topics:** Growth Mindset, Student Engagement and Motivation

## What do we mean by *efficacy*? Efficacy for whom?

Efficacious people believe that they have both the capacity and the ability to reach challenging goals successfully. Obviously, it's important for learners to have efficacy as they strive to accomplish robust learning goals. If learners don't believe they are capable of doing the work, they will readily disengage when the challenge feels insurmountable.

But the same can be said for educators. Unless teachers believe they are capable of moving *each* of the learners in their care—even the difficult or unmotivated learners—to high levels of learning, they too can give up in hopelessness. Educators with a high level of efficacy believe they can control, or at least positively influence, student motivation and achievement.

Because beliefs inform action, efficacious teachers and learners are more likely to commit to a challenge, persist through obstacles, rebound through failed attempts, and focus on successes to reflect on and then refine their strategies for future use. Efficacy is critical for the success of teachers and learners alike.

**Connected Tenets:** Student Investment

**Topics:** Growth Mindset, Student Engagement and Motivation

# How can I increase hope and efficacy without building a false sense of entitlement?

Being hopeful and efficacious has nothing to do with entitlement. When learners are hopeful, they believe success is still within reach. When learners experience self-efficacy, they believe they can reach goals. Hope and efficacy are the characteristics of confident learners (Hattie, 2012). Confidence is *grounded optimism* (Kanter, 2004), where there is an authentic belief that success is inevitable, but that focused effort toward success is still necessary. When learners believe success is possible (hope) and believe they can do it (self-efficacy), learning happens.

*Entitlement,* on the other hand, indicates success without merit; that one is entitled to success without producing the necessary evidence to justify the proclaimed success. Entitlement has no place in any assessment system since teachers should measure learning on the quality of the evidence learners produce. So, there should be neither a sense of entitlement nor a false sense of entitlement. That would be counterproductive to any environment where developing a deep understanding of learning and developing a strong work ethic are parallel goals.

Strategies to increase hope and efficacy in learners include the following.

1.  Provide clarity around learning goals and success criteria to help students see the path toward success but still require them to do the work to get there.

2.  Offer timely and specific feedback to let students know when they are on the path or when they have strayed off it.

**Connected Tenets:** Instructional Agility, Student Investment

**Topics:** Feedback, Formative Assessment, Self- and Peer Assessment

# What would I need to change for my evaluation practices to support achievement for all?

Evaluation (summative assessment) practices that support achievement for all contain the following characteristics.

- Evaluation occurs only *after* explicit instruction, plenty of practice, strong feedback, and time to set goals and adjust efforts in order to grow.

- Evaluation is limited to only the most important kinds of learning (critical skills and understanding).

- When new evaluation evidence indicates increased proficiency of a learning goal, new evidence replaces old evidence.

- Learners have the opportunity to be reassessed when additional practice and learning occur.

- Academic achievement is evaluated separately from behavioral factors, and both types of learning are supported.

- When appropriate, learners have flexibility in the method of evaluation so they can leverage personal strengths and interests.

Evaluation is only accurate when it certifies the true level of proficiency a student attains by the end of the marking period. The concluding preponderance of evidence upon which the score is based must be tied directly to the learning expectations and criteria for quality and must be completely free from the penalties of early mistakes and all nonacademic factors, such as compliance, attitude, aptitude, or effort.

**Connected Tenets:** Assessment Architecture, Student Investment
**Topics:** Reporting, Summative Assessment and Grading

# How can I use assessment practices to develop a growth mindset in my learners?

The *growth mindset* is, as Carol Dweck (2006) describes, the inherent belief that the mind is a muscle that can be developed, that one's mind can *grow*, and that one's current state is simply a starting point. Using assessment to develop a growth mindset with learners is seamless when the focus of assessment is to elicit evidence in ways that make clear the next steps toward proficiency for each and every learner. A *fixed mindset*, on the other hand, would have one believe that intelligence is a fixed commodity; that one is either smart or not. The idea of a fixed mindset runs counter to the purpose of education—that at its most efficient and effective, learning is focused on growth; that learners can know more, do more, or understand more through the instructional process.

A key to ensuring a growth mindset over a fixed one is to use assessment as a springboard for instructional decision making. Assessment is simply eliciting ongoing evidence of learning in its most actionable form, evidence that identifies areas of strength, aspects in need of strengthening, and the subsequent actions necessary to advance learning. D. Royce Sadler (1989) identifies the three essential assessment questions that drive this process.

1. Where am I going?

2. Where am I now?

3. How do I close the gap?

*Closing the gap* has two benefits: (1) it makes obvious to learners the necessary steps to develop their learning, and (2) the process of developing their learning gives learners firsthand experience in *growing* their minds or expanding their intellect.

The key to using assessment to develop a growth mindset is for teachers to create assessment practices and processes that most seamlessly lead to subsequent action. Using assessment *formatively* is how teachers develop the growth mindset in learners. One of the arguments against formative grades is that grades aren't informative of next steps. While grades often do inform learners about their current status, they rarely specify what subsequent action is necessary to keep learning. By focusing assessment on *what's next* instead of *what was*, teachers can create the necessary conditions for growth.

> **Connected Tenets:** Assessment Purpose, Instructional Agility
>
> **Topics:** Feedback, Formative Assessment

# Relationships, Teacher Confidence, and Assessment Practices

## How can I protect the relationships I have with students when making assessment decisions?

When teachers recognize the power of assessment to either nurture or diminish relationships, they can design assessment tools and processes that support the former and prevent the latter. The role of a teacher is to support and develop learning for individual learners, and one of the best ways to do this is through strong assessment practices.

When assessment is primarily used to inform instruction and identify student strengths and needs, it can enhance the relationships teachers are developing with their students.

As with any good relationship, there has to be mutual respect and genuine caring. Using assessment as a catalyst for conversation and an open exchange of information can support the teacher-learner relationship. Giving learners a voice in decision making and choice in how to advance specific aspects of their own learning can be a great way to leverage the information an assessment delivers and foster mutual respect. For example, empowering learners to choose how they will practice and develop new knowledge and skills engages students in the learning in a deeper way. It also requires them to truly understand what success looks like. Communicating optimism and belief in a student before, during, and after an assessment process reflects genuine caring. Pairing this with targeted and specific instruction and feedback puts the teacher in the advocate and support roles, which is one of the best ways to ensure assessment supports the relationship through the challenging moments in the learning process.

When assessment processes carry the weight of judgment and value without a balance of support, growth, and risk taking, the relationships between people involved in the assessment process can falter. On the other hand, when assessment is viewed as an opportunity to support learning, it can help teachers relate to students and students relate to teachers.

**Connected Tenets:** Communication of Results, Student Investment
**Topics:** Formative Assessment, Relationships, Student Engagement and Motivation, Student Efficacy

## How does assessment build teacher confidence?

Assessment contributes to teacher confidence when the resulting evidence (namely, student achievement) shows that the teacher's use of formative assessment results and artifacts helped them leverage their professional judgments to make effective instructional decisions that then drove achievement gains for all of their students. When assessment leads to increased learning for students, it builds confidence in a teacher's own ability to create highly effective learning environments. There is nothing more empowering than having clarity about learners' current learning states and subsequently knowing exactly what to do to create an enhanced future state. Quality assessment practices lead to improved student learning *and* improved efficacy for the teachers designing and employing the practices.

**Connected Tenets:** Accurate Interpretation
**Topics:** Professional Judgment

## Does the focus on accountability stifle creativity in the classroom?

It's important to separate *intent* from *execution*. It is, on the surface, hard to argue with the point that schools, teachers, and learners are accountable for the results of the education system—especially public schools, where millions of dollars are invested to ensure learners are reaching identified outcomes. Of course, one may make arguments in reference to whether there is enough funding and whether that funding is equitably distributed, but conceptually, being accountable for results is a reasonable expectation for any organization or jurisdiction to have of those within the system.

That said, it is true that the execution of *accountability* has often inadvertently led to creativity in the classroom being stifled or sometimes outright lost. Too often, *standards* and *standardization* are conflated, which leads to an opaque view of what the goals of an accountability system could be. The conflation of these two terms often results in an oversimplified assessment system, but unfortunately such systems fall short of the lofty goals that most jurisdictions strive for due to assessment processes that restrict student creativity. While this stifling of creativity is likely not intentional, it has been a residual effect nonetheless.

*Standards* are about outcomes; they are the knowledge, skills, ways of thinking, and dispositions that are the goals of the education experience at each grade level. However, they most often don't, in and of themselves, demand that learners present their learning in a *standardized* way. Standardized assessment is easier to score, especially if the assessment is dominated by binary questions of recall or instances where every learner is asked to respond to the same performance task. Now, there are good reasons for some standardization since large-scale assessment is designed to, among other things, draw large-scale conclusions about a cohort of learners. The accuracy and meaningfulness of these overarching conclusions depends on assessments that are both *valid* and *reliable*. Reliability speaks to the consistency with which an assessment measures what it is intended to measure (Heritage, 2010b); if an assessment is reliable, its results are repeatable. Without a reliable measure, the interpretation of the assessment results can't be valid, or accurate.

There are two things to note about this point. First, it is possible for standardized assessments to infuse opportunities for learners to creatively respond, especially where the focus is on a skill, a mindset, or a dispositional attitude. For this to work, criteria would have to be clear, and formal processes for scoring would have to be consistent, but the variety that results from student responses could still satisfy the same learning goal. Formal protocols to accommodate such assessments are already in place in some jurisdictions. Next-generation assessments that integrate content and skills in authentic ways and encourage student choice and personalization are becoming more prevalent (see, for example, Schimmer, 2019).

Second, it might be wise to begin working to disconnect large-scale assessment results from the judgment of the quality within the school-based experience. Large-scale assessment results are limited in scope and do not provide a complete picture of the system or of individual students. Focusing on a balance of different types of assessment creates a more complete picture of learning. Large-scale assessments have only ever shown a moderate (0.5) correlation to classroom grades (Bowers, 2019), which means the expectation that a school-based grade will seamlessly align with large-scale accountability tests is misguided. This disassociation from a hyper-focus on standardized testing would perhaps allow classroom teachers the freedom to expand opportunities for creativity for learners, without fear that the standardized results would result in negative outcomes for themselves and their learners (see, for example, Allensworth, Correa, & Ponisciak, 2008; Wiliam, 2013b).

**Connected Tenets:** Accurate Interpretation, Assessment Architecture

**Topics:** Accountability and Standardized Tests, Assessment Design, Criteria, Critical Competencies, Standards

## How would my assessment practices be different if they supported productive failure and intellectual risk taking?

Learning something new is risky because it's rife with opportunities to fail early. If assessment practices are to support productive failure and intellectual risk taking, hope must be cultivated for students. Hope is not simply warm feelings; rather, it can be connected to concrete actions on the part of both learners and teachers that cultivate efficacy, such as the following.

- A belief that assessment should be used to power through the *danger zones*, to get to the real learning; this authentic learning requires learners to move beyond what is comfortable and familiar into the new and unknown, which inherently requires risk taking for both learner and teacher. This means assessment processes must be future-focused, formatively supporting both teacher and student decision making in the improvement process. The connection between formative assessment and enhanced, responsive instruction must be visible at all times to both teachers and learners. This ongoing formative assessment and instructional response helps both learner and teacher navigate the unknown. When learners see that assessment serves their own learning needs, it takes on a different meaning for learners.

- Assessment that focuses on and utilizes strengths; it is from a position of strength that next steps emerge. Assessment that highlights only deficits stifles risk taking. When assessment includes specific feedback for the learner that provides information about what has been mastered and what is yet to be learned, this information can be used to identify next steps by both the learner and the teacher.

- Assessment that honors not only learners' intellectual needs but also their physical, social, and emotional needs (White, 2017); learners will only take risks if it is safe to do so. Three things can facilitate the sense of safety required to grow between assessments: (1) time to recover from mistakes or errors, (2) opportunities to make new decisions and improvements, and (3) teacher and peer support in doing so. We must make sure that our assessment practices provide both the feedback and the time and support necessary to use them effectively.

- Reflective opportunities that are built directly into the assessment system; learners also need time to reflect on what worked and what didn't and to design approaches that will lead them to more successful outcomes (White, 2019, 2022). For example, a reflection process might be implemented following a first attempt at a product, when students consider the decisions they have made so far and whether those decisions are leading them to their desired results. Learners may then select a goal to focus their next set of actions as they work to refine the product.

- Feedback that focuses on enhancing skills and knowledge and not on increasing numerical values; the language connected to assessment has to be a language of quality learning and not a language of quantity and value. It is insufficient for feedback to simply be stated in terms of a percentage or a number; rather, it should include more specific and actionable information for the learner to effectively use it.

- Scoring practices that do not factor in earlier, unsuccessful attempts with later proficiency when determining grades; learners will not take risks when they believe that unsuccessful attempts will negatively affect their overall grade. Averaging old evidence with new will both shut down risk taking and communicate a score that does not reflect the actual degree of learning attained.

When teachers activate the conditions, they use formative assessment practices in the manner intended while simultaneously creating a growth-mindset classroom.

**Connected Tenets:** Communication of Results, Student Investment
**Topics:** Formative Assessment, Growth Mindset

# If I have to increase the amount of formative assessment I conduct, what should I stop doing to make time?

There are some assessment or even instructional practices that can steal valuable time because they do not deliver rewards that balance out the cost of engaging in them. Some things educators might stop doing include the following.

- Interrupt learning momentum to engage in an assessment process that does not reflect the learning currently being addressed. Formative assessment is not a *thing* that teachers do. Rather, it is an embedded process that gives teachers real-time information and lights the path to immediate next steps. Stopping learning in its tracks to engage in something that seems unrelated steals learning time.

- Do the thinking for the learners in the name of feedback. It is possible to give too much feedback, especially if it overwhelms the learners and makes the task of revision seem too daunting. Furthermore, when feedback is completely directive, it places all the thinking in the hands of the person giving it and little thinking in the hands of the person receiving it. Teachers can leverage time with focused feedback that invites decision making by the learner; teachers can save time by writing less feedback and, instead, planning for responses to the assessment evidence they gather that re-engages the learners in the concepts and skills they are exploring.

- Assign a lot of practice work with no plan for (1) providing feedback, or (2) using the resulting evidence to inform next steps. Instead, try using a few quality questions intended to deepen the learning and explore plausible errors and misconceptions so learners can improve their efforts between practice opportunities.

- Place the greatest assessment focus and spend inordinate amounts of time on standardized test preparation. When students learn well (with rigor and depth), they test well. Focusing on the learning goals and the strategies that equip learners to succeed in a wide variety of contexts is a good use of time.

- Teach learners those skills and knowledge they already possess. Some of the strengths of timely formative assessment are that it identifies learners' areas of strength, prevents educators from repeating things learners have already mastered, and honors the natural process of reassessment that should be already built into the spiraled assessment pathway. When teachers design instructional units, they should intentionally plan assessment processes and build in flexibility to use the information gained from them to provide additional instructional support and possibly reassessment. This is explored further in the chapter about assessment architecture (page 71).

- Engage in whole-class lecture for the majority of instructional time. Instructional strategies that maximize connection making and learner dialogue also maximize the transference of learning from surface acquisition to deep learning (Hattie & Donoghue, 2016). A well-considered instructional approach can save time in interventions later on.

- Fail to co-construct the learning goals and success criteria before and during each learning experience. When learners (and teachers) are unfocused and unclear, valuable time can be wasted practicing things that aren't important, engaging in tasks that aren't meaningful, and spending instructional time on areas that are not vital.

The important thing to remember is that any process that maximizes learning *saves time* in the end—intervention time, reteaching time, reassessing time. Formative assessment is a process essential for achieving optimal learning in the shortest amount of time.

> **Connected Tenets:** Assessment Architecture, Communication of Results
>
> **Topics:** Feedback, Formative Assessment

# Is it fair to assess English learners in the English language?

Assessing accurately means that the assessment evidence has a high likelihood of providing clear information about a learner's degree of proficiency in relation to the standards or learning goals a teacher intends to assess or measure. Assessing fairly means that all factors are considered when designing the assessment (for example, background knowledge, language proficiency, vocabulary, content, skill, and so on) and when analyzing the results.

There are many factors that determine whether it is fair or not to assess learners in their non-native language. If a learner is new to the language, assessing in English will not yield accurate information for the learner, the teacher, or the team. For example, a learner may struggle to solve mathematics problems on an exam, but the factor that had the greatest influence on their demonstration of mathematics skill was the volume of written English language within the mathematics problems; assessing in the language of instruction would, as a result, not be indicative of their true level of mathematics aptitude. When educators assess, especially when the purpose is formative, their goal is to get information to understand a learner's strengths and plan next steps. To do that, consider the following when fairly assessing English learners.

- Clarify the targeted learning (standard or competency) and identify the language needed to engage in the assessment.

- Analyze the item or task. What does a learner need to know and be able to do to demonstrate mastery on each task or item? Consider what is intended to be assessed and provide support for additional skills needed to show mastery beyond what was intended to be measured.

- Identify a learner's level of English language proficiency, and choose appropriate supports to remove potential barriers beyond subject-area skill and understanding. There are many factors to consider to help with this.

  - If learners are new to the country and the language, using English to assess standards will not be fair or accurate. In this case, if the learner can demonstrate the learning in their first language, then do that, and the assessment will be more accurate.

  - If they have some language proficiency (for example, they are conversationally fluent but have yet to develop academic language proficiency), certain accommodations can help (such as additional time, talking through the meaning of questions and tasks with a teacher or another person, using sentence frames and images, preteaching vocabulary, and more).

  - If the learners are proficient with English, tease out which aspects of the assessment may be language specific and which may be unintentionally creating a barrier to showing their actual proficiency on the learning goal. If learners have the academic language proficiency to engage in the item or task, then it is appropriate to have learners independently engage in the assessment. However, this determination may not be clear until individuals or teams of teachers have analyzed the learners' work. Be ready to offer the learners another assessment opportunity or change the support students need to get a clear sense of their proficiency on the intended learning goal.

- Use observational protocols to gather more comprehensive understanding of the English learner's content, skill, and language proficiency. Consider the following list of questions from Margarita Calderón (2007).

- Does the student use the first language to make meaning?

- Does the student require more than one explanation?

- Does the student use pictures to help understand meaning?

- Are objects and manipulatives helpful to the student?

- How often does the student ask peers for help?

- What type of help does the student ask from peers? From the teacher?

- Does the student read the problems aloud?

- Do examples help the student? How?

- Does the student prefer written or oral directions?

- Does the student check classwork for accuracy and completion before submitting it?

The fairness and accuracy of using the English language to assess English learners is contextual. Consider all of these factors, and keep in mind what the learning goal is and possible ways evidence of mastery may be collected on that targeted learning goal. English language will always be developing and expanding, so teasing out what is specific to the language, what is specific to the concept or skill, and what is specific to the learner will be a process in which individual teachers and teams continuously engage.

**Connected Tenets:** Assessment Architecture, Communication of Results
**Topics:** English Learners, Summative Assessment and Grading

# Hope, Efficacy, and Achievement in a Remote Learning Context

The most important thing to remember when making assessment decisions in a remote learning context is that any decision and process must support hope, efficacy, and achievement for learners. This means that when teachers communicate assessment results, they must ensure learners remain confident and optimistic in the face of the information they receive. When learners feel able to respond to assessment information on assessment tasks that hold meaning for them, they remain both hopeful and efficacious. When learners have the opportunity to engage in meaningful feedback and then revisit, review, and revise efforts that fell short of the goals, their achievement will increase. By observing student responses to assessment, teachers can determine whether their decisions are supporting both the achievement of the learners and their beliefs about who they are and what they can accomplish.

Such efforts on behalf of the teachers became even more challenging during periods of virtual learning, such as during the COVID-19 pandemic. In a remote learning context, consider the following.

- Design methods for collecting feedback from learners before, during, and after an assessment experience. Let learners know how long an assessment should take, and ask them to rate their confidence level going into the assessment. Also, give them a space to share any concerns or questions they may have.

- Offer timely and specific feedback about both the assessment task itself and the processes the learners used during the assessment in order to self-regulate and provide strong assessment information. Then, allow time for learners to reflect on the feedback, set goals, and revisit and revise their efforts.

- Celebrate specific strengths often. Relate these celebrations to decisions learners made that led them to strong learning. By acknowledging strength that is explicitly connected to actions learners took, teachers can fan the flames of hope and efficacy.

- Engage in processes that allow learners to track their progress in achieving important learning targets. Make growth tangible and invite reflection consistently.

It might come as no surprise that what works best in a face-to-face environment will also work best in a remote environment. Educators can streamline their efforts by designing for remote learning and employing such practices with consistency in all environments (virtual, hybrid, and face to face). The external environment learners are asked to navigate—namely, remote or hybrid environments—makes the work of developing hope, efficacy, and achievement even more pertinent for educators.

# CHAPTER 2
# A CULTURE OF LEARNING

Building relationships that support learning means deliberately attending to culture. A school's culture is made up of the beliefs, assumptions, expectations, and habits of the people within it; it is visible in the unspoken norms for conduct, the language those within a school use, and the narratives that emerge from shared histories. If schools and educators do not carefully craft and monitor culture, they cannot sustain the future-focused work of assessment. The power of the culture (what is done in the learning space) will always override intentions (often indicated by what is said in the learning space). Teachers have to intentionally align their words with their actions; their beliefs with their assessment systems.

It cannot be overstated that when teachers and learners are engaging in effective assessment practices, teachers must pay careful attention to their word choice, tone, timing, supports, and instructions, while also monitoring learners' levels of independence, their confidence, and their reactions. These factors are critical in building the trust that is essential for growth, risk taking, and deep thinking.

Considering how to build learning-rich cultures in classrooms and schools is a critical focus that grounds *all* assessment decisions. Questions that invite educators and leaders to reflect on the necessary conditions for this shift remain an important part of establishing effective assessment systems.

# The Shift Away From Traditional Assessment Culture

## How do assessment and school culture intersect?

The way teachers assess, the way they give feedback, and the opportunities they offer for redemption (or no redemption) following a mistake dramatically influence students' learning experiences and the overall perception of the school culture in which they learn every day.

Culture is found in the words, deeds, and feelings of everyone in an educational context. Just as positive energy breeds more positive energy, so does negative energy generates more negative energy. In a positive school culture, there is a sense of belonging, an overarching feeling of optimism, a focus on well-being, and a commitment to supporting learning for all.

Assessment has a direct link to the characteristics of positive culture. When teachers believe students can learn, they approach the assessment systems with great care and ensure their assessment decisions build hope and efficacy while increasing achievement. School culture impacts how learners interact with and respond to assessment, and how learners engage in assessment impacts the school culture. Assessment and school culture are interdependent.

> **Connected Tenets:** Assessment Purpose, Communication of Results, Instructional Agility
>
> **Topics:** Feedback, Formative Assessment, Growth Mindset, School and Classroom Culture and Climate

## How can I shift my classroom climate away from competition and compliance and toward learning?

A culture of competition emerges when there is a sense that grades are scarce, that there are, for example, only so many As available, and that one must be truly special to earn one. While it is true that there is competition for spaces at universities and that competition is global and is beyond any learner's sphere of control, what *is* within their sphere of control is reaching their highest level of performance. Some teachers may see this competition as a motivator, and maybe for some learners, it is, but the downsides to this competition often outweigh any potential upside.

Research indicates that peer assessment is a powerful learning experience (Topping, 2013), but the benefit may be neutralized if the result is a kind of leap-frogging through the achievement scale, where learners compete for the top spot. For example, learners may see peer assessment as an undesirable exercise and may not fully invest in the process when the result *may* be that other learners perform better than they do. Why would they purposefully assist others in outperforming them if access to the highest level of achievement is limited?

Compliance can also have a counterproductive impact. To be sure, behavioral compliance is part of living in a society. Compliance is important when certain societal expectations ensure a focus on safety and fairness (for example, red lights, stop signs, assigned seats at concerts, and so on). But compliance as an achievement indicator misses the mark, as simply completing an assignment or assessment does not ensure that learning has occurred. *Quality* is what matters, so educators should determine achievement based on the quality of what was produced, not simply because it *was* produced. Being compliant, for the most part, is a social norm and can be a part of rating any learner along their social competence continuum, but a compliance approach to assessment and grading would likely result in some learners settling for *done* instead of striving for higher levels of performance.

To avoid this, focus on developing clear performance criteria that identify progressions of quality. Students should be able to see multiple points of learning and levels of quality throughout the journey toward proficiency; it should not just be the beginning and the end. Teachers should analyze the task and expectations to identify and clarify these different steps. This will help undercut both unhealthy compliance and competition for two reasons. First, learners will see that their only competition is against the learning goal and established criteria, and that how they compare to their classmates is of no concern. Second, clear performance criteria establish that the quality of what they produce or perform is the exclusive measure of success; that completing it matters, but completion is the minimal expectation prior to assessment. Establishing rigorous criteria that articulate descriptions of excellence allows for a transparent culture where the collective can work together to reach each individual's personal best.

**Connected Tenets:** Communication of Results, Student Investment

**Topics:** Criteria, Self- and Peer Assessment, Summative Assessment and Grading

## Can assessment and creativity coexist? How can I incorporate creativity into my assessments?

Traditional assessments of testing memorization have, historically, failed to engender creativity. However, not only can creativity coexist with assessment, but also creativity is actually dependent on assessment in order to flourish. Assessment, especially modern assessments, must move from creating knowledge consumers to producing knowledge creators—the very root of creativity (Erkens et al., 2019; White, 2019).

Learners need the opportunity to experience the effects of decisions that move them toward personally meaningful goals and those that move them away from their goals. They need room to take risks, try on ideas, and stretch their current worldview. It is for this reason that effective assessment design and opportunities for self-assessment are the currency of imagination and creativity.

Foster creativity by placing decision making in the hands of learners and giving learners responsibility for exploring, elaborating, curating, expressing, and reflecting on their own ideas. Teachers can intentionally create these types of reflective prompts and actions for students throughout the learning journey. They may do this through reflection and goal-setting sheets, structured peer conversations, or conferring sessions between the learners and their teacher. (For more ideas, see White, 2019.) This will help learners move beyond imagining what they think adults want them to imagine or creating only what they hope will satisfy their teachers and instead will elicit true creativity. Self-assessment and peer assessment both create a level of engagement and efficacy for learners that is inherently different from simply trying to guess the expectations of the teacher. Creating these opportunities for learners and allowing them to have input on the creation and expansion of criteria benefit both learners and teachers.

> **Connected Tenets:** Communication of Results, Student Investment
> **Topics:** Critical Competencies, Formative Assessment

## How can I make failure okay in my classroom? My students won't take risks.

Students often define failure as a low grade, score, or mark. To redefine failure as an opportunity, educators must help learners reframe how they interpret their scores (when given) and ensure that their own communication methods focus on feedback and describing qualities of learning, as opposed to simply quantifying. The following ideas outline a few concrete and practical strategies educators can implement to make failure and mistakes within the assessment process not only okay but also moments that inspire learning.

- Share any score or symbol by learning goal. If learners receive a quantitative mark such as a letter grade, a rubric score, or a smiley face, it should be defined in terms of qualities of learning in relation to a specific goal or goals. When learners only receive a number, such as 5/10, they do not have enough information to know what they have learned and what is yet to be mastered. Instead, provide that information by learning goal to indicate specifically what is yet to be learned.

- With essential standards and learning outcomes, guide learners in self-reflection by identifying the learning goals in which they hold strength (criteria on a rubric or sections by learning goal on a test) and learning goals or criteria that are in need of strengthening. Require action on the areas of growth, and provide time for recovery.

- Only provide the more summative, quantitative score after learners have taken action on an area needing growth and have met a level of proficiency. If there was a score prior to this point, then replace the old score with the new score. With new evidence of proficiency on the same learning goal or standard, scores should never be averaged; the score should represent the current truth about the learner's full depth of understanding. Thus, educators should determine scores using the more recent or more consistent evidence.

- Have learners track their growth over time, and help them reflect on the growth they have made and what caused this growth. This process can help them see how their mistakes are actually opportunities for more learning.

- When using an assessment formatively, delay determining a grade as much as possible; grades and scores can interfere with learner willingness to reengage in learning. No matter what, provide one or two manageable next steps and require action on those next steps. Formative assessment and the feedback that is generated by it should incorporate concrete actions to strengthen the learning. The next steps could happen during instruction or outside of class, but it is the action that will lead to growth. Then, have learners reflect on this action and their growth. This will help them start to reframe mistakes as opportunities to learn more.

- Learners who don't take risks very often have little confidence in their potential success, or feel like the risk will lead to more evaluation as opposed to growth. In either case, provide learners with strength-based feedback only, for a period of time. Frame strengths in terms of learners' learning goals, and describe them using specific success criteria so they build confidence. This confidence will then lead to learners being more open to critical feedback and growth.

- The action educators take when learners make a mistake will determine the culture of learning that is present in the classroom. A culture of risk taking and recovery means that taking risks is safe, brave, and encouraged. When learners make mistakes, educators must establish a tone of inquiry ("What led to this mistake or this response?") and an opportunity and requirement to take action ("What do you need to learn to move forward? How and when will you take action on this next step?"). It is essential that learners take action, no matter how motivated or unmotivated they may appear. Taking a step into something that one is not confident in is not easy, and so it will take time and multiple strategies to help and guide learners to take the next step.

Creating a culture where learners take risks and see mistakes as opportunities to grow takes intention, time, and patience. Continue to frame risk taking as a positive step for learning and mistake making as an essential part of the process. This will help learners reframe their thinking. It is just as important to provide time and space for learners to dig into their mistakes, take action, and reflect on what it means for their next steps. Taking these next steps and then reflecting on their growth will be key to creating a healthy culture for learning. A tone of possibility will lead to learners understanding that faster is not always better and that perfect is not the only way to achieve success.

**Connected Tenets:** Assessment Architecture, Communication of Results, Instructional Agility

**Topics:** Formative Assessment, Growth Mindset, School and Classroom Culture and Climate

# My students are afraid to ask questions because they believe their peers will think they are unintelligent. How can I encourage them to take risks and ask questions?

Simply encouraging learners to take risks and attempt answers to teacher queries will not work, at least for the majority of learners, and it will not work in a manner that extends beyond the individual classroom or time frame in which the reassuring nudges occurred. Moreover, the tendency to avoid public, intellectual risk taking spans a wide array of learners, not just the timid or struggling learners, so encouragements to a few will not address the systemic issue. Consider it this way: would learners who frequently raise their hands do so in a moment when they knowingly *don't* have an answer for the teacher? Are they actually taking much of an intellectual risk if they have the answers?

Surprisingly, the strategies teachers use to protect learners from revealing their own discomfort, like only calling on learners who've raised their hands to indicate a level of confidence and readiness to answer a teacher prompt, often work *against* creating a learning culture that promotes intellectual risk taking. In fact, the public display of rewarding those who already know the answer builds winning streaks that turn into accumulated advantages for the students who volunteer while also discouraging other students in the classroom from participating since the unintended message is that all students already know the answers. The resulting effect of widening the chasm between the *haves* and *have nots*—a concept coined by Merton (1968) known as the *Matthew Effect*, based on the adage *the rich get richer and the poor get poorer*—exposes inequities that make risk taking even more terrifying for learners who are trying to keep up with the pace. Researchers found that applying this principle to reading acquisition helped to explain how learners who master decoding processes widen the gap in reading because they are better able to concentrate on the meaning of texts than learners who have not developed those skills (Neuman & Celano, 2006).

A far better solution involves creating a culture in which *all* learners are engaged in intellectual risk taking (Wiliam, 2014). Consider the following alternatives to a rapid-fire call-and-response approach to questioning in the classroom.

- Predesign questions that will require learners to engage in complex thinking and productive struggle. Use the emerging results to guide instructional maneuvers.

- Randomly call on all learners. Do not allow hand raising unless it is to have learners seek teacher permission or offer questions or challenges of each other.

- Offer learners alternative responses or strategies to employ when they are at a loss for how to answer a query (for example, "May I have a minute?" or "Can I ask a friend?").

- Increase wait time after asking the question and before soliciting responses.

- Seek multiple answers to a single question, showing no indication of right or wrong answers until many students have offered their opinions.

- Engage learners, especially those who already had the answer but have not yet explained the *why*, in backing their own or each other's answers with evidence and justifications.

- Treat mistakes, errors, or misconceptions as opportunities to deepen the learning for everyone.

Intellectual risk taking is the hallmark of a thriving and safe learning environment. Rather than encourage a few to speak up more, educators must create an equitable environment where everyone is challenged and mistakes are cherished as opportunities to continue learning.

> **Connected Tenets:** Instructional Agility
>
> **Topics:** Questioning, School and Classroom Culture and Climate, Student Engagement and Motivation

## Don't grades motivate students to do well? How can I motivate my students within a culture of learning?

Grades can (and do) motivate *some* learners. On the surface, learners know that grades are the currency that allow them to apply to the postsecondary institution of their choice. Provided this pathway is important to a learner, grades might seem to be a motivator. Even younger learners may learn that their parents and caregivers place much attention (sometimes disproportionately) on the grades learners receive on their report cards. As long as learners care what their families think about their school success, grades may seem to be motivating, regardless of age. The power and influence of grades has historically been a strong narrative throughout families and societies.

The challenge is that not all learners hold the same goals for themselves, not all families value high grades as a source of pride, and not all learners believe they are capable of achieving high grades. Furthermore, often the motivation for high grades seems to be more about *acquiring* than *earning* (or *learning*), and the meaning of the grades is often unclear. Traditionally, grades have been a product of points *acquired* in a variety of ways (such as extra credit or bonus questions), which could inadvertently— or intentionally—send the message that *getting the points* is all that matters.

Teachers may not ever completely eradicate the emphasis on acquiring high grades, but sometimes working *with* learners to clarify expectations and success criteria can be a more effective and efficient way to bring things into alignment. If, for example, grades are only a reflection of learning, then the motivation for a higher grade is far less problematic since there is only one pathway to achieve the learning; learners would have to know more, do more, or understand more. This, of course, is really about the summative purpose of assessment, where evidence is used to verify that learning has occurred and then to report to others about student achievement. Within the formative purpose, it's a different story.

Research shows that grades, scores, and levels can inhibit student learning rather than motivate it. Students who receive lower grades are not more motivated to achieve at higher levels (Guskey, 2011). When learners are fixated on grades, using grades during the formative process could lead them to settle for *good enough*, which is counterproductive to a continual learning process. This is why assessment *purpose* is so vital. (For further information on assessment purpose, see chapter 3, page 41.) The purpose of formative assessment is to initiate more learning through the use of descriptive feedback that identifies *what's next* for the learner. Clarity about next steps as well as about the learning goals themselves helps motivate learners through the efficacy that they can achieve a target that they fully understand. Teachers should make sure that their practices enhance motivation rather than diminish it. One of the strongest practices is to ensure that grades are only a reflection of learning and not other factors. This brings the two groups of students in your classroom—those motivated by grades and those motivated by a culture of learning—closer to alignment.

**Connected Tenets:** Accurate Interpretation, Communication of Results

**Topics:** Feedback, Reporting, Student Engagement and Motivation, Summative Assessment and Grading

# Isn't a grade the best way to celebrate achievement? How can I meaningfully celebrate achievement in the classroom?

Grades can be a good way to celebrate achievement. If educators determine grades solely on the quality of what learners produce, and if they represent the most accurate and current level of proficiency, then yes, higher grades can celebrate student achievement. But those are two big *ifs*.

First, over one hundred years of research has consistently shown that teacher-assigned grades mix academic and nonacademic factors (Bowers, 2019). This means that, despite the collective advancements in assessment literacy in the 21st century, teacher-assigned grades typically also include (directly or indirectly) aspects like attitude, effort, overall conduct, and growth. Add in the fact that teachers don't typically include all those factors to the same degree, and what results is inconsistent grades that are, at best, opaque. With opaque grades, one would have to wonder what exactly is being celebrated.

Second, even if the grades weren't inconsistent, how teachers determine grades would also be a factor. Consider that the traditional practice of grade determination often includes averaging old and new evidence (such that every 40 needs an 80 just to earn a 60). When done, the results rarely reflect a learner's true skill or understanding. To ensure that learners earn full credit for their learning, teachers would have to reengineer how they determine grades to ensure that student grades reflect what they know about student proficiency (Schimmer, 2016). This would include valuing more recent scores as stronger evidence of proficiency and not penalizing early learning errors.

Grades, when they are a true reflection of student learning, can be a source for celebration. However, there are better—or at least more detailed—ways to celebrate all that learners have accomplished. *Growth*, for example, can also be a meaningful source for celebration. Although some learners may not rate high on the achievement scale, they may have authentically made tremendous progress throughout the year. This growth needs to be celebrated too, as the discipline and work ethic required to persevere despite low achievement results are honorable characteristics. Other ways that grades can be celebrated include recognizing learners who make unique connections to other learning and learners who apply learning in new and unique ways, and focusing on the work itself rather than just an arbitrary score. For example, when students are invited to set personal goals that focus on interim steps in the learning process, they can celebrate their achievement of these goals often and in ways that are personally meaningful for each learner (White, 2022).

It's not that grades shouldn't be celebrated; they should. But pinning all the celebrations on a singular summary symbol (or several) loses sight of all that can be celebrated in terms of what learners have accomplished and, maybe more importantly, who they've become.

**Connected Tenets:** Communication of Results, Accurate Interpretation

**Topics:** Growth Mindset, Reporting, Summative Assessment and Grading

# Why can't we just grade or assess students on growth or personal bests?

Standards-based education was intended to ensure that all learners get access to and are held to high expectations. In the absence of these standards, bias and low expectations lead to achievement disparities and inequities in educational experiences and learning. Assessments and the communication of these results must be focused on learning and reflect what learners know and can do in relation to those standards. Any time educators start to deviate from this path, communication becomes inaccurate and ultimately unfair. When educators are sharing information about learners' learning, it should reflect that learning in relationship to the standards. Using the standard as the basis also eliminates the norm-referenced approach to grading—that there are only a certain number of learners who can achieve at the highest level and that the scale will be manipulated to make sure that the largest number of learners fall somewhere in the middle.

This does not mean that teachers cannot communicate information about growth or improvement in addition to how learners performed in relationship to the established standard; they certainly should. But educators don't have to view this decision as either/or. When teachers average multiple measures into a single grade, or when they include extra credit or behavior in that grade, the true level of the learner's learning is unclear. Including information about a learner's growth on a learning progression—for example, by providing feedback on each individual learning goal within the standard—helps learners know where they are in relationship to that standard. Information about personal learning growth should be part of the journey for the learners, but not the destination itself.

**Connected Tenets:** Accurate Interpretation, Assessment Purpose
**Topics:** Standards, Summative Assessment and Grading

## How can I assess students on grade-level material if they are not at grade level?

It is critical to start from a place of high expectations and to believe that all learners need to learn grade-level standards or competencies. "Students can rise no higher than the assignments and instruction they are given" (Dysarz, 2016), so it is essential that individuals and teams of educators review their instructional lessons, assignments, and assessments to ensure that the level of thinking aligns to grade-level requirements. This step is the foundation of high expectations and sets the stage for providing instruction using the most powerful, high-leverage learning strategies that learners need to thrive and ultimately learn at high levels.

Once educators establish the grade-level expectations, individuals and teams of teachers should create a learning progression. A progression asks, What are all of the knowledge and skills needed along the way to achieve the grade-level expectation? This process allows teachers to design summative assessment processes at the grade level and create formative assessment processes that capture learner needs along the way. Teachers can analyze student work to understand where learners need additional time and support to take their next step. In most cases, learners' misconceptions and next steps will emerge from completing a grade-level task. If they struggle to do so independently and need prompting, that is also an indicator of where learners need support. It is okay if they do not do well on the grade-level task; the formative information gathered lets the teacher know what kind of reteaching or feedback the learners need to take their next step forward.

There are moments when it can feel overwhelming to start at grade level and with a rigorous focus. Learners come with many different experiences and skill levels. It can be tempting to assess learners where they are, feeling they are not ready for grade-level assessment. In so many cases, learners who are far below grade level are never exposed to grade-level goals and end up being drilled on the basic or prerequisite skills.

If learners are to engage at high levels, they must see the end first to know what their destination is. Then, educators can provide the steps along the way to get them there. This means educators must believe in themselves and their colleagues, and they must leverage formative assessment to support their decision making during the learning process. Educators have the knowledge and skills to be able to guide learners to achieve high expectations. By engaging in a robust process of determining grade-level expectations, designing assessments that reveal student needs, and building in time to address these needs, every learner can reach grade-level learning.

**Connected Tenets:** Assessment Architecture, Instructional Agility

**Topics:** Differentiation, Formative Assessment, Summative Assessment and Grading

## When is it okay to move on to teaching new content?

While the goal is for every learner to master every essential standard, the reality is that some learners may not master that essential learning in the time provided. When teams of teachers create an assessment plan, it is part of their overall instructional plan. They embed time for learners to have multiple opportunities to share what they know. This plan identifies which assessments the team will analyze to determine the impact of a teacher's instructional decisions on learning and to make adjustments in instruction before the end of the unit or allotted time frame. If some learners do not master the essential learning in the time given, educators should still allow them to move forward with the curriculum and engage in the next important learning. The teacher and team monitor progress on those essential learnings and embed opportunities for learners to continue to revisit the most important learning. By clarifying the essential learning, the teachers can identify points in time to revisit that content based on its connection to new units of study. Learners can also be provided with additional opportunities to demonstrate proficiency on that previous unit. For example, in a mathematics class, chapter test scores could be replaced by unit test scores that are broken down by chapter learning goals, and later evidence could replace previous scores. This may require some additional support during the subsequent content, but teachers should not deny learners the opportunity to learn that new information. Often, learners may master the previous standards once they are exposed to new information and given extra time. Providing another opportunity for learners to demonstrate that mastery at a later date and using that updated assessment information will provide the most accurate picture of the learners' current levels of understanding.

A team of educators can have conversations about how best to support these learners and how to continue to provide supplemental instruction on previously taught standards. The priority should be ensuring learners' access to grade-level standards and preparing them to learn and get the support they need to learn through a recursive approach. When teachers intentionally plan opportunities for reteaching and reassessment prior to starting a new unit of instruction, those opportunities are more likely to be available for learners. These can be designated times for review or extension or simply reviewing previous content through formative assessments and in-class learning activities. It is certainly a challenge to keep learners moving forward when others are still struggling to master previous content, but to keep classrooms both rigorous and equitable, teachers must continue to provide learners with the opportunity to learn grade-level essential standards and to get the support they need to master them.

> **Connected Tenets:** Assessment Architecture, Instructional Agility
>
> **Topics:** Intervention and Instruction, Pacing Guides, Reassessment, Summative Assessment and Grading

## When does an assessment become "old"? How do I know when it is time to change things up?

The traditional cycle of teach—test—teach—test can quickly get old for learners and teachers alike, especially when testing is limited to a paper-and-pencil test that results in an evaluative score but does not allow for improvement over time. In addition, when the results of assessment processes do not reflect the skills and understanding of the learners, it may be time to explore new ways of gathering assessment information.

When designed well, assessment should never get old. Rapid changes in both technology and available information demand that educators remain fresh and current in assessment strategies, specifically when striving to engage learners in the way things are done in the world beyond the school walls.

When teachers are interested in gathering evidence of student readiness, their assessment questions, prompts, cues, and tasks will be authentic and timely. They should use the evidence they solicit from formal and informal activities in meaningful ways that support continued improvement over time. This evidence can include formative assessments, observations of students, conversations with students, student work, and countless other artifacts of learning.

When learners feel as if their efforts make a difference in their long-term results and their feedback is invaluable, the assessment experience becomes less of a focus and more of a natural process for learning and succeeding. This approach never gets old.

> **Connected Tenets:** Assessment Architecture, Assessment Purpose
>
> **Topics:** Formative Assessment

## Isn't part of my job to prepare students for life after school? How can assessment within a culture of learning do this?

The purpose of education is to provide learners with the skills and knowledge they need to be independent and productive citizens. The reality of what learners need to meet that goal varies from student to student. Frequently, people will say that providing learners with the opportunity to retake an assessment or to revise their work "doesn't prepare them for the real world." In truth, there are very few instances in life when a person cannot retake a test or try again to get better, whether it's a driver's license test or the medical board examination. In fact, doing these things is demonstrating the skill of learning how to learn and examine the situation or assessment information to determine how to move forward. In those situations, the learner must take responsibility to make that retake happen and to continue to study in order to be successful. However, educators must teach learners how to do that—and this must be part of the assessment design within a culture of learning.

To teach learners how to persist, consider some of the following strategies.

- Teach learners how to reflect on their experience that did not meet the expectations the first time (a test, a project, or so on) and then invite them to revise or try again after some new learning. The results should indicate that learners have truly mastered—or at least progressed toward—the knowledge and skills that teachers have identified as essential.

- Help learners understand that the learning is essential, and that learning to learn is what prepares them for life after high school. The real world

requires learning how to respond when we fail or don't do as well as
we want or need to do. When learners don't get things right, provide
the time and support to ensure they grow and revise their learning
(focusing on the essential standards, not on everything). Teach learners
to be responsible by providing them with the opportunities to practice
responsible actions like relearning and demonstrating mastery of
missing skills prior to a retake option.

These strategies ensure that learners learn the content as well as valuable lessons
regarding self-efficacy and responsibility—lessons they will need to know in life
beyond the classroom.

**Connected Tenets:** Assessment Purpose, Student Investment
**Topics:** Reassessment, Rigor and Cognitive Complexity

## How might I recognize assessment changes within a classroom setting? What might I see?

Productive changes in classroom assessment practices will result in more positive
experiences for teachers and learners—such as learners and teachers partnering effectively to master learning goals—because assessment decisions will power learning the
majority of the time. Learning and assessment will visibly connect to standards and
other learning goals. Done well, assessment processes support the development of
skills and knowledge that intentionally lead to proficiency. This march toward proficiency or mastery will be visible in lesson plans, in assessment tools, and in displays of
student work. Teachers and learners should experience the criteria for proficiency as
they are embedded into practice, self-reflection, and formative assessment processes.
An aligned, healthy assessment system will enable learners to approach summative
assessment experiences with confidence. With deliberate sequencing and scaffolded
support, learners will feel prepared, and this will be evidenced in their demeanor and
language, as shown through a variety of assessment tools (such as exit cards, anecdotal
records, rubrics, or checklists).

Teachers can use assessment experiences to make decisions and provide feedback,
such as to create flexible and varied lessons and groupings of students. Learners will
clearly understand the purpose of their grouping and what learning goals are trying to
achieve. They will have clear direction and strong investment. Their language will be
positive and their choices purposeful, and they will demonstrate increased independence. They will be in charge of their own learning, with the teacher acting as a partner.

If learners don't experience learning differently as a result of shifting assessment practices, then more shifts are necessary to make the entire assessment system work appropriately. In the end, best practice changes in assessment practices and belief systems can only lead to profound and meaningful learning for students.

> **Connected Tenets:** Assessment Architecture, Assessment Purpose
>
> **Topics:** Formative Assessment, Student Engagement and Motivation, Summative Assessment and Grading

# A Culture of Learning in Interventions, Collaborative Teams, and Leadership

## What is the connection between assessment and response to intervention (RTI)?

Assessment is what drives a response to intervention (RTI) continuum. The fundamental idea behind RTI is that the *intensity of any intervention must match the intensity of the presenting challenge.* The identification of the necessary interventions at the appropriate intensity level hinges on accurate assessment information to guide decision making. RTI is about correctly identifying learners who need intervention and for which specific needs, designing and then delivering interventions efficiently and effectively, monitoring the success of the interventions, and making the required data-based adjustments, should they be necessary. It is also important to know that an effective intervention system must be built on a strong core instruction (Buffum, Mattos, & Malone, 2018). At Tier 1, sound assessment and grading practices are part of a universal approach to instruction that creates an environment where the greatest number of learners can be successful. Without the most promising practices at Tier 1, teachers and schools may be left with an inflated number of learners needing secondary intervention. Through ongoing instruction, assessment, and differentiation— as well as periodic and intentional monitoring—teachers and schools can ensure they are maximizing success for the greatest number of learners.

Learners who, despite all best efforts, emerge as having additional need for support beyond Tier 1 core instruction will require secondary supports, usually in the form of targeted, group-based intervention. Beyond just second opportunities within the typical learning cycle, Tier 2 interventions focus on the specific, targeted needs of the learners, and sound assessment practices reveal these needs. These interventions are often group based since it is quite likely that several learners have the same learning needs, making the group-based approach to Tier 2 more efficient for both learners and teachers. Not only does assessment reveal which learners are in need of Tier 2 interventions, but the increased frequency of monitoring within Tier 2 needs to produce accurate and reliable information to ensure teachers are implementing evidence-based practices with fidelity and that these practices are producing the desired results.

Learners who again reveal a need for support beyond Tier 2 interventions (as indicated by assessment results) will require Tier 3 interventions, personalized to each learner. At this tier, the frequency of intervention will need to increase—Tier 2 interventions often occur two to three times per week, and Tier 3 interventions most often occur daily (Buffum et al., 2018). While Tier 3 supports *can* be group based if more than one learner emerges with the same needs, these groups are kept smaller to ensure an increasingly personalized approach. The learners who demonstrate needs beyond that which Tiers 1 and 2 can provide require specific, detailed assessment (such as Functional Academic Assessment) to determine the most effective and efficient strategies for addressing their significant needs.

Again, *the intensity of any intervention must match the intensity of the presenting challenge*. If it does not, the intervention is doomed to fail. Sound assessment practices are what provide teachers and schools with specific information about how *intense* the interventions must be and which specific needs they must address. Assessment is the engine that drives an effective and efficient RTI continuum.

> **Connected Tenets:** Instructional Agility, Accurate Interpretation
>
> **Topics:** Feedback, Intervention and Instruction, Response to Intervention

## What can I do to ensure a culture of learning within my collaborative team?

The collaborative work teams engage in within a school- or districtwide professional learning community (PLC) is some of the most challenging work that educators will ever do. Like most challenges, successful collaboration requires shared commitment and preparation as well as monitoring and feedback. Far too often, educators believe that time is the only obstacle to collaboration, and that once systems create the shared time, collaboration will naturally follow. Educators are used to working with people all day long but are not necessarily used to collaborating with others in a way that is focused on learning and results. To realize the power and potential of effective collaboration, teams must take some formal steps.

One of the first steps that a collaborative team should take is to *establish norms*, which formally describe the work that the team will do and how it will do it (DuFour, DuFour, Eaker, Many, & Mattos, 2016). Basic norms such as arriving on time and participating are important, but teams should also have conversations about the more difficult aspects of collaboration, such as managing conflict, building on each other's strengths, and sharing information freely with each other. Cassandra Erkens and Eric Twadell (2012) describe four important aspects of norm development: (1) creating consistency around nebulous terms such as *respect*, (2) making sure that all members of the team agree to the norms, (3) discussing how the team will hold each other accountable to the norms, and (4) deciding how the team will proceed when one member does not agree with the rest of the team.

Another challenge that can often stall the work of a collaborative team is a lack of clarity about the kind of work in which the team will engage. Teams should constantly review their purpose and what they are trying to accomplish. For example, the purpose for teams examining assessment results (student work from common assessments and data by student and by target) is to understand the effectiveness of the instructional strategies the teams employed, to determine the learning needs of individual and groups of learners, and to plan instruction to ensure learners achieve the essential standards. Assessment data review is not about evaluation to determine who is a better teacher. When challenges and difficulties arise, these *discussions about purpose* can help the team get back on track. *Leading by Design* (Erkens & Twadell, 2012) reminds us that productive teams move beyond written norms to the deep conversations that impact student learning (see page 34).

Finally, a team of educators working collaboratively should continue to monitor the effectiveness of that collaboration and attend to emerging needs over time (DuFour et al., 2016). The creation of norms and purpose statements are often activities that take place when collaborative teams initially form. The reality is that teams should nurture and attend to their collaboration as though it were a delicate orchid. As conditions or team members change, the team should revisit those founding documents and not be afraid to make the changes necessary for continued success. Teams can use these documents throughout the years that teams work together, and they can be powerful tools for helping new members understand the purpose and the work of the team.

**Connected Tenets:** Assessment Purpose, Instructional Agility
**Topics:** Collaboration, Professional Learning Communities

## What role do leaders play in assessment reform?

Leaders have to know what they're talking about. To engage in *instructional leadership* is to be a leader of change, and it requires a level of competence to effectively and authentically engage in the conversation about what's changing. Leaders need not be the experts in the building, and over time, as teachers implement new practices, they certainly won't be, but there needs to be enough depth and breadth of understanding for leaders to be able to meaningfully contribute to the change efforts. Leaders will often be the first to identify needs within their schools and systems and should also be a primary source of celebration when desired results occur. In this context, being assessment literate is non-negotiable.

As well, leaders are the gatekeepers of the essential structures and supports that teachers depend on to be able to collaborate, ensuring there is internal alignment that supports assessment reform. Those opportunities can often have monetary implications, which means leaders will signal priorities through budget allocation—if assessment reform is a priority, then leaders will allocate time and money in service of that change.

Finally, leaders can advocate for the assessment reform efforts. Almost without exception, when assessment and grading systems change, questions from parents, learners, the community, and even others within the system (such as district staff or other schools) will arise. Sometimes these questions are about clarification, but sometimes the questions are criticism clothed as inquiries. As pushback happens, however small or large, leaders can stand in sponsorship of the reform efforts and clear a path for teachers exploring more accurate and meaningful ways to maximize the use of assessment in service of learning.

Obviously, context and position will matter significantly in terms of what obstacles leaders must clear, but by being assessment literate, creating internal opportunities to expand assessment reform, and providing external sponsorship of the new ideas, leaders will play a monumental role in ensuring assessment reform efforts are successful.

> **Connected Tenets:** Assessment Purpose, Communication of Results
>
> **Topics:** Collaboration, Leadership, Professional Learning Communities

# Creating a Culture of Learning in a Remote Learning Context

A context in which teachers are not seeing learners face to face for the entire school day adds its own challenges, to be sure. However, teachers can achieve a learning-rich culture when they are intentional with their language around expectations for learners, when their assessment systems align with essential learning goals, when they share and even co-construct success criteria with learners, and when the focus of all planning and instruction remains firmly on targeted growth and support.

To ensure that remote learning truly focuses on *learning* and not just *doing*, teachers might consider the following.

- Determining a few targeted essential learning goals and communicating these goals with learners and families in connection to both learning experiences and assessment processes

- Co-constructing success criteria (descriptions of quality) with learners, using exemplars and student-accessible language

- Exercising care with language—avoiding compliance and completion language and, instead, framing each task and experience with the intended learning (skill and understanding); for example, instead of using the phrase "Today, we will be doing _____," shift to "Today, we will be learning _____."

- Providing ample opportunity for learners to take risks, make decisions, and recover from mistakes; when the focus remains on high levels of achievement for every learner, it is hard to deny that the culture is about rich learning.

While there may be many factors over which teachers feel they have little control in a remote learning context (equity, access, accuracy, and so on), they do have control over the culture they develop and nurture.

# CHAPTER 3

# ASSESSMENT PURPOSE

Assessment can serve multiple purposes. It can be the process that provides insight into student thinking and skill development so targeted instruction and support can advance achievement (formative assessment). It can be a springboard into self-reflection and goal setting for learners (formative self-assessment). It can offer insight into the development of independence, confidence, and decision making (formative assessment). It can allow teachers to make professional judgments and verify degrees of skill and understanding (summative assessment). It can be used to form generalizations about achievement in targeted areas for the purposes of reporting and systemic decision making (summative assessment).

Moreover, the purposes for an individual assessment can morph over time, allowing formative information to become summative and vice versa. The malleable yet tight alliance between assessment purposes requires the interplay between formative and summative assessment activities to be interdependent to maximize learning and verify achievement.

Clarity about the purpose assessment will serve is critical to ensuring it lives up to its potential. As part of a strong assessment system, teachers, learners, families, and stakeholders must be clear about the purpose of each assessment process and use each assessment in ways that reflect its intended purpose. This alignment between purpose and use is indicative of a strong assessment system that sustains hope, efficacy, and achievement for learners.

# The Purpose of Assessment

## What do we mean by *assessment purpose*?

The purpose of an assessment relates to how teachers *use* the results of an assessment. The purpose is not determined by how large or small the assessment is, whether or not scores are recorded in a gradebook, or when the assessment occurs. Typically, every assessment reveals aspects of student strengths and areas that need strengthening, but how teachers *act on* that information defines (even in retrospect) the purpose of that assessment.

Prior to any assessment, the fundamental question a teacher should ask is *why*— *why* do I want the information that an assessment will elicit? The answer to that one question will reveal the intended purpose, which in turn, provides clarity on how to act following an assessment.

If the teacher determines that the reason for an assessment is to identify specific strengths and needs and to provide learners with specific feedback on how they can advance their proficiency, then the purpose for the assessment is *formative*. However, if the teacher determines that the reason for the assessment is to verify that learning has occurred and communicate that to the students and other stakeholders, then the primary purpose for the assessment is *summative*.

> **Connected Tenets:** Accurate Interpretation, Instructional Agility
> **Topics:** Feedback, Formative Assessment, Summative Assessment and Grading

## Why is it important to clarify purpose ahead of design?

Assessment informs action, so knowing the purpose of the assessment clarifies which subsequent action teachers will take when results are revealed. Clarifying the purpose ahead of design allows teachers to know how granular or holistic in focus an assessment should be, based on what information they need to gather and what decisions might follow.

What's required with the *formative* purpose is great specificity, so teachers are likely to design assessments that seek specific information related to learning targets, aspects of strength, and areas that need strengthening. Assessment items seek to isolate knowledge, skills, and understandings in order to provide teachers with *why students might be experiencing challenge* and *what's next* for the learner. While the formative purpose can certainly apply to the standard (outcome, competency) level, more often it is focused on the curricular underpinnings that support students along their learning trajectories toward meeting the standards.

What's needed with the *summative* purpose is synthesis and cognitive complexity, so it is paramount that teachers design assessment items that ask learners to pull together all of the individual underpinnings at a level of sophistication in keeping with what the standards articulate. While unpacking standards is a common approach to the formative purpose, less common is the practice of repacking standards for the summative one. Summative assessment is not just the sum of the formative parts in isolation; rather, it is the holistic demonstration of all of the isolated skills and understandings through application and synthesis.

> **Connected Tenets:** Assessment Architecture, Instructional Agility
>
> **Topics:** Feedback, Formative Assessment, Summative Assessment and Grading

## Why do we assess students, and what can we learn from them?

Teachers assess learners to gather evidence that will support decision making with regard to both instructional responses and building student investment (formative assessment), and to verify degrees of proficiency on standards (summative assessment). It is important to be clear about the purposes assessment can hold so teachers can frame assessment experiences clearly for both themselves and their learners. Some questions teachers might ask themselves about an assessment are as follows.

- In which areas of this assessment evidence do learners show strength?
- What areas of this assessment evidence indicate student needs? What are those specific needs?
- What is the root cause of challenges learners are experiencing? Why did they make the decisions they did?
- What degree of skill and understanding are learners demonstrating?
- What does this assessment evidence reveal about engagement? Motivation? Independence? Student interests? Student confidence?
- How might the information gathered be used (by teachers and learners) to adjust upcoming learning experiences? Do learners need feedback? Practice? Additional instruction?
- How might learners extend their thinking and skill? How might they engage more deeply in the learning goals when they are proficient early or when they indicate a desire?

- How is behavior impacting academic achievement and vice versa? How is it impacting confidence and engagement?

- When it comes to reporting, what does the evidence indicate? What is it revealing about most recent and most consistent strengths and needs? How might assessment evidence support valid and reliable professional judgments?

It is important to remember that, ultimately, assessment offers clarity about where student skill and understanding are in relation to articulated goals at a particular moment. When educators gather and analyze assessment information, it can serve as the basis of all decision making. Assessment that works this way is a natural part of daily routines. Clarifying the purpose of assessment allows teachers to efficiently and effectively utilize assessment results.

**Connected Tenets:** Communication of Results, Student Investment

**Topics:** Formative Assessment, Summative Assessment and Grading

## How can I make sure my assessments aren't just another grade in the gradebook?

If teachers want assessment to propel learning forward, and if they want their gradebooks to reflect the most current state of learning for learners, then the decisions teachers make and the actions they take in relation to the assessment information they gather will need to reflect this end. Assessment becomes just another grade in the gradebook if educators do nothing with the information they gather. If they assess and then simply enter a score, assessment becomes about entering that grade and nothing more.

However, when teachers assess and then group learners the next day to meet their specific needs, they have transformed assessment. When educators invite learners to reflect and set goals after an assessment experience, assessment processes reflect a purpose that shifts from summative scores to formative responses. When teachers use gradebooks as just a small part of a larger conversation with families, the grades act as catalysts for deeper, richer conversation. In the end, teachers decide what assessment will mean to them, to their students, and to their students' families. Teacher actions will communicate intent.

**Connected Tenets:** Communication of Results, Student Investment

**Topics:** Formative Assessment, Reporting, Summative Assessment and Grading

# Isn't the focus on assessment literacy just another educational fad?

Absolutely not. For as long as there will be teachers, students, and required learning expectations, there will be assessment. Developing a strong understanding and competence with all aspects of assessment is foundational to teaching effectiveness. The work of assessment requires accurate, thoughtful instructional inputs that ultimately culminate in invaluable outputs to facilitate continued, deep learning. Because assessment is never perfect, there will *always* be the need to study and refine the educator's craft, knowledge, and skill.

Assessment sits at the *center* of anything to do with the learning process. It's tied to curriculum decisions, instructional maneuvers, standards requirements, grading and reporting, differentiation, systems of intervention, and so on. Given that, it is imperative that educators are always highly skilled and informed about assessment literacy.

**Connected Tenets:** Assessment Architecture

**Topics:** Leadership, Standards

# What is a balanced assessment system?

A balanced assessment system occurs when the classroom experiences of students reflect assessment used for both formative and summative purposes. When an assessment system is balanced, it means there is enough formative assessment, feedback, reengagement, and recovery to ensure optimal learning so that when summative assessment, or verification, occurs, students are well prepared and have learned the most important skills and developed the appropriate understanding to ensure successful summative results.

The notion of a balanced assessment system can be extended to a district level. In this case, a system collects a broad range of assessment evidence to make strategic decisions that support optimal learning for each and every student in the system's care. This evidence may include any standardized assessment that could be used for decision making. However, a balanced assessment system at the district level also reflects an acknowledgement that assessment designed by teachers will have the greatest impact on student learning. In a balanced system, teachers engage in daily formative assessment, common formative assessment, and summative assessment of their own design to advance learning.

**Connected Tenets:** Communication of Results, Culture of Learning

**Topics:** Formative Assessment, Summative Assessment and Grading

## As an administrator, how do I help my teachers understand the different purposes of assessment?

Aside from the array of professional learning opportunities that could be engineered through book studies, workshops, conferences, and so on, administrators can ensure that there are no policies or common practices—written or unwritten—that inhibit a teacher's opportunity to create a balanced assessment system in their classroom. For example, policies that require teachers to enter a minimal number of grades per week may inadvertently create a distraction from what truly matters. As well-intentioned as these types of policies might be for keeping parents updated via an online gradebook, the artificial nature of the number (such as two grades per week, per class) may result in teachers creating summative moments not because it's the optimal time to verify learning, but because they have to update their gradebooks. This is an insufficient reason to summatively assess. That said, it would be equally inappropriate for updates to be sparse and irregular. That's why balance is the key.

Maintaining the collective focus on *learning* instead of *compliance* is how administrators show teachers that while the grading might be a necessary part of assessment systems, grading shouldn't drive or dominate the culture of learning. Inviting teachers to work together to clarify flexible ways to verify learning when the time is right (summative purpose) can support equity and clarity for teachers and learners. Working together to create assessment systems that utilize assessment primarily as an instructional exercise (formative purpose) will tamp down the anxiety that can emerge with restrictive policies. Creating opportunities for teachers to collaborate on ways their assessment practices can result in instructional action can focus attention on the next steps in learning instead of the next update of a gradebook.

> **Connected Tenets:** Assessment Architecture, Communication of Results
> **Topics:** Leadership, Reporting, Summative Assessment and Grading

## How do I help stakeholders understand the different purposes of assessment?

It's not important that stakeholders—especially learners—understand the technical language of the teaching craft (formative versus summative assessments). However, it *is* important that they understand assessment as a journey, allowing for student improvement to happen over time. The good news is anyone who has watched someone learn to walk or read or count, or who has themselves learned to drive, honed a skill, or perfected a hobby, intuitively understands that growth naturally happens over time and the timing is different from person to person.

The first challenge educators face is helping learners and parents alike understand how they are monitoring for and allowing learners to improve over time and ultimately, achieve a degree of mastery. The second challenge involves how educators share the information in a visible format so all stakeholders can watch the trajectory of growth and intervene appropriately when growth flatlines at a less than proficient level or takes a downward spiral.

To answer the first challenge of engaging learners in using assessments to improve their own results, three things must be in place: (1) engaging and purposeful assessments; (2) targeted, responsive assignments; and (3) diagnostic feedback (not scores).

1.  Educators create student investment when assessments are engaging (interesting, focused, and able to be completed in a timely fashion).

2.  Educators create student agency when learners are allowed to use their own data to make decisions about what they need next in the learning.

3.  Educators generate commitment to mastery when they employ diagnostic feedback that advances the learning for the learners and positions them for ultimate success. So, *if* scores are provided, learners need to know that they can grow past the initial proficiency levels over the course of many assessments. Powerful diagnostic feedback (insightful, pointed, and supportive) should leave learners motivated to continue trying.

The second challenge of sharing the information in a visible and timely format that allows for a visible trajectory of growth also requires three things.

1.  A grading policy that allows for mastery using the particular mode in the later samples of work

2.  Grading software that empowers the teacher to use the more robust professional discretion than standard number-crunching algorithms to make final grade decisions

3.  Grading software or a web-based communication system that transforms data into visible tools to show trajectories

It's far more important that the results learners get from each assessment point to what comes next in the learning journey. When teachers use feedback and proficiency levels that focus learners and parents on the learning expectations and clear next steps, then stakeholders are less likely to care about the purposes of the assessments.

**Connected Tenets:** Culture of Learning

**Topics:** Feedback, Homework, Summative Assessment and Grading

# The Purpose of Preassessments

## Does every teacher have to preassess? Is it required to support learning?

Preassessment has the potential to support learning, but it is not required all the time. Most commonly, educators will employ a preassessment to measure both prerequisite knowledge (conceptual understanding) and skills that should be in place or to gather a baseline of what needs are to be developed in a unit of study.

Teachers can design a preassessment in any number of ways, and preassessments can serve many purposes and vary in structure, intent, and use from one discipline to the next. Perhaps science teachers want to know what learners know about an atom, or maybe they are more interested in how strong learners are at developing an argument. In this case, approaching the preassessment process from a learning stance will help to ensure it serves learners and teachers in both the short and long term. A mathematics preassessment could identify student readiness by checking for prerequisite skills. In language arts, however, the summative results from the last submitted essay may provide teachers with a clear indication of where to go next in their instruction, so no formal preassessment would be needed. In social studies, where concepts are brand new and prerequisite skills are less delineated, educators could employ a preassessment to pique curiousity and identify naïve theories or common misconceptions before launching instruction. What information is needed and how the information will be used should dictate whether or not educators need to use a preassessment.

> **Connected Tenets:** Assessment Architecture, Student Investment
> **Topics:** Preassessment, Student Engagement and Motivation

## Why would I preassess when students haven't been taught the material? What could it tell me?

Far too often, preassessment is seen simply as a first step in demonstrating growth. One would anticipate that student learning should improve following instruction. Instead the emphasis for preassessment should be on generating information to improve the effectiveness of teaching and learning and to focus on the learning needs of learners. Preassessment can and should take different forms based on the standards, the learners, and the learning targets.

Preassessment can provide valuable insights for teachers as they plan and refine their instruction. Teachers and collaborative teams should spend time unpacking standards and content to create clarity around the expectations. This helps to identify the prerequisite knowledge and skills that learners need to master the new materials. A preassessment incorporating the previously taught content or standards provides teachers with important information to guide and maximize the effectiveness of instruction.

If the standards address something like a comprehension skill (main idea or inference) that has been taught in previous years, courses, or even units, but will involve a more complex text in this course, the preassessment might address the skill using a simple text. This will help teachers know and understand the level of proficiency of learners and how much background knowledge they are bringing to the new lessons.

Preassessment can take many different forms. It might be a quiz at the beginning of the unit, or it might emerge from a brainstorming session in small groups. Teachers may even ask a question related to the prerequisite knowledge of the next unit during an exit ticket in the current unit. Exit tickets that include previous content can provide learners with an opportunity to review what they've learned and also make connections between standards.

Preassessment may also be part of the instruction itself. Teachers can incorporate purposefully planned discussion questions into their daily lessons to get a better idea of the level of knowledge learners are bringing to the new content.

> **Connected Tenets:** Assessment Architecture, Instructional Agility
> **Topics:** Preassessment, Summative Assessment and Grading

## How do I use a preassessment?

The *pre-* in preassessment indicates when teachers might give this kind of assessment and what they might do with the results. Preassessment should occur prior to significant instruction in a particular goal area, with the purpose being to ready teachers and learners in anticipating instructional needs.

Preassessment has, in some cases, morphed into an assessment given before instruction as a comparator to an assessment given at the end of instruction, presumably to show growth. However, this use serves adults more than learners. Certainly, systems hope to track growth throughout a learning cycle, but the most authentic and applicable purpose of a preassessment is to predict student strengths and needs so that responsive instruction can be designed as early as possible.

Teachers may use a preassessment to intentionally group learners to meet very specific learning needs. Learners themselves may use a preassessment to track their own progress in relation to learning targets over the course of a unit. A preassessment can identify the presence or absence of precursor skills learners will need to explore a topic deeply. In this case, teachers may use the preassessment to plan interventions that will close gaps in readiness for specific learners. They can also use preassessment to identify strengths and to position learners as supports for each other as learning develops.

The important thing to remember about preassessment, as with any formative assessment process, is that it is only as useful as the actions teachers take in response to the information they gather. If the results do not serve future learning, the process of preassessment is vastly limited. Reciprocally, when educators use the results of preassessment to engage learners in assessment conversations, to inform instructional design, to flexibly group learners in ways that power learning, and to celebrate strengths learners already possess, they are harnessing the power of preassessment in learning-rich ways.

> **Connected Tenets:** Assessment Architecture, Communication of Results, Student Investment
>
> **Topics:** Preassessment, Student Engagement and Motivation

# The Purpose of Standards

## Why do we choose essential standards? Aren't we supposed to teach all standards?

It is appropriate to choose essential standards. However, it is also important to understand what this choice does and does not mean. Essential standards are not the only standards that are taught, but they are the standards teachers guarantee will be learned. Essential standards are really a determination of how teachers will distribute their instructional minutes.

Teachers can't teach and ensure students learn it all. When standards are covered, there is often a lack of deep understanding and skill with some students; it is easy to fall back on the sentiment, "I taught it, but they just didn't learn it." In a culture of learning, educators position essential standards as guaranteed learning, meaning those standards will receive a disproportionate amount of attention until all learners reach proficiency. This comes at the expense of the time allotted for the other standards. Collaborative teams identify essential standards that spiral into future units and future grade levels, that are critical skills that cross content areas, and that last beyond any single unit or test. If a large-scale assessment exists, it is also helpful to understand which standards are heavily assessed. Teachers do not ignore the standards that are not essential; they are simply prioritizing what they are going to ensure all students learn.

The guarantee that all students will learn the essential standards has important implications when it comes to teaching and learning. These essential standards are where collaborative teams will provide the most feedback, targeted instruction, and intervention. Essential standards (and even the most targeted within the essentials) will be the focus of common formative assessments and the most heavily assessed on a common summative assessment.

Educators should intentionally sequence all essential standards across all units. Teacher teams work relentlessly to provide learners feedback and intervention on these essentials, letting those standards that are not as important be taught and integrated, but not necessarily emphasized. This helps students learn and develop confidence because their teachers are focused on the most important—or essential—learning.

There are simply too many standards to guarantee that all learners will reach mastery on every single one, and the standards are much less a checklist and more of a holistic learning experience. So, while all standards are placed within units, teacher teams choose essential standards and commit to providing more feedback and assessing these more thoroughly. Essential standards provide a focus such that when learners are demonstrating specific needs in relation to these essentials, they get additional time and support. Teacher teams also spend collaborative time developing innovative lessons to ensure every student learns the most essential standards.

**Connected Tenets:** Assessment Architecture, Instructional Agility

**Topics:** Common Assessment, Essential Standards, Formative Assessment, Intervention and Instruction, Response to Intervention, Rigor and Cognitive Complexity, Summative Assessment and Grading

# Is the goal to get all students to proficiency or beyond proficiency?

The answer to this question depends on whether the question is an assessment and learning question or a grading question. First, if educators are thinking about learners and a desire to invite them into the kinds of learning experiences that engage them in as much deep thinking and extended learning as possible, then the answer is *beyond proficiency* when the time and means are available. Certainly, stopping learning in its tracks simply because a learner has demonstrated proficiency adheres to learning plans that resemble a march through each learning goal as through it is an isolated entity. Expanding and extending learning is good for everyone.

The answer is a little more nuanced if this question is connected to grading and reporting decisions. While teachers want student learning to be expansive, a learner's chance of receiving a high grade cannot be tied to moving beyond proficiency. A grade-level proficient understanding and demonstration of skill should be enough to ensure a grade that opens the door to all future possibilities (admission into post-secondary education, scholarships, and so on). Once a learner has demonstrated proficiency, goal-focused learning can continue, but this proficient demonstration should result in a high grade.

> **Connected Tenets:** Communication of Results, Student Investment
>
> **Topics:** Enrichment and Extension, Student Engagement and Motivation, Summative Assessment and Grading

## Is there a correct way to unpack standards?

The purpose of unpacking standards is to create a deeper understanding of what is expected of learners in order to plan both assessment and instruction. The process of collaboratively unpacking standards facilitates valuable professional conversation that establishes common expectations for learners. There is no one way to unpack standards because standards are written in different formats for different content areas in different locations. The essential components of the process are to determine the complexity of learning students are expected to master (often indicated by the verbs) and the common, shared definitions of the important terms within the standard. These descriptions of standards provide a road map to achieving the standard and to the student work and assessment that will lead to a common understanding and achievement of the standard. Once a team has had these important conversations, the next steps of planning instruction and assessment are far more productive because of shared understanding of the learning.

> **Connected Tenets:** Accurate Interpretation, Assessment Architecture
>
> **Topics:** Intervention and Instruction, Professional Learning Communities, Unpacking and Learning Progressions

# Formative and Summative Assessments

## Are there different kinds of formative assessment? It seems like some are short and some are complex. Is this accurate?

Formative assessment can happen in a wide variety of ways, and it can vary in length and complexity. What never varies is the need to take action as a result of what is learned from formative assessment.

When formative assessment occurs closer to the introduction of new concepts and skills, it may include less complex questions. This kind of formative assessment process is intended to quickly and efficiently catch gaps in knowledge or skill, important for readying learners to take on more complex thinking as the goals deepen in complexity. Perhaps an early formative assessment might include vocabulary terms, a review of previously learned concepts, or foundational skills. This kind of formative is akin to *drills*, which focus on smaller targets performed in practice sessions before an actual game is played. These drills allow coaches to respond to player needs early, before counterproductive habits are formed. Feedback emerges from this kind of formative assessment, followed by regular practice. These short formative assessment processes allow for quick correction and reinforcement.

When formative assessment occurs closer to the end of the exploration of learning goals, it may become more complex and ask more from the learner. At this stage, learners are likely combining several targets within more complex tasks. They are moving toward the complexity of learning goals, rather than focusing solely on one target at a time. They may even combine skills and understanding across several goals. This kind of formative is like a *scrimmage* or practice game. It looks a great deal like a game, and it combines skills and understanding into complex maneuvers, but there is still time to respond to instructional needs and offer feedback as skills are revealed during play. This more complex formative assessment is important because it tells teachers and learners how well learners are able to engage in the deeper thinking and skill application the learning goals require. It captures the combination of individual targets into contexts where application and decision making are needed.

Both of these types of formative assessment are essential for preparing learners for the summative assessment, or the big game or recital. During summative assessment, independence and consistent proficiency are required, and learners are asked to apply their understanding and skill on their own. This doesn't mean there is never any coaching, but this support does not happen during play.

**Connected Tenets:** Assessment Architecture
**Topics:** Formative Assessment, Unpacking and Learning Progressions

# If the results of a summative assessment should not be a surprise, then why do I need them?

The results of a summative assessment will not be a surprise if both teachers and learners, throughout the formative process, develop a clear indication of how student proficiency is advancing. In the most optimal circumstances, success is not a surprise because learners have been effectively preparing for their summative demonstration through the use of formative assessment and effective response and support. That said, assessment is about evidence, which means learners must demonstrate proficiency on the learning goals in their complexity. It's not about guessing based on past performance or practice—a great week of practice does not automatically give one team a victory prior to playing the game. The lack of surprise should not be conflated with the importance of summative assessment.

When assessment is focused on the granular underpinnings or targets within learning goals, assessment should be exclusively formative since the assessment tasks are most often set at a cognitive complexity that is *less than* the standards themselves. Any *proficiency* determined from the resulting formative information would likely not encompass the totality of the standard.

At the standard level, the formative-summative distinction is unnecessary. While teachers might still have a predetermined purpose (for example, "Today we will be engaging in summative assessment"), it is quite possible for teachers to simply assess their learners on the standard and then make the formative-summative distinction after the fact. For those learners who demonstrate proficiency, the resulting information is used summatively to verify that proficient learning occurred. For those learners who are not yet proficient, the information is used formatively to guide the next steps to reach proficiency.

> **Connected Tenets:** Accurate Interpretation, Assessment Architecture
> **Topics:** Rigor and Cognitive Complexity, Unpacking and Learning Progressions

## Is it fair to only include summative assessments in a gradebook when I know some students freeze or perform poorly at the summative level?

In truth, if formative assessments are used to ensure learner readiness, confidence, and competence, and if summative assessments are comprised of the exciting performances that serve as a public celebration of learning, then freezing or performing poorly on a summative assessment shouldn't happen. Students fear summative assessments when they are mysterious (for example, when learners are surprised by the content), high stakes (when learners cannot continue the learning and replace old data with new data as learning progresses), and memorization-dependent (when learners must regurgitate specific details or perfect procedures on demand). In these kinds of summative assessments, learners are being judged as knowledge consumers rather than inspired as knowledge producers.

If a learner experiences anxiety before an exam that reduces the validity of evidence an educator collects, it is appropriate to wonder if there might be a better way to collect evidence. The good news is that evidence can be collected in any number of ways—projects, performances, oral presentations, demonstrations, labs; the list goes on and on. As long as the teacher honors the rigor of the learning goals and effectively elicits the skills and understanding they require, the assessment is valid. Therefore, if teachers need to make an adjustment in how they collect summative evidence, they can. At the end of the day, their grading decisions are firmly grounded in strong professional judgment—of both their subject areas and their learners. Teachers don't just calculate degrees of proficiency; they *determine* them. Educators can offer learners choice and voice in the assessment practices and work with them to get the best and most accurate evidence possible.

In gradebooks where summative evidence is the only evidence a teacher uses in making a determination about grades, it is fair to question how an educator may ensure that the grades that emerge from this collection of evidence accurately reflect a learner's skill and knowledge in relation to learning goals. If gradebooks are set up by standards or skills, and if older summative data are allowed to decay so newer data replace older evidence, then learners have multiple summative data points that can lead to their ultimate success.

> **Connected Tenets:** Communication of Results, Student Investment
> **Topics:** Professional Judgment, Summative Assessment and Grading

# Behavior and Critical Competencies

## Why is it important to keep academics and behavior separate? Aren't they related?

Academics and behavior are certainly connected. Research shows that there are student behaviors (like attitude, engagement, and motivation) that contribute to student learning (Hattie, 2009). Because these specific behaviors can contribute to student learning, educators should attempt to both understand them and measure them effectively. When educators combine these behaviors with the academic goals they seek to measure, they create a picture that is much less clear. All stakeholders will have difficulty separating the two—they will not be able to get a clear idea of either what learners know and are able to do or the behaviors that contribute to learning.

Imagine, for example, that a learner's final grade in a mathematics class is determined by a combination of daily homework or practice and his or her performance on summative tests (probably not a big stretch to imagine for many educators). Now imagine that a learner makes a decision to not turn in homework each day (whether he or she completes the practice problems or not) because the teacher does not provide any specific feedback on it other than a check mark at the top. As a result, that section of his or her grade is now very low. The learner then performs at or above the standard on all of the summative assessments. The teacher, who believes that the daily homework is important both for the practice it provides and to teach learners to be responsible, decides that the student's grade should include both the zeros for missing homework and the proficient and advanced scores for the summative assessments. The student's final grade for the class is lower than any of the summative assessment scores. Later, when asked at a parent-teacher conference about the grade, the teacher responds that the student was irresponsible and the grade reflects that. The parent presses and asks how that would be obvious to someone who did not know the teacher's grading practices, as such a person may assume that the learner does not understand the mathematics concepts in the class. The teacher is left with a valid and difficult question.

There are a couple of important points to consider in this example. First, the learner did not demonstrate high degrees of responsibility by not turning in required work. Responsibility, attitude, and motivation are important skills for students to learn and master. However, when those behaviors are combined with measures of mathematics skill in a mathematics grade, the feedback the teacher provided to the learner about both behavioral decisions and mathematics skills are unclear. The assertion is not that behaviors and skills like collaboration and communication are not important; quite the opposite. These skills are so important and so relevant for learners that they deserve to be featured separately rather than included in an academic grade.

**Connected Tenets:** Accurate Interpretation
**Topics:** Behavior, Reporting, Summative Assessment and Grading

# I have heard that we should separate behavior from academics, but what if my standards are about behavior?

First, there is a difference between a behavior and a skill. The kind of behavior that is best kept separate from academic score is classroom behavior—the behavior that guides learners to make strong learning and self-regulation decisions during class time. Certainly, many academic standards require learners to take action (engaging in strategic play, performing a play, constructing an item), but these are skills, different from classroom behavior.

Perhaps one way to differentiate between behavior and skills is considering when a teacher might send a learner from the classroom—for example, to the principal's office for a decision they made. This would indicate a behavior. An educator would never send a learner to the office for continuing to play after the whistle was blown. They would simply correct the behavior through instruction—in other words, they would teach the student the skill. However, if a learner persistently threw a ball at another student's head, teachers might consider this a behavior issue beyond the scope of academic learning.

Teachers should ensure that a learner is not penalized for poor behavioral decisions within their academic grades. Things like poor attendance, difficulty during transitions, and the inability to bring or organize materials should be addressed and shared with families when necessary, but these behavioral struggles should not impact the assessment of academic goals.

> **Connected Tenets:** Accurate Interpretation
>
> **Topics:** Behavior, Summative Assessment and Grading

## How is assessing behavior different from assessing academics?

Assessing anything requires clarity about two things: (1) clarity about the specific learning goal, and (2) clarity about current state in relation to the goal. Whether the goal is behavioral or academic, clarity of both aspects is essential.

Academic standards require clarity of evidence about the academics alone, so behavior features (compliance, timeliness, participation, effort, attitude, and so on) can never be included; academic grades can only reflect academic performance.

This is not to suggest that behavioral expectations are not important; rather, it is to note that (1) such desired behaviors must be taught before they can be assessed, and (2) behaviors must be assessed based on a set of clear criteria and shared expectations for proficiency. Many school systems include scores for citizenship, responsibility, and other desirable behaviors as separate scores on the report card; this is a clear and appropriate use of behavioral assessment.

> **Connected Tenets:** Accurate Interpretation, Assessment Architecture
>
> **Topics:** Behavior, Reporting

# Are there such things as essential behaviors?

Decisions around what is to be deemed *essential* are always made by the educators within the system. Like those who set academic standards on the national level, educators should look to the behavioral expectations learners will encounter *next*. Beyond academic standards, businesses, universities, and military branches expect certain behaviors from their incoming members, like the ability to think and work independently and collaboratively as well as the ability to problem solve, communicate, persevere, inquire, and so on.

Erkens, Schimmer, and Dimich (2019) recommend seven critical competencies to prepare all learners for success beyond their schooling: (1) self-regulation, (2) communication, (3) critical thinking, (4) creative thinking, (5) collaboration, (6) digital citizenship, and (7) social competence. It can be argued that all seven competencies involve behaviors and attitudes that support students in their ability to learn through the assessment process.

**Connected Tenets:** Hope, Efficacy, and Achievement; Student Investment
**Topics:** Behavior, Student Engagement and Motivation

# How important is it to assess critical competencies?

It is as important to assess critical competencies (self-regulation, communication, critical thinking, creative thinking, collaboration, digital citizenship, and social competence) as it is to assess anything that serves as an instructional goal and focus. As schools and districts throughout the world purposefully place the development of critical competencies at the core of their learning priorities, a balanced and robust assessment system will be essential to ensure that learners either are on the trajectory toward or have reached proficiency.

There is no teaching and learning without assessment, so developing learners as *critical thinkers*, for example, still requires the same fundamental skills of identifying clear learning goals, transparent criteria, sophisticated tasks, accurate interpretation, effective feedback, periodic verification, and so on. While it is true that the nature of assessment may shift toward performance assessment, where learners are asked to demonstrate the critical competencies within a context that replicates the authentic circumstances in which the knowledge and skills are actually applied, the principles and practices of sound assessment remain.

If schools or districts (even states and provinces) are going to proclaim that they are *developing 21st century thinkers*, assessing the critical competencies is the only way to develop and then verify this lofty goal. Whether assessing an individual learner or a large cohort of students, being able to authentically verify and communicate that learners are developing the skills and dispositions needed for 21st century success will provide the substance behind the claims that schools and districts are so rightly making.

> **Connected Tenets:** Accurate Interpretation, Assessment Architecture, Student Investment
>
> **Topics:** Authentic Assessment, Criteria, Critical Competencies

# Assessment Practices

## What roles should accountability and high-stakes testing play in our assessment decisions?

In education, accountability is used to reference the policies, practices, and metrics used to hold educators and educational systems accountable for consistent, acceptable levels of students' academic achievement. Such metrics are important to ensure that all learners have equal access to a quality learning experience and to provide transparency to all stakeholder groups that schools are living up to their commitments to their communities. Every parent or caregiver and every community wants to ensure that learners get what they need to be able to contribute in a meaningful way when they leave the educational system.

But accountability systems must be the floor, not the ceiling. The data from any accountability system should inform the *schools* on areas for program improvements. Schools that maintain robust learning expectations that are tightly aligned to their local standards and embedded in highly engaging instruction and rigorous assessment activities will most likely achieve high levels of success in any accountability system.

However, the term *high stakes* holds a different meaning altogether. The stakes are high when the risk is significant and those engaged either win or lose. In a high-stakes accountability system, schools can deny graduation for students and states can withdraw funding if a "win" is not achieved. Any time the impact of an assessment process holds influence over decisions that directly affect the lives of the people who engaged in the assessment, the assessment can be considered high stakes.

Most often, these decisions are made by people not directly engaged in the assessment process (namely, not teachers or students), and students and teachers alike perceive these decisions as unfair, untimely, and unreflective of their needs. For this reason, when teacher teams make decisions about students and how to support their learning before a high-stakes standardized test, it is appropriate to examine sample assessments and student results from previous assessments to direct attention to particular skills teachers may need to focus on that will support student success. However, many of these same skills (stamina, clarity of written language, conceptual understanding) also support the development of skills and knowledge contained within the expected learning goals.

Seeking clarity about expectations for learning and the articulation of proficiency is good work when it takes into account all sources of information available to teachers and learners. It is even better work when the needs of learners, aligned with the provided expectations, *lead* the conversation and the high-stakes or accountability systems are worthy checkpoints but not the directors of the conversation.

**Connected Tenets:** Communication of Results
**Topics:** Accountability and Standardized Tests, Essential Standards

## When is it too soon to assess?

Decisions about when to assess are inextricably linked to the reason for assessing (the assessment purpose) and how educators communicate that reason to learners. At the formative level, when evidence is solicited for the purposes of supporting continued learning, it's never too early to assess. Even when a learner knows very little or has skills that lack refinement, a formative assessment may be timely because it allows teachers to focus in on exactly what each student needs.

However, at the summative level, when teachers are documenting and holding learners accountable to levels of achievement, there can be times when it is too soon to assess. This purpose presumes that learners have had ample learning and relearning time, filled with feedback and reflection. Engaging in a summative assessment process too early can diminish confidence, hope, and the opportunity to create and reflect as much learning as possible. To meet the hope that most learners will demonstrate proficiency during summative assessment, teachers should seek evidence that learners are independent, accurate, and consistent in their practice demonstrations of the required expectations. The timing of a summative assessment should reflect as much strength as possible.

**Connected Tenets:** Assessment Architecture, Communication of Results, Student Investment
**Topics:** Formative Assessment, Summative Assessment and Grading

# How do I assess students who rarely attend?

When learners do not attend school regularly, it challenges teachers' efforts to gather assessment information and respond in consistently supportive ways. However, it is important to remember the difference between lack of evidence and evidence that demonstrates academic struggle. This is the difference between clarity about achievement and clarity about behavior. Student attendance is critical for teachers to make strong instructional decisions based on current and accurate evidence, and so when students are not attending, teachers might consider a few approaches.

- Refrain from documenting a lack of skill or understanding in a gradebook as a result of lack of attendance. Instead, document lack of attendance as a behavioral concern and note the lack of sufficient evidence (incomplete or insufficient evidence) to make grading decisions when necessary.

- Refer the attendance concern to school teams who have been tasked with supporting behavioral challenges (RTI or MTSS teams) and work to clarify the root cause for the lack of attendance.

- Engage the student's family in a conversation about attendance when possible. A team approach to resolving the issue is optimal.

- Collect or document all evidence of learning when the student is at school. Do not depend on them to hand in work, if this is proving to be difficult. Instead, make copies of in-class efforts and engage in formal observation whenever possible.

- Stay focused on essential learning goals. Monitor progress in relation to the most important skills and knowledge and collect evidence whenever it is available. Proficiency can be assessed in a wide variety of ways. Select the methods that are most accurate and efficient for these learners until the attendance challenge is resolved.

At the end of the day, teachers must ask themselves whether, in their professional judgment, they have enough evidence to justify failure and how they might communicate gaps to future teachers in the most accurate and helpful way possible.

**Connected Tenets:** Accurate Interpretation, Student Investment
**Topics:** Behavior, Response to Intervention

# Do I really need to assess if I know students are struggling?

This question speaks to the purpose of assessment in two ways: (1) it invites teachers to consider what an assessment tells them about what their learners need, and (2) it also invites them to wonder what their assessment practices tell them about their own instruction.

Sometimes, when teachers work with learners for extended periods of time in various contexts, they may come to believe that they can predict student difficulties. It may seem like a waste of time to assess when students and their learning patterns appear predictable. However, this dilemma relates to the purpose of assessment. When assessment is treated not only as a tool to determine degrees of student proficiency but also as a means to determine whether instruction and learning plans have been effective, it becomes clear how it might be important to continuously collect assessment information. The challenge lies in how to treat the evidence that emerges from a struggling learner.

Knowing that learners are struggling is a great first step in responding to their needs. Knowing how to respond when learners are finding learning difficult is when assessment really earns its stripes. Assessment is a process that teachers should employ precisely at the point of needing to identify challenges and strengths. If teachers grant themselves permission to use assessment to support their instructional efforts, then it is to realize struggling learners likely need *more* assessment work, just not the *same* assessment work as others in the room. A really great assessment reveals the root cause of various learner challenges so educators can plan how to address these root causes in the most efficient and meaningful ways, *alongside* learners.

**Connected Tenets:** Accurate Interpretation

**Topics:** Formative Assessment

# Should assessment in high school be different from assessment in elementary school?

The answer is both *yes* and *no*. No, assessment should not be different because assessment fundamentals are universally applicable in grades K–12. Of course, as learners get older, *what* is being assessed will increase in complexity. However, ideally, teachers would still utilize a balanced assessment system where the formative and summative purposes of assessment would have a seamless relationship, much like the practice:game or rehearsal:performance dynamic most are familiar with. The impact of effective, descriptive feedback knows no age restriction.

However, the answer is *yes*, it might be different, since there may be aspects of assessment at the high school level unnecessary at other levels of schooling. The direct interface with higher (postsecondary) education is unique to high school, which means a great level of synthesis will be necessary when it comes to grade determination. While it does still occur in some places, the determination of a singular, overall grade is educationally unnecessary at the elementary or middle school level. However, it currently remains necessary for most high schools to produce a traditional transcript for college application. This means assessment at the high school level will be more focused on assessment within strands, categories, and domains that ask students to demonstrate their learning with multiple standards simultaneously, rather than in isolation. In other words, differences are more likely to emerge within the summative purpose where, like in high school, grades might take on a more significant role in the lives of learners.

**Connected Tenets:** Assessment Architecture, Instructional Agility

**Topics:** Feedback, Formative Assessment, Summative Assessment and Grading

## Should I assess the same way as my grade-level or course-alike partners?

Teachers do not have to assess the same way (namely, using the same method) as their grade-level or course-alike partners—one teacher may choose to assess comprehension of a main idea and supporting detail through a constructed-response question on a test, while a different teacher may choose to assess it through a blog post—but teaching colleagues should definitely agree on the following items.

- The criteria for quality when assessing the main idea and detail
- What the various levels of proficiency will look and sound like in relation to learning goals (standards, outcomes, competencies)
- What will be deemed on-grade-level work within the various defined levels

The criteria should be consistent between educators; this makes assessment reliable. Once colleagues have clarified the rigor and accompanying criteria for essential learning goals, they are free to design assessment experiences that reflect their own learners' strengths, needs, and preferences.

**Connected Tenets:** Assessment Architecture, Accurate Interpretation

**Topics:** Collaboration, Essential Standards, Unpacking and Learning Progressions

# Can I design assessment ahead of time in a play-based, emergent context, such as early learning?

In any context in which the organization of learning experiences is emergent and dependent on in-the-moment decision making (for example, some early learning environments, inquiry-focused environments, creative environments, and performance-focused environments), assessment should still guide decision making. However, how assessment fits into these environments might look, sound, and feel a little different from traditional assessment processes.

In emergent contexts, student preference, questions, and decisions guide the learning. However, this does not mean that the experiences are without guiding goals or success criteria. Teachers still assess very specific, predetermined goals (for example, cooperative play, strong questioning, pattern making) and use the information they gather to guide conversations, resource selection, student groupings, and feedback—all aspects of effective instruction in any learning context.

Assessment in emergent contexts can often occur through purposeful observation and conversation. Teachers engage learners in organic but intentional discussions to determine student progression toward any number of process or product-related goals. For example, a teacher might watch two elementary-aged learners making patterns out of blocks during center time and may ask the students to identify the core of the pattern (a learning target). The teacher may then invite the students to introduce new materials into their pattern and create a new and more complex core. This intentional conversation in the middle of emergent play assesses current understanding and advances the complexity of learning within a context determined by the students themselves. Teachers can then document this kind of assessment information and use it to plan instruction and environments that support learner growth. In addition, teachers may use student artifacts (brainstorming sheets, research papers, or drawings) to further assess growth in relation to specific criteria.

Learning requires clarity about a learner's current state in relation to goals, and teachers work alongside learners to plan next steps. In emergent contexts, these steps are often co-constructed with learners, with learners holding the primary responsibility for exploration. Strong assessment throughout these processes ensures student success.

**Connected Tenets:** Accurate Interpretation, Assessment Architecture
**Topics:** Early Learning, Formative Assessment

## Are assignments different from assessments?

If assignments are created to elicit evidence of learning for either formative or summative purposes, then they function as assessments. For example, if an assignment is given to allow learners to practice a particular skill or apply knowledge, and a teacher intends to then examine the students' work and plan for future instruction, then the assignment is serving as a formative assessment. If an assignment is given for the purpose of capturing and verifying independent skill or understanding in relation to a standard, then this assignment is acting as a summative assessment.

Assignments are *not* assessment-oriented if the evidence they elicit has no impact on the instructional decision making by teachers or students or on the students' final scores. If teachers give an assignment to invite learners to wrestle with thinking or generate ideas and do not use the results to inform instruction or verify degrees of proficiency, then in this case, the assignment is not the same as an assessment. And, if a teacher is merely providing check marks for completion of tasks, then the assignment is not being used as an assessment of learning. It all depends on how the teacher uses the assignment.

**Connected Tenets:** Communication of Results

**Topics:** Formative Assessment, Summative Assessment and Grading

## My district has a policy that I put grades in the gradebook three times a week. Both formative and summative grades count toward the final grade. How can I make my assessment practices accurate with such a policy in place?

It is a best practice to ensure all key stakeholders in an individual learner's life (including the learner) are constantly informed about that learner's progress toward the learning expectations. Frequent updates are important so that early intervention, on everyone's behalf, is possible. However, learning is not algorithmic, so guidelines like "Enter three grades per week" generate contrived assessment evidence that educators may or may not have needed at that time. The greater issue is the grading software, which treats formative and summative assessment data equally.

Here are some ways teachers have bypassed the grading software challenges.

- Check the preferences or settings of the online gradebook to see if it's possible to turn off automatic averaging of all scores. If so, document the scores and then look for the *mode* in the later samples of work (for example, the most consistent number or letter grade that the learner generates at the end of the learning experience).

- Enter each formative assessment as a zero value but record the score the learner earned. This way the learner can watch the trajectory of growth, but the grades don't count in the final scores because the assessment had zero value.

- Use alternative scoring codes like NY (not yet), +/–, or P (progressing), for example, on all formative work.

- Digitize student tracking forms so parents can see how learners are self-tracking their progress, and share those links with parents.

- Digitize feedback systems (for example, use Seesaw, Student Feedback App, Google Classroom, and so on).

No matter what options educators use, it is always important to help all stakeholders understand the new system: What do the codes mean? How is the final grade calculated? Putting those critical factors in writing and sharing them in many places (on the school or teacher webpage, in a letter to the parents, in signage at parent-teacher conferences, and so on) is paramount to the success of such changes.

> **Connected Tenets:** Culture of Learning, Instructional Agility
> **Topics:** Formative Assessment, Reporting, Summative Assessment and Grading

# How should I critically examine my assessments to make sure they are good?

Developing quality or "good" classroom assessments is a process (Willis & Adie, 2016). Understanding the purpose of classroom assessment as generating and analyzing evidence of learning is central to identifying how often to examine assessment tools and processes and how to engage in critical analysis. If a tool is not serving its purpose, it may need some critical examination.

Critical analysis of assessment involves several considerations. Often, educators organize learning by units or themes. When this is the case, each unit usually contains a focused set of standards or critical competencies learners must master to some level. Any assessment can be used to provide learners feedback to learn more (formative) or to describe a level of proficiency at a given moment (summative). It is the action taken that makes the assessment formative or summative. Assessment validity (for either formative or summative use) reflects confidence that the items and tasks on the assessment have a high likelihood they will reveal what was intended to be learned and measured. To ensure this, there are actions individual teachers and, ideally, collaborative teams can take to achieve validity (the end goal of a critical analysis).

Before the unit or assessment:

1. Determine essential standards and competencies for that unit or time frame and unpack each goal to articulate learning targets and clarify the learning progression.

2. Choose or align items and tasks to the standards or learning targets you intend to measure. Be sure the rigor of the assessment matches the grade-level expectation the standard reflects. The verb used in the learning description is a strong indicator of the cognitive level and demand that must be present in the items; immediately after the verb is typically the depth of thinking the learner must demonstrate. Together, the cognitive rigor and depth of thinking make designing the assessment task much clearer. For example, be sure not to confuse *identify* or *select* with *analyze*, *assess*, or *explain*. If the verb is *explain*, learners must do the explaining in the item or task, and that task needs to ensure that the learners are doing the explaining. If learners are providing an explanation of something factual, they may be explaining, but the depth of thinking is quite low. In any case, a constructed-response item would be required since *choosing* an answer would provide insufficient evidence. Learners will need to share their thinking through a graphic, an essay, a video, or a blog post.

After the assessment is administered:

1. Analyze the student work to determine students' strengths and next steps. Analyzing a (common) formative assessment informs instruction before the end of the unit (sometimes called Tier 1 prevention). Analyzing an end-of-unit assessment, or (common) summative assessment, identifies learners who have not mastered the essential standards for Tier 2 intervention.

2. Reflect on learners' responses to understand if anything in the design of the assessment led to poor results—perhaps confusing wording, unclear directions, or vocabulary that was unfamiliar. Revise the task or assessment items to avoid this misinterpretation or confusion the next time you give the assessment. Use caution when changing the assessment—ensure that you do not inadvertently reduce rigor or diminish the expectations of the assessment simply because learners were not able to achieve at the assessed level. In this case, keep the items and tasks at grade level and use instruction to meet learners where they are.

Ideally, every assessment experience would be planned and organized by learning goal prior to the unit. Each assessment (student work) would be (1) analyzed to inform additional instruction and intervention on essential standards when needed, and (2) revised, if items and tasks are deemed to be in need of refining.

Collaborative teams or teachers should only administer as many common formative assessments as they can analyze and respond to; *using* the evidence matters more than simply gathering it. It adds way too much work and too little impact if educators give assessments but take no action as a result. Collaborative teams should also always analyze end-of-unit or common summative assessments to ensure that learners who need additional time and support get it. In both cases, this analysis should always include questions about the structure or design of the items and tasks and what might need to be changed to make the assessment and ensuing results more accurate.

**Connected Tenets:** Accurate Interpretation, Assessment Architecture

**Topics:** Common Assessment, Essential Standards, Formative Assessment, Intervention and Instruction, Response to Intervention, Summative Assessment and Grading

# Assessment Purpose in a Remote Learning Context

When education shifts to a less familiar format, both teachers and learners may find themselves focusing more on the practicalities of day-to-day operations and less on the nuanced purposes of assessment. However, it is important to remember that assessment is the process by which strong instructional decisions are made. In order for both teachers and students to design daily learning experiences that are grounded in both student strengths and needs, educators must produce and analyze evidence of the current state of skill and understanding regularly. This formative purpose for assessment becomes critically important in a remote learning context, where the observational assessment to which teachers have become so accustomed (for example, checking in-the-moment for students who are struggling to get started, for those who are missing important strategies, or for those who are having difficulty self-regulating) is far more challenging. Spontaneous check-ins of any sort are more complex when students are no longer situated in close physical proximity to teachers at synchronous times.

In addition, verification of student learning (the purpose of summative assessment) has its own layer of complexity in a remote context. Teachers may have the intention of checking on independent skills in relation to goals, only to find themselves concerned about the level of independence learners actually exhibit when they cannot watch the learners during assessment. They may find it essential to differentiate their assessment methods to meet the needs of learners, and so assessment record keeping looks different in a virtual environment.

Part of addressing these increased challenges requires everyone involved to be crystal clear about the purpose of each assessment, how the results will be used, and whether learners are expected to be working on their own (summative assessment) or whether they can seek supports, which formative assessment not only allows but encourages as part of a strong response. It is for these reasons that addressing the purpose of assessment in a remote learning context is essential *before* the assessment is ever administered to learners.

To support clarity around assessment purpose, teachers might consider the following.

- Intentionally labeling an assessment as for practice and feedback or for certification of learning and ensuring students and families understand the difference in terms of how it will be used and the level of independence expected when engaging in the process

- Explicitly connecting the purpose of the assessment to the instructional decisions that immediately follow; for example, if an assessment is formative, the educator will structure the following day's breakout room conversations to address the student needs revealed in the assessment.

- Establishing a healthy balance between formative and summative assessment, with a far greater emphasis placed on formative assessment; to further clarify the difference for learners, consider withholding scores on formative assessment and focusing on feedback and goal setting instead.

Assessment
Purpose

# CHAPTER 4

# ASSESSMENT ARCHITECTURE

Like the blueprint of a house, assessment architecture provides a layout of the plan teachers will use to monitor learning throughout a unit of instruction. The plan includes strategic formative assessment opportunities that will lead to success on summative assessments. Just as the building of an actual house is often modified from the original plans, assessment blueprints are malleable in that teachers will likely need to add, modify, or delete some formative activities as they respond to the emerging evidence of student learning. Assessment architecture, when mapped out in advance, provides teachers with opportunities for the intentional design of assessments, implications for daily instruction, and possible responses to use to maximize effectiveness.

Being able to respond to student needs accurately and efficiently is highly dependent on collecting the right evidence that reflects the actual, current state of learning. This is why assessment architecture is so critical to any assessment system. Without strong design, assessment interpretations, communication of results, and development of student investment will be extremely challenging. Being clear about the characteristics of strong assessment architecture is a great place to start.

## Assessment Architecture

### What do we mean by *assessment architecture*? Why is it so important?

Assessment architecture is simply the designing of assessments to ensure assessment evidence accurately measures the intended learning. It involves individual teachers and teacher teams engaging in identifying the learning and choosing assessment evidence to craft an assessment plan. When individuals or teams of teachers engage in assessment architecture, they do the following.

1. Choose the standards (or competencies or outcomes) learners are to learn within a targeted unit of study or time frame.

2. Analyze the standards to identify the more specific and granular learning targets needed to achieve the standard (unpacking or deconstructing standards). The verbs in the standards signal the cognitive complexity a standard requires and how the learners might demonstrate this skill or understanding as described in the standard. The depth of thinking typically follows the verb and provides essential insight as to the depth and breadth of the expected demonstration of learning.

3. Identify, based on the cognitive complexity, the methods of assessment (for example, selected response, constructed response, performance assessment) that will most accurately provide evidence of where learners are in achieving these learning targets, and eventually the standard. For example, if the verb identified in the standard is *analyze*, the method must ensure learners are actually analyzing and not just simply identifying or recalling the best analysis.

4. Ensure, if assessments already exist, that the current items or tasks on any given assessment provide accurate information on the learning targets or standards intended to be learned and assessed. Checking directions, phrasing, and organization is part of this process. The items, tasks, and rubrics are critiqued based on how learners interpreted the design and implementation of the assessment. There are times when an item is unintentionally misinterpreted or poorly written. This means that teachers need to analyze the evidence and reflect on the assessment design, ensuring that they revise any formatting, wording, or method if these things are determined to be the reason learners did poorly.

5. Intentionally plan the assessment evidence gathered and analyzed throughout the unit or time frame and determine how the information from the assessment evidence will be used—formatively or summatively. Planning assessment for a formative purpose means intentionally identifying what kind of analysis will happen with the evidence, what kind of feedback the learners will receive, and how students and teachers will act on what they learn from the assessment evidence. When evidence is used summatively, teachers identify how to share results with learners (symbol, comments, ratio) to communicate accurately the degree to which

learners have met the learning goals. In addition, teachers ensure that a summative grade or score accurately represents a level of achievement based on that evidence.

Assessment architecture is very similar to the planning and instructional design process that Grant Wiggins and Jay McTighe (1998) describe in *Understanding by Design* or *backward design*, where teachers begin with the end in mind. Assessment architecture takes assessment planning to a deeper level because it ensures that assessments are valid and accurate as well as intentionally planned in advance, to drive lesson planning and decision making.

**Connected Tenets:** Assessment Purpose, Communication of Results

**Topics:** Formative Assessment, Preassessment, Summative Assessment and Grading

## How can strong assessment architecture encourage learners to get involved in the learning process?

The key to student involvement in both learning and assessment processes is to plan for it in an intentional way. When teachers dig deeply into their standards and learning goals and design assessment tools and methods that capture student learning as it develops, they are simultaneously planning ways to invite learners into the assessment and learning conversation. Assessment can serve both teachers and learners when it is designed well.

Perhaps a teacher plans to assess the foundational skills a learner brings into a learning context through a preassessment. At the same time, they may also plan how they will use the preassessment results as a way to frame learning each day with students, or how to use it to invite learners to track their own growth over time. While the preassessment provided the educator with the information needed to address specific student needs, it also provided a vehicle through which to engage learners in their own quest for skill development.

Strong assessment architecture supports the development of skills and understanding over time when it is built on a deep understanding of the learning goals as well as the targets and criteria within those goals. Once teachers have developed this depth of personal understanding and have explicitly planned how they will assess learners both formatively and summatively, they can also plan times within the learning experience when it makes sense for learners to self-assess and set goals or engage with peers in feedback processes. As teachers develop their own assessment architecture, they can

Assessment
Architecture

plan how to share the assessment process with learners. Assessment and learning are intertwined, and so when learners are engaged in assessment, they are also engaged in their own learning.

**Connected Tenets:** Assessment Purpose, Student Investment

**Topics:** Self- and Peer Assessment, Student Engagement and Motivation

## What is the difference between a standard, a target, and criteria?

*Standards* are the specific outcomes learners are supposed to achieve; they are primarily assessed summatively at appropriate intervals. *Targets* are the underpinnings that, when intentionally sequenced, lead learners to achieve the standards. The teaching and assessing of targets is one priority of formative assessment, whereby teachers will come to know when learners are ready for the next level of sophistication as they scaffold their way to reaching a more complex standard.

If, for example, a standard is at the *analyzing* level of Bloom's Taxonomy (Bloom, 1956)—or depth of knowledge level 2, or DOK 2 (Webb, 1997, 1999)—the teacher would know there are knowledge, comprehension, and application *targets* that lead learners to fully develop and reach the standard. Educators often use a framework or model to analyze the cognitive demand of instruction and assessment. Depth of knowledge is one common framework used to describe the cognitive demand of any given item or task. For more information on DOK levels, consult Eileen Depka's (2017) *Raising the Rigor: Effective Questioning Strategies and Techniques for the Classroom*; Cassandra Erkens's (2019) *The Handbook for Collaborative Common Assessments: Tools for Design, Delivery, and Data Analysis*; or Erik M. Francis's (2022) *Deconstructing Depth of Knowledge: A Method and Model for Deeper Teaching and Learning*. Standards and their underpinning targets are intentionally sequenced to form a learning progression, which is the foundation for creating effective and efficient units of study.

Whether the assessment focus is on standards or targets, *success criteria* support both the development and verification of proficiency. Success criteria are a description of the quality of what learners will perform or create to demonstrate their success with the standards or targets. When success criteria are made clear and transparent, teachers and learners understand how to achieve the learning goals of each individual lesson, a lesson sequence, or ultimately the standards within the unit of study. Often, teachers choose to use rubrics to articulate multiple aspects of quality (success criteria) along several degrees of proficiency, when the standards or targets are complex (for example, writing a narrative essay). When a target is less complex (for example, recognizing the numerals 1–10), teachers might simply articulate the singular version of correctness (perhaps in a checklist).

**Connected Tenets:** Accurate Interpretation, Assessment Purpose

**Topics:** Criteria, Formative Assessment, Summative Assessment and Grading, Unpacking and Learning Progressions

## What is the difference between rigor and difficulty?

Understanding this difference can be confusing when the terms *rigorous* and *difficult* seem to equate to *hard*. But it is important to know that they measure different things.

Rigor measures the level of cognitive complexity required in a task. What are the mental processes required to accomplish the task or answer the question at hand? Rigorous questions require learners to balance their conceptual understanding and procedural fluency in a complex application that requires extended or strategic thinking.

A difficulty index measures the degree of challenge a learner experiences while engaging in the tasks or questions at hand. The difficulty of an item varies based on whether or not learners find the task to be easy or hard. A difficulty level is determined after learners have taken the exam, and the data reflect how many learners were accurate. The difficulty index is determined by dividing the number of students who answered the item correctly by the total number of respondents, and the resulting score is called a difficulty, or discrimination, index. A discrimination score of 0.40 and higher is considered ideal in the testing industry (Renner, 2018; Vallesi, 2020). In other words, a test item is considered difficult, and thereby successful, when several learners are unsuccessful. This normed approach is in direct conflict with a school's mission to ensure all students are successful at high levels; the metric will just keep moving as more students are successful.

An assessment task can have both a rigor level and a difficulty index. Rigor levels remain stationary, but difficulty levels vary. In other words, a rigor level 3 task is level 3 for *everyone*, whereas the difficulty indices will change based on the learners' readiness and overall experience with the task (some learners will find the task easy while others might think it's hard). For example, imagine all learners have the task of pushing the same rock uphill. The size, weight, and shape of the rock as well as the slope of the hill (rigor) is the same for everyone, but the challenge of the experience (difficulty) will vary; some people will find the task harder than others based on their own degree of physical strength and fitness.

**Connected Tenets:** Assessment Purpose

**Topics:** Formative Assessment, Rigor and Cognitive Complexity, Summative Assessment and Grading

## What is the difference between a learning progression and a proficiency scale or rubric?

A progression of learning delineates the instructional pathway to proficiency in relation to a single standard or a cluster of standards. In other words, the learning progression is most often (but not always) found in the individual learning targets of a complete standard, and it highlights the scaffolds that must be in place in order for a learner to achieve proficiency. Progressions of learning can be used to (1) isolate and clarify learning targets for learners, (2) inform the assessment pathway, and (3) apprise the sequencing of instructional steps.

Progressions of learning are often embedded in a proficiency scale, which delineates *how much* of a standard has been mastered. Unlike progressions of learning, proficiency scales add qualifiers to which parts of the standard have been accomplished and to what degree of dependency and accuracy. Robert J. Marzano (2010) suggests the following qualifiers for each level of a proficiency scale.

- **Level 1:** Student is completely dependent on support. Student can complete only the simple parts with partial accuracy.

- **Level 2:** Student is independent of support. Student can complete the simple parts with a high degree of accuracy.

- **Level 3:** Student is completely independent of support. Student can complete both the simple and complex parts with accuracy.

- **Level 4:** Student is completely independent and advances beyond provided instruction. Student extends complexity to include in-depth inferences or extensive connections.

It is the sequence from the simple to the complex parts of the standard that reveals the progression of learning, which by itself does not add qualifiers to levels.

Where proficiency scales indicate *how much* of a standard learners achieve and to what degree of independence and complexity, a rubric indicates *how well* the learner has mastered the entire standard through an assessment that was written at the expected level of proficiency (typically the level 3 of a proficiency scale) for that standard. Rubrics use quality criteria that also have various levels (typically 4 or 5). Even though the number of levels might be the same, the tools serve different purposes. Schimmer (2016) uses the analogy of a standard for making pancakes to explore how a scale is different from a rubric on the same standard. Figure 4.1 offers a simplified version of the difference between a proficiency scale and a rubric and places the rubric on par with the required level of proficiency on a standard for making pancakes.

| Scale | 1 Initiating | 2 Developing | 3 Achieving | 4 Advancing |
|---|---|---|---|---|
| **Level 4** <br> • Adds unique ingredients to make new types of pancakes | | | | |
| **Level 3** <br> • Uses proper technique <br> • Makes pancakes | | | | |
| **Rubric** <br> For an assessment written at the desired level of proficiency | Visual Appeal | | | |
| | Taste | | | |
| | Aroma | | | |
| | Texture | | | |
| **Level 2** <br> • Reads recipe <br> • Accurately measures <br> • Uses appropriate tools | | | | |
| **Level 1** <br> • Names ingredients <br> • Explains what each ingredient does in the recipe | | | | |

*Figure 4.1: A visual representation of the relationship between a scale and a rubric.*

**Connected Tenets:** Accurate Interpretation

**Topics:** Unpacking and Learning Progressions

# Don't common assessments restrict my ability to be creative and do what I know is best for my students?

A teacher's prowess hinges on his or her ability to be flexible within the confines of precision. There is a need, then, for common assessments to ensure that the entire team (department or grade level) is exact in its interpretation of the standards and consistent in its achievement of the desired results. While precision is the end goal, it does not preclude a teacher's opportunity to be creative or flexible in both assessment and instruction.

In terms of assessment, *common* does not mean *exactly the same* (Erkens, 2016). Common assessments must measure the same standards, with same expectations for quantity and quality, at the same level of rigor, and with the same criteria for analyzing the results, but the assessments themselves need not be exactly the same. It is possible to employ different passages, prompts, questions, or tasks and still measure student mastery on the expected standards. Be aware, however, that differences in the design of a common assessment will require an additional step when reviewing the data to ensure the assessment variations were not a cause for achievement variations.

As for instruction, common assessments should never infringe on a teacher's instructional maneuvers within the team's established timelines and shared expectations. All teachers must find their best instructional options—aligned with their personal preferences and unique style—to maximize learning in their individual classrooms. Collaborative teams are strongest when their individual instruction is agile yet precise, and their individual choices generate diverse and invaluable options to meet the full range of student needs.

Creativity is a really important part of the teaching process. No protocol or policy should ever attempt to take away a teacher's license to be creative or compromise a teacher's ability to meet the needs of his or her learners. Still, every teacher *owes* it to their learners to guarantee their accurate and comprehensive attainment of the standards.

**Connected Tenets:** Instructional Agility

**Topics:** Common Assessment, Professional Learning Communities

# Assessment Design

## At what point in my planning process should I think about assessment?

Teachers must consider accurate assessment design and effective use at the very beginning of the unit design, and even with the long view of the overall course design. When teachers have created their summative assessments in advance of the instruction, they can experience the following gains.

- Creating a meaningful pathway for the entire assessment system, focusing the feedback from formative assessments on developing readiness for the summative assessments

- Employing a laser-like focus in instruction, sometimes modifying or removing content that will not be helpful to student success on the summative

- Ensuring their assessment system is truly aligned to the identified standards involved in the unit of study

It's even important to map out a few key questions to employ during each day of instruction that will (1) challenge the learners' thinking at the appropriate level of rigor, and (2) elicit learner insights that will guide the teachers' instructional maneuvers. In other words, assessment of all kinds (formal and informal) can never be an afterthought.

**Connected Tenets:** Assessment Purpose

**Topics:** Formative Assessment, Professional Learning Communities, Summative Assessment and Grading

## Is it possible for teachers to write valid and reliable assessments?

Absolutely. While assessment literacy is rarely included in either undergraduate or graduate programs for educators, understanding the purpose of assessment and how to create the assessment architecture that informs the process is both critical and attainable. To enhance these important assessment design skills, teachers should work together to engage in the process of creating assessment plans and the assessment tools and supports that move the plan forward. When teachers collaborate on assessment design, they enhance their own knowledge and improve student achievement (Hattie, 2009; Moss & Brookhart, 2019).

The process starts with collaborative conversations about the standards themselves. Understanding all of the components, sometimes called unpacking, and how the components fit together (repacking) is critical. Learning progressions then help to define each of the steps the learner must master before ultimately meeting the standards. The success criteria help to define what proficiency looks like as well as the steps to proficiency and beyond, enabling teachers to give more precise feedback than simply saying "not yet."

Selecting the best assessment method helps to make sure that educators are measuring the standard and targets (and not other things). For many assessments, teachers must also create measurement tools to help define those levels of quality (for example, checklists or rubrics).

Teachers should work together both in the creation of these assessments and in the scoring of them. This helps to establish inter-rater reliability and shared understanding of whether the assessment truly measures the standard and effectively uses the success criteria. Valid assessments measure what is intended. Reliable assessments measure consistency. When this collaborative process is followed, assessments are more likely to meet these criteria, and teachers are better able to understand the effectiveness and limitations of both assessments they have created and assessments created by others.

**Connected Tenets:** Accurate Interpretation, Assessment Purpose

**Topics:** Assessment Design, Collaboration, Unpacking and Learning Progressions

# Do I really have to create all my own assessments? Can I use assessments created by someone else or from a textbook or program?

Planned and purposeful assessment should be grounded in standards with clarity around the success criteria. There should be a match between the standard and the type of assessment used. Once all of that is in place and clear for the teacher or teachers who will be administering the assessment, educators can use any number of resources to create the assessment tool itself.

Starting with an assessment provided by a textbook or other instructional material can provide a valuable and time-saving starting point. Teachers should review commercially produced assessments with a critical eye and evaluate all materials to determine if they truly assess the standards in the best and most efficient way and at the level of rigor necessary, and if they ultimately provide both the learner and the teacher with the information needed. Teachers should expect that some editing or adjusting of the assessment will likely be necessary to meet these criteria. The inclusion of assessments in commercially published materials does not guarantee that these assessments are of the highest quality or that they meet all standards. Teachers' professional knowledge is invaluable in making these kinds of decisions.

The more teachers can engage in this process collaboratively, the better; the professional conversations will help to ensure clarity around the expectations, the success criteria, and the assessments themselves. Teachers may effectively use assessments created by someone else under these same conditions. The criteria of well-designed and well-planned assessment architecture should be the focus of the work.

> **Connected Tenets:** Assessment Purpose, Instructional Agility
>
> **Topics:** Collaboration, Formative Assessment, Summative Assessment and Grading

## How can I know if an assessment I have already created is a good one?

The following categories and subsequent questions provide guidance in examining the effectiveness of an assessment.

Be precise:

- Are there learning targets on the assessment, and are they clear to learners?

- Does the assessment method match the learning target? Is the method effective? (For example, if the verb in the learning target says *explain* or *analyze*, are the items actually having learners do those actions at the appropriate depth of thinking?) If unsure, align items to each learning target to check. For an example, see the sample unit assessment map in figure 4.2 (page 82).

- Is what learners need to know and be able to do clear on the assessment?

- Is the vocabulary familiar? Will learners have the needed background knowledge?

Take action:

- When an assessment is used formatively, learners get feedback, revise, or get instruction to move their learning forward. If it's a common formative assessment, when will the data and student responses be analyzed? When will intervention and extension occur?

- When an assessment serves a summative purpose, will communication through scores or grades provide clear information on the level of proficiency (strengths and next steps)?

| Standard | Learning Targets | Items/Tasks on Assessment (End of Unit OR Common Formative Assessment) |
|---|---|---|
| **Example:** Write informative or explanatory texts in which they name a topic, supply some facts about the topic, and provide some sense of closure. | I can write information about a topic. I can explain information about a topic. I can supply accurate facts about the topic. I can provide closure about a topic. | Items 1, 2, 5, 6 |
| | | |
| | | |

*Figure 4.2: Sample unit assessment map.*

Get students invested:

- How are learners reflecting on their strengths from the assessment?

- How are learners reflecting on their next steps or challenges from the assessment?

- How are learners reflecting on what keeps them persisting and what shuts them down (self-regulation)?

Learners are excellent sources of feedback when examining assessments to determine their effectiveness. Consider asking learners to reflect on the design and implementation of the assessment by asking the following questions.

- To what extent did you feel the assessment provided you an opportunity to demonstrate an accurate picture of what you know and can do?

- How did you prepare for this assessment?

- What went well in your preparation for the assessment?

- What would you do differently if you could do it again?

- Were there any surprises on the assessment?

- How would you change the assessment to represent a more accurate picture of what you learned during this unit?

- Share anything else you feel would be important in order to demonstrate your understanding.

**Connected Tenets:** Assessment Purpose, Communication of Results

**Topics:** Formative Assessment, Preassessment, Summative Assessment and Grading

# How can I know that my assessments are aligned with state, provincial, or national tests? How much should I teach to the test?

Educators should teach to the test insomuch as their instructional progression leads learners toward the opportunity to meet the identified standards at their full cognitive complexity. Teachers know that state tests and other forms of standardized tests may assess learners at the full depth of knowledge. If teachers do not at least provide the opportunity for learners to reach the appropriate DOK level (for example, they only teach to DOK 2 when the standard is DOK 3), then learners will be underprepared for state tests. As well, teachers would be wise—to the best of their ability—to provide learners with the opportunity to experience the question types and formats that are likely to occur on state tests. This isn't about replicating the question content but rather about replicating the *format* so that format, for example, can be eliminated as a potential mitigating factor in demonstrating proficiency. After all, it is unfair to test that which hasn't been taught, and to test in ways for which learners have never been prepared.

On the other hand, teaching to the test crosses the line when classroom assessments are reduced to a kind of *test prep* that reveals a disproportionate obsession with practicing the test questions and formats. As the old assessment adage says, *you don't fatten the pig by weighing it*. Learners immersed in a rigorous learning environment where the expectation of reaching the full depth and breadth of standards is the norm will be prepared for state tests. Full mastery of the required understanding and skill is the best kind of preparation, so while teachers replicating the format and cognitive complexity of state tests could certainly be somewhat helpful, it is more effective and efficient when the instructional focus is on creating an environment where learners authentically develop and then demonstrate their understanding of the standards in ways that are engaging and meaningful.

> **Connected Tenets:** Accurate Interpretation, Communication of Results
>
> **Topics:** Accountability and Standardized Tests, Rigor and Cognitive Complexity

# How much should instructional innovation impact my assessment design?

It is important to have a shared definition of instructional innovation. Some readers may believe that instructional innovation is any new or current educational idea that focuses on instructional quality. Others may view instructional innovation as research projects conducted by higher education to identify the evidence-based strategies that have the most significant impact on student learning. Regardless, there is certainly a place for thinking about, planning, and implementing effective and innovative instructional practices within strong assessment architecture, when those practices have the potential to positively impact student learning.

The metaphor used frequently to illustrate the components of effective assessment architecture is the building of a house. The assessment plan is the blueprint. The standards and criteria for quality are the specifications that guide the design. The curriculum and content become the materials through which the structure is built, like the concrete and the walls. The instruction, which typically comes last in the plan, is the design that makes the house unique. A home with three bedrooms and a main floor master bedroom is a specific plan, just like a standard that requires learners to demonstrate mastery of reading informational text is a specific standard. The blueprint helps to identify where structural supports, plumbing, and electrical work are needed, and the assessment plan helps to identify important learning checkpoints so that students and teachers can monitor learning progress. The concrete foundation, framing, and roof help to protect the house from the weather, and the curriculum and content help to make sure that learners can demonstrate comprehension skills in a variety of texts. Ultimately, that home can look very different when the final design is completed by two very different designers. It could be contemporary or traditional or something in between. At the same time, the fundamentals of the blueprint, materials, and assessment are consistent.

Instructional design is an important part of the assessment planning process. However, it should be considered only after the learning expectations are clear and decisions have been made about the best ways to measure the learning. Further instructional design will follow when assessment evidence reveals a need. Individual or innovative differences in how instruction is delivered can still facilitate the meeting of those goals, as long as there is shared understanding of the expectations, the levels of complexity, and the learning progressions.

**Connected Tenets:** Instructional Agility, Student Investment

**Topics:** Collaboration

## What is the best way to make sure the questions I ask align with what I taught?

The best way to ensure complete alignment is to invert the question and begin with designing the assessment *before* instruction begins: *What is the best way to ensure teaching will support student success on the assessments?* First, teachers must begin with the learning goal itself. Once educators have thoroughly determined the intention of the learning goal, including the required skills, knowledge, and criteria by which proficiency will be verified, they can design the assessment tools, prompts, and questions that will get to the heart of this intention. It is only *after* designing assessment that teachers should plan instruction. They will then give consideration to the steps learners may need to take in order to master the learning goal. This is the essence of backward planning or *Understanding by Design* (Wiggins & McTighe, 2005)—assessment guides instructional planning. When teaching follows assessment design, teachers can feel confident that the questions asked will align with what was taught.

**Connected Tenets:** Assessment Purpose, Instructional Agility

**Topics:** Formative Assessment, Summative Assessment and Grading, Unpacking and Learning Progressions

## Do I need to make a rubric for every learning experience?

As with any assessment decision, the design and use of a tool is dependent on the purpose of the assessment and the context in which it is given. Rubrics are created in order to make clear degrees of skill or understanding in relation to the success criteria for a learning goal. By describing how criteria will look and sound at various degrees of proficiency, teachers and learners can not only recognize the current state of learning but also make plans to develop skills and understanding even further. In effect, well-designed rubrics make the path for future learning very clear.

However, it is not necessary or even possible to create a rubric for every learning experience. Firstly, not every learning goal is easily described through a rubric. For example, in the early years, learning goals are often a case of yes or no. In these cases, teachers may choose to create a rubric around frequency as opposed to quality, or they may prefer to utilize checklists or anecdotal records instead of rubrics. Secondly, too many varied rubrics become too challenging for teachers and learners to navigate. When teachers work with learners to co-construct criteria or make degrees of proficiency clear through exemplars, they can be very helpful, but when there is not time to engage in this depth of work, other assessment tools may be easier for learners to understand.

**Connected Tenets:** Assessment Purpose
**Topics:** Formative Assessment

## How do I choose the assessment method? When should I use selected response, constructed response, or performance assessment?

Part of being assessment literate is understanding that every assessment method has both strengths and limitations in what it can offer. Accurate assessment evidence emerges when the assessment method is an appropriate match for the full cognitive complexity of the standard or target and when it informs next steps, when appropriate.

The advantage of *selected response* is the ability to assess a large amount of material in a relatively short period of time. As well, responding to assessment evidence can happen rather quickly since educators can analyze the information efficiently. With standards or targets where there is clearly one correct response, selected-response questions offer immediate clarity that is lost with the other two methods. However, as learning becomes more complex and versions of quality begin to emerge (often assessed with the help of a rubric or proficiency scale), selected response becomes a less effective method for eliciting evidence.

The advantage of *constructed response* is that it provides a more thorough explanation of what learners are thinking; selected response won't allow that. Constructed response has a wide range of formats (everything from *fill-in-the-blank* to *projects*), but the common thread is that the teacher requires much more sophisticated evidence of learning than simply choosing the right answer. Typically, as the cognitive complexity of standards and targets increases, teachers will choose constructed-response questions, since with greater complexity comes multiple versions of correctness. In addition, evidence of thinking is required to know *to what degree* learners have met the standards or targets and to determine how best to support learners in their next steps.

*Performance assessment* is about demonstrations of proficiency that attempt to replicate the authentic context within which learners are meant to apply the intended learning. While a constructed response *can* be a performance assessment in the strictest sense (for example, scientists write research papers), performance assessments are often demonstrations that a teacher needs to *see* or *hear* in order to assess. Authenticity comes from combining multiple standards, from the replication of context, or from the creation of something other than an extended written response. While performance assessment often requires more time than the other two methods, the evidence that is generated from a performance assessment can inform decisions in relation to multiple standards or targets. Finally, performance assessments create enriching learning experiences and are not just an alternative demonstration of learning. The experience of *doing* the performance assessment can be equally as enriching and rewarding as the *done*.

> **Connected Tenets:** Assessment Purpose, Accurate Interpretation
> **Topics:** Assessment Design, Criteria, Questioning

## How many questions should appear on each assessment?

The answer to this question is contextual. A general rule of thumb is that a learning target should have at least five to ten points of evidence before educators can accurately determine a level of proficiency. However, educators can gather evidence over time. If a teacher uses formative assessment to gather evidence in advance of summative assessment, then the summative assessment might only need to have two or three key questions to offer confirmation of the previous evidence gathered.

In the primary grades, a teacher naturally gathers evidence over time. It would be inappropriate to give a young learner a long test, and it would be inaccurate to assume learners really knew letters, for example, if they simply had to find a letter seven times in a single setting. At the middle and secondary levels, it might be appropriate to have five to ten questions about a single target to ensure mastery of the target.

**Connected Tenets:** Assessment Purpose

**Topics:** Assessment Design

## Can I measure more than one standard or target in the same assessment or even the same prompt, or should I split them up?

The answer to this question depends on the purpose of the assessment. If the assessment is formative, and a teacher is using it to *improve learning*, then a single-standard assessment might well be in order. Single-standard assessments make the following processes more manageable: (1) isolating common misconceptions or errors, (2) diagnosing student readiness, and (3) providing the necessary intervention to advance the learning for each learner. On the other hand, if the assessment is summative, and a teacher is using it to *prove learning*, then a multi-standard assessment would likely be most beneficial as the integration of standards will (1) lead to a more robust and integrated assessment design, (2) reveal a learner's grasp of the entirety of the knowledge and skills involved, and (3) provide more structured opportunities for teachers to observe higher-order thinking.

**Connected Tenets:** Assessment Purpose

**Topics:** Assessment Design, Formative Assessment, Summative Assessment and Grading

## Can I ask some really easy questions on an assessment so every student gets at least some points?

This questions speaks to the important relationship between formative and summative assessment. Avoid giving easy questions for this purpose most of the time. It is better to build confidence through a strong and recursive formative assessment process that allows learners to see both the complexity of questions increase and their own proficiency grow as the unit progresses. By the time learners get to a summative assessment, they are ready to receive questions that reflect the complexity of the learning goal; building their confidence during the summative assessment is far too late.

That being said, the following are some practical considerations around complexity when designing an assessment tool or process. First of all, it is effective to group together all items or tasks assessing one standard or learning target. There is no need to mix the assessment of learning goals because learners' brains then have to jump all over to make sense of each item. This can lead to fatigue and inaccurate results. Instead, develop enough questions to assess each standard or target and place them together, when appropriate.

Building confidence is certainly a strong strategy for ensuring learners stick with an assessment—with confidence, learners will do better. However, teachers do not want to wait for the summative assessment to build that confidence. Throughout a unit, learners should be tracking their confidence and success with individual learning targets. When they get to the end-of-unit assessment, learners will be prepared and will not need lower-level items. When learners recognize learning they have practiced, they will approach the assessment with confidence.

The exception to this rule is in the case of formative assessment. If simpler items lead to insight into whether a learner is achieving the standard, which specific knowledge or skills are still causing difficulty, and why, then less rigorous questions may be useful. However, teachers will want to ensure their learners are building up the knowledge and skills they will need to engage in grade-level work by the end of the unit, so they will spend most of their assessment energy on items that reflect the whole standard during those summative moments.

> **Connected Tenets:** Accurate Interpretation, Assessment Purpose, Communication of Results
>
> **Topics:** Preassessment, Summative Assessment and Grading

# How important is vertical alignment between grade levels and courses for curriculum and assessment?

Vertical alignment is an important part of the bigger picture of both curriculum and assessment alignment. As organizations engage in curriculum development work, teams should plan vertical conversations about alignment throughout the process. Educators should not assume that commercially produced textbooks have the vertical alignment necessary to address all the required standards. Very often, these vertical conversations help to identify gaps that can exist both in the materials and in the standards themselves.

When educators participate in collaborative conversations around vertical alignment, it helps them gain a better understanding about the expectations of both previous grades and courses as well as the grades and courses that come after theirs. This knowledge can help inform the unpacking process and criteria development for teachers as they learn more about the standards in their grade level and course. This information can also help identify the prerequisite skills that learners need to be successful as well as ways that they could potentially extend the learning for learners who are proficient early. Educators may share essential standards or learning with grade levels or courses before and after them and have conversations about the differences among and between the learning described, including how a strand of the learning changes and grows from one grade level to the next. Sharing assessments vertically can also contribute to deep understanding of the vertical alignment and what is important to emphasize and how learning may progress.

**Connected Tenets:** Accurate Interpretation, Assessment Purpose
**Topics:** Leadership

# How might I use technology as part of my assessment architecture?

Technology, when used intentionally, is a tool that can provide *accurate* assessment information that informs both teacher and student decision making. Technology can also offer an *efficient* way to collect information, making both the administration and analysis of the assessment occur more quickly. Lastly, technology can offer learners *a way to create* something as part of a performance assessment (for example, a learner-created blog, infographic, website, and so on). All three reasons support strong assessment architecture.

At its most basic level, technology tools can replace paper-and-pencil options—learners can type an essay on a Google Doc or create a presentation on Google Slides instead of a physical poster. In its more sophisticated form, technology can allow for collaboration that leads to sources, ideas, and products or performances that would not have been available without technology. For example, learners may be able to collaborate with scientists, authors, or organizations that can provide firsthand accounts of what they are studying. In one of its most advanced forms, learners can use technology tools to create websites or products that they share with an audience outside of their peers and their teachers. They may be able to collect surveys from people around the world, using Twitter and other social media outlets. And, they may be able to create something posted on a website to inform others of an issue that is critical to local or global citizens. This is technology at its most powerful.

Technology also provides avenues for feedback that can be authentic and inspiring. Learners may be able to gather feedback from other learners, community members, or experts to further enhance what they are trying to accomplish. Teachers can also use technology to provide feedback in the moment. There are many applications (such as Orange Slice, Vocaroo, or Mote) that allow for teachers to review student work and provide both audio and written comments to guide learners in identifying their strengths and their next steps.

Both the potential for technology to be a method of assessment and its potential to enhance feedback can provide deeper engagement and a more authentic audience as part of authentic assessment architecture. With an intentional purpose in mind, the following questions can guide the effective use of technology in assessment architecture.

- What is the targeted learning to be measured?

- How will technology enhance the materials, the method, and the look and feel?

- Do all students have access to the technology needed to engage in this method?

- What kind of learning about the technology will students need to be able to do this successfully?

- Are there any downsides to using the technology that could take away from the focus of what is to be learned? Is there a possibility that technology might diminish the accuracy and reliability of assessment results?

- How will I check to be sure the technology does not act as a barrier to students showing their proficiency?

- How will I make sure the technology isn't included simply because it seems flashy or trendy?

These questions can help guide the effective use of technology in assessment architecture so it enhances learning, avoids the outward appearance of efficiency or shininess, and maintains the depth and effectiveness necessary for valid assessment architecture.

**Connected Tenets:** Accurate Interpretation

**Topics:** Formative Assessment, Summative Assessment and Grading

# How do I make my assessments culturally responsive?

Culturally relevant and sensitive assessment is not just for racially diverse contexts. All learners benefit from multiple perspectives and a strength-based view of culture. Culturally responsive performance tasks and instruction can be informed by the work of Geneva Gay (2002) and Gloria Ladson-Billings and Mary Louise Gomez (2001). According to Gay (2002):

> Culturally responsive teaching is defined as using the cultural charac-teristics, experiences, and perspectives of ethnically diverse scholars as conduits for teaching them more effectively. It is based on the assumption that when academic knowledge and skills are situated within the lived experiences and frames of reference of scholars, they are more personally meaningful, have higher interest appeal and are learned more easily and thoroughly. (p. 106)

Educators make assessment culturally relevant and responsive by ensuring that the sources come from multiple perspectives, show strength-based examples of diversity, and represent meaningful and authentic (to the learners) scenarios and opportunities to engage in real issues.

Ladson-Billings (2009) further describes "culturally relevant teaching [as] a ped-agogy that empowers learners intellectually, socially, emotionally, and politically by using cultural references to impart knowledge, skills, and attitudes" (p. 20). With this in mind, teachers might ask themselves, "How might an assessment pose an authen-tic problem for learners to explore? How might assessment design invite learners to study multiple perspectives and pose solutions? How could a performance task or other assessment process cultivate a sense of social justice and change?"

Culturally responsive methods of assessment mean critically analyzing the assump-tions being made in the tasks themselves. Whose perspectives are being shared? Are they shared with a feeling of singularity, meaning there is only one way to experience or look at this event, person, story, or context? When considering the cultural rele-vance of a task, consider the following questions.

- Is it clear which standards or learning goals are being assessed? Is it clear why these goals might be important, interesting, and meaningful to learners?

- Are multiple perspectives referenced and explored? Is there a balance of strength-based perspectives of race and culture as well as examples of oppression? Are there examples of freedom balanced with moments of oppression?

- Do the sources used provide evidence for the claims and counterclaims of their position?

- Are learners able to explore their personal, cultural understanding? Are the learners' worldviews, learning preferences, beliefs, and values reflected in the assessment process?

- Is the task's introduction clearly formulated for each and every learner? Do one or more introductory sentences set the stage or provide context for the task?

- Is there a focused task with an appropriate verb that directly reflects the intended learning (*produce* versus *explain*; *create* versus *identify*)?

- Is the task authentic? Does it empower learners to generate solutions? Does it inspire social change? Does it seek to educate?

- Are tasks achievable within the time frame and context of class? Are criteria outlined for learners so they know what quality looks like? (Consider rubrics and scoring checklists.)

- Does instruction teach skills so that learners are able to succeed during the assessment process?

- Is the teacher aware of the communication patterns of the learners in the classroom (both in instruction and in task design)? Has the teacher removed barriers for learners?

Being culturally responsive means being acutely aware of both the goals for learning and the learners who will engage in those goals. Opening up the contexts for assessment, the resources and texts used, the ways learners might demonstrate their learning, and the approaches teachers use to honor learners are critical steps to building culturally responsive assessment.

> **Connected Tenets:** Accurate Interpretation, Communication of Results
>
> **Topics:** Assessment Design, Summative Assessment and Grading

# Assessment Use

## How do I balance authentic assessments with traditional assessments?

The answer to this question hinges on a shared understanding of the terms *authentic* and *traditional*. In general, authentic means assessment that is grounded in real-life or applicable experiences. Similarly, traditional most often implies test or selected-response items that are scored based on right and wrong answers.

Perhaps the way to view assessment is through the lens of learning. What needs to be assessed to support next steps or certify proficiency? From there, what is the most accurate and efficient way to gather the information? Both authentic and traditional assessments serve purpose toward the end goal; the challenge is selecting the best approach for the desired outcomes. There are times where concise, accurate responses (traditional or selected response) will provide the best means to attain the information. The challenge lies in not assuming speed and efficiency will lead to comprehensiveness and accuracy. Most learning standards are written at a performance level, so the selected-response assessment will never be able to comprehensively assess a learner's ability to put all of the learning together in a meaningful performance. When assessing the comprehensiveness of the standards at the point of mastery, it's important to consider more of the authentic (or constructed response) assessments.

**Connected Tenets:** Assessment Purpose

**Topics:** Assessment Design, Authentic Assessment, Formative Assessment, Summative Assessment and Grading

## How do I balance assessment architecture and instructional agility?

Balancing *architecture* and *agility* is about planning for the most common misunderstandings and being ready to make an instructional maneuver, should it be necessary. Being instructionally agile is not about flying by the seat of one's pants; it's about making instructional maneuvers, most of which can be anticipated by teachers. The need for mid-lesson assessment is predicated on the question of how a teacher, in the middle of a lesson, knows that the learners are still learning. Too often in the past, teachers would find out days later on an assessment (such as a failed quiz) that the learning from a few days ago was missed. By *planning with precision*, teachers can most efficiently and effectively *respond with agility*, so what appears as an assessment dichotomy actually can work seamlessly to accelerate learning.

For maximum agility, teachers' architecture would consider the following three things: (1) What are the most common misunderstandings that typically emerge when I teach this lesson? (2) How will I know whether one or more of those misunderstandings is emerging during the lesson? and (3) What will I do instructionally, should one or more of those misunderstandings emerge? The first question identifies areas where formative assessment might be beneficial. What results from the second question is the strategic placement of an assessment moment, while the third question is about agility. Now, the mid-lesson assessment may not reveal any misunderstandings, which allows the teacher to know that moving ahead in the lesson is the most favorable course of action. On the other hand, there may be learners who would definitely benefit from clarification or additional practice. The point is to make maneuvers *should they be necessary.*

This same process can occur on a larger scale with common formative assessments, where teams collaborate to determine next steps for their learners. While anticipated misunderstandings can be planned for, it is also possible for an assessment to reveal a misunderstanding not anticipated, which makes the collaborative process amongst teachers even more valuable and important. In this case, teachers can work together to design instructional responses that will address the newly identified student need. The point is that at any level, assessment architecture (precision) and instructional agility (flexibility) can work in harmony to allow teachers to be at their learner-responsive best. (For more information on instructional agility, see chapter 7, page 149.)

**Connected Tenets:** Instructional Agility

**Topics:** Intervention and Instruction, Questioning

## Should my collaborative team members all use the same assessments?

PLCs are organized around three big ideas: (1) a focus on learning, (2) collaborative culture and collective responsibility, and (3) a focus on results (DuFour et al., 2016). Common assessments provide the data necessary for that focus on both learning and results that fuel effective collaboration. It is difficult to imagine how a collaborative team would work effectively without common assessments because this common assessment evidence ensures collaborative teams interpret the standard in a similar way. The methods a team chooses to assess the standards is part of what educators use to determine learner expectations. Assessing a standard using a multiple-choice item is very different than asking learners to produce their own response. This shared decision about what types of items will lead to understanding mastery is essential for the team to examine student work in relation to shared goals and success criteria. Analyzing the evidence from those common assessments leads to understanding learners' strengths and learning needs, which informs a team about which instructional practices worked and what instruction they need to design for individual and groups of learners moving forward. Common assessments are, in effect, a shared language and a process to get to clarity regarding what mastery looks like. The collaborative team can work together to create the assessment plan to determine how to assess and when it makes the most sense to assess learners, in terms of both learning and how to support the learners.

While a collaborative team should spend time and energy on utilizing the information from common assessments, that does not mean that individual teachers cannot make decisions about formative assessments based on the needs of their learners. Teachers are certainly not limited to utilizing only common assessments to determine what learners know and are able to do.

**Connected Tenets:** Accurate Interpretation, Instructional Agility

**Topics:** Collaboration, Professional Learning Communities

## How should my collaborative team members make sure that we are scoring assessments with a rubric consistently?

Rubrics are valuable tools for both the learner and the teacher because they describe student performance with specificity. As with any tool, they must be used effectively and appropriately to truly realize their potential. If a collaborative team decides to use a rubric to score a common assessment, then time should also be spent making sure that the tool is being interpreted consistently.

The first step would be to engage in collaborative conversations about both the rubric and the task that learners will be asked to complete. Collaborative team members should be clear about what is expected of learners and what the language of the rubric means.

After the learners have completed the task, the team engages in collaborative scoring. Ideally, each student's work would be *double scored*, or reviewed and scored by two educators, particularly in the case of an assessment being used summatively. If time does not allow for this, the team should set aside some time to calibrate, where a sample of evidence is scored individually by each team member and then collaboratively discussed so team members come to consensus on each piece of student work. This leads to more precision in interpreting the rest of the assessments that may be scored by only one teacher. There should also be time spent reviewing the scoring for exact and adjacent matches on scores as well as reviewing the rubric during that process. Each time the rubric is used, time should be spent reviewing it and considering how learners interpreted the rubric and if the rubric clearly distinguishes between levels in terms of qualities. This is particularly helpful when new team members are added to the team or when teams revise student tasks.

**Connected Tenets:** Accurate Interpretation, Instructional Agility

**Topics:** Collaboration, Student Engagement and Motivation

# Can I have groups of students complete assessments together?

Cooperative learning has research-proven benefits for student learning. When used in the context of assessments, it can, however, make assessments very unclear. That is not to say that it cannot be accomplished, but teachers must take very explicit steps in planning both assessment and scoring to make sure that the assessment is an accurate reflection of each student's learning. Not every standard or learning target lends itself to cooperative learning. Once a teacher determines that there is a match between the learning and a collaborative assessment, then certain design steps should be taken.

- There should be opportunities for each learner to demonstrate his or her learning on an individual basis as well as collectively throughout the collaborative process.

- Reflection tools are essential for both learners and teachers in order to provide insights into both learning and the contributions of all group members.

- Observation checklists or rubrics can guide data collection while cooperative learning is occurring.

- Summative assessment can occur after collaborative learning, so the group works together to develop learning, but individuals are responsible for demonstrating skill and understanding at the end of learning.

**Connected Tenets:** Assessment Purpose, Student Investment

**Topics:** Collaboration, Critical Competencies

# Is it okay to assess through observation alone?

Some standards and learning targets can certainly be assessed through observation as learners perform the skills articulated in the standards. Teachers should establish clear success criteria as well as a process for collecting information about student performance during observations prior to the assessment. One example of this may occur in preschool or primary grades, when a dependence solely on writing is not possible (or preferable). The teacher may use a data collection sheet organized around a specific standard with spaces to collect data about each learner. As he or she interacts with learners throughout the classroom during independent work or centers, the teacher can collect evidence of student performance related to that standard.

Observation can be a valuable method for collecting individual student performance for certain standards. Teachers should be clear about the expectations and success criteria and use an efficient method for collecting that information about each learner individually.

> **Connected Tenets:** Assessment Purpose, Student Investment
> **Topics:** Authentic Assessment, Early Learning

## How do I handle assessment in special education and with language learners?

Learners in special education and learners who are language learners are entitled to and deserve high-quality assessment experiences and methods that accurately reflect their learning and do not reduce the cognitive level because of the different ways they process information or are learning another language. Teachers use the assessment plan to articulate the learning goals and note the specific language learning goals that learners learning the language would also need to engage in the assessment. This signals to the teacher team and any other teachers who are working with learners learning the language that instruction and formative feedback should focus on those language targets to ensure learners are on the path to achieving the standard. The assessment plan is also a place to note accommodations that learners with special learning needs may need to engage in instruction and assessment. Tapping into colleagues who have expertise in learning a language and supporting neurodiverse learners in special education is essential to ensure that instruction and assessment are set up accurately. This assessment plan is the foundation for learners and their teachers to get accurate information about knowledge and skills. Using assessment formatively along the way is essential for all learners, and even more so for the learners with divergent learning needs or those learning a language. The process of providing descriptive feedback and ensuring learners act on that feedback will help them make progress and achieve the standard. These are the environments that benefit all learners.

Learners with specialized or language needs should be assessed on grade-level standards and participate and engage in the learning experiences associated with those grade-level standards. These learners may need additional accommodations or supports to help them showcase what they know and are able to do. Making decisions about accommodations can be incredibly difficult and complex for teachers, which is why collaboration with other educators can be very beneficial. For language learners, identifying language targets and ensuring learners have ample dialogue to learn and explore vocabulary and context is part of the instructional process. Conversations among educators are essential to determine what accommodations still allow the learners to demonstrate proficiency and to determine the point at which accommodations become modifications of the expectations or the standard itself.

The creation of detailed learning progressions is an important part of the assessment design process. These progressions are descriptions of the more sophisticated ways learners think and act (Erkens et al., 2017). It is important that the progressions do not simply reflect the proficiency level but also reflect the steps along the journey as learners move toward proficiency. These learning progressions help to guide assessment design and also help both teachers and learners alike pinpoint a learner's place on that journey. It is important for language learners and learners with special needs to see both where they are in relationship to the standard and what steps come next in order to meet it.

**Connected Tenets:** Assessment Purpose, Communication of Results

**Topics:** English Learners

## How do I handle assessment in a multi-grade setting?

In a multi-grade setting, assessment architecture depends on the same—if not more explicit—clarity as the traditional setting. The difference is that learners in a single classroom will be working toward different learning goals at the same time. This means that teachers will need to spend time clarifying targets and success criteria for more than one grade level. The processes for doing this remain the same, but the volume of work increases.

However, there are a number of steps a teacher can take to make assessment design, administration, and analysis more streamlined in a multi-grade environment. First, teachers may decide to map the learning goals and targets to allow them to align similarities between two (or more) different grade levels for the purpose of planning and instruction. For example, a teacher may notice that while her fourth- and fifth-grade learners have some different learning goals, they share the goals of creating narrative texts, comprehending informational and literary texts, and formal speaking. By mapping the areas that overlap, assessment and instructional pacing on these goals can occur at the same time, making the classroom environment feel less fractured. Assessment tools may look similar for these shared goals, and while the rigor will shift for learners as they get older, the criteria for success may look quite similar.

Teachers in a multi-grade environment may also find it helpful to align the tools and methods they use to assess learners. Even when learners are working on different learning goals at the same time, it can be helpful to invite the learners to engage in similar assessment processes. For example, if one group of learners is exploring environmental sustainability while another group is working on acids and bases, the tool by which learners are assessed could be the same (for example, the creation of a flow chart or a table). This means that the teacher can issue the same oral instructions, applied to different content, thus reducing the amount of time the teacher has to spend moving from one group to the next.

When teachers in a multi-grade environment are responding to assessment information, they may find it helpful to group learners by similar needs. In this way, learners who are in different grades may find themselves in the same group because they share a similar need. For example, a ninth-grade learner may need additional help and practice with supporting responses with evidence from a text, and a tenth-grade learner may share the same need. This means that even though the learners are in different grades, the response to assessment may be the same, and they may be grouped so they can practice this skill together.

Many teachers working in a multi-grade environment may feel like they spend their days rushing back and forth between groups of learners. However, if they can make time to design assessment and responses processes that leverage the similarities between learning goals, they can reduce this feeling of being overwhelmed. They can also help their learners understand that learning is not about isolated bits of content at different grade levels. Rather, it is a continuous process of adding new learning on top of old learning. This is a healthy perspective that a multi-grade environment can support.

**Connected Tenets:** Accurate Interpretation
**Topics:** Differentiation, Unpacking and Learning Progressions

# If I am held to a pacing guide but I know my students are not ready for an assessment, what do I do?

Pacing guides are well-intended tools to ensure learners have all of the necessary knowledge and skills they will require to be successful with upcoming learning experiences. But pacing guides are tools, not rules, so it's important to implement with integrity rather than fidelity—sticking with the spirit of the tool rather than the rule of the tool. Pacing guides highlight the educators' best guesses as to the amount of time it will take for learners to grasp concepts, but learning is not algorithmic and cannot be scripted.

The best approach to this dilemma is a proactive one. When teaching teams work together to create their summative assessment in advance of instruction, they can begin making strategic decisions that enable them to *find* time to respond to potential learner needs during the learning schedule by streamlining, abbreviating, or even eliminating curricular components that will not ensure student readiness for the standards.

If, after this proactive planning, additional time is still required and it will extend the timeline dramatically, then it's helpful to work within the team to solve the problem, modifying the pacing guide accordingly so the most significant components are still allowed the appropriate amount of attention. Together, teams can begin to identify pacing components that can be embedded elsewhere, altered, or shortened, or any other strategy that can allow the team to cover the significant components within the required timelines.

> **Connected Tenets:** Instructional Agility
>
> **Topics:** Common Assessment, Pacing Guides

# If I have a performance assessment and students are absent, what should I do?

When learners are asked to create, produce, or replicate the authentic context within which the learning is meant to be applied (performance assessment) and they are absent, educators have a few options. The options depend on a number of factors, and careful consideration of these factors lead to the best action to take. Consider the following.

- If the learners' absence was legitimate (for example, illness or family crisis) and not based on a fear of the assessment itself, then having learners complete or present when they return is the best way forward. If this is not possible due to time constraints, then perhaps the method of assessment could be streamlined (for example, instead of performing an entire play, the learners are interviewed or record their portion for the teacher). There are usually multiple ways skills and knowledge can be assessed.

- If they are absent and they were part of a group, while this can be tricky, it is still optimal to have the group finish and present when the learner returns. If the group went forward without the absent member, then the absent member must still present or record a portion of the presentation. In any case, all learners should be individually scored on the intended standards, measured with little to no part of the overall score dependent on another group member. As an alternative, the learner who was absent could share another perspective or another aspect of the work as well—in a video or in a small interview.

- If the reason the learners were absent is related to the assessment itself (for example, they were nervous or fearful), then a more nuanced response is necessary. Talk to the learners about their reason for the absence. Acknowledge their anxiety and consider alternative options such as presenting only to the teacher, recording it, or writing it (if the end goal is not speaking). If there is another method of assessment that would gather accurate information on that learner's level of proficiency on the standard to be measured, then consider providing an alternative method while assessing the same criteria. It can be advantageous to ask the learners how they might like to demonstrate their understanding.

- If learners were absent and it was because they were unprepared, then a conversation about the process of designing and planning a performance assessment can help guide the learners in reflecting what led to being unprepared and what they might do differently next time. Then, the learners must still perform, present, or produce the assessment. If the standard is essential, then assessment is not optional. However, the nonacademic criteria dealing with preparedness would be scored lower to indicate more work needed.

Absence is nuanced and so paying attention to the reason for the absence contributes to a response that leads to accurate inferences and interpretations about learners' proficiency on the intended standards as well as their nonacademic behaviors such as timeliness and preparation.

> **Connected Tenets:** Accurate Interpretation, Communication of Results
> **Topics:** Assessment Design, Authentic Assessment, Behavior

# What role should homework play in assessment?

Anyone who has mastered a craft will confirm that a *lot* of practice—which often included some struggles and a plethora of mistakes—preceded his or her success. Malcolm Gladwell (2008) suggests it takes ten thousand hours of practice to become an expert at something. The value of targeted practice is both common sense and rigorously documented. But there are guidelines to make practice effective. As the saying goes, *practice doesn't make perfect; practice makes permanent.*

Homework is most frequently applied as an opportunity for practice, and it can be highly effective in the assessment process *if* it is employed the right way. There are several guidelines to make homework as invaluable practice to the assessment journey.

1. Practice should begin with a clear and transparent goal. When it comes to homework, the goal should be *student-generated* and directly linked to the academic standards being studied.

2. Practice should allow for risk taking and mistake making. If practice work goes into the gradebook, then it counts. If mistakes happen during the learning, and such scores are documented and included in final grades, then there is no chance to achieve mastery later. Why practice if the option to achieve mastery is off the table early in the learning process?

3. Practice should generate focused, diagnostic feedback that will advance the goal and precipitate success in the final product. Marks, grades, or scores do not tell a learner what or how to improve; they only document what happened. If the opportunity to practice is intended to generate improvements, then learners require penalty-free, factual evidence of what worked and what didn't, so they can make the necessary adjustments and maintain the motivation to try again.

Many teachers bemoan the fact that learners will not engage in practice work if it doesn't add value in the gradebook. But learners have proven time and again that they will actually engage in *more* practice than was assigned *if* the feedback is so valuable they couldn't succeed without it and *if* the feedback fed forward so success was imminent.

**Connected Tenets:** Assessment Purpose

**Topics:** Formative Assessment, Homework

# Assessment Examination

## How often should I critically examine my assessments to make sure they are good? How do I do this?

Critical examination of assessment tools and process can occur anytime. For example, there may be a moment during instruction when a teacher and the learners gain insight about a learning goal and an assessment is adjusted to reflect this new understanding. Or perhaps, after a teacher observes learners engaging in the assessment and notices a large degree of hesitation and uncertainty by learners, the teacher may decide to explore the assessment itself to determine possible causes of the difficulty. That being said, the process of ensuring assessments are strong will likely occur *most often* at two times during the learning process.

The first time is prior to beginning the unit. At this time, teachers select standards and determine learning targets for the unit. If they are using assessments from a specific resource, from a previous year, or from a different teacher, teachers should analyze and align the assessments to the identified standards to ensure they match what is intended for students to learn. Sometimes, teachers will revise given items or tasks and add another part to ensure the assessment accurately reflects what was intended for students to learn and achieve. This analysis before instruction ensures that instructional moves and formative feedback along the way (during the unit) are clear and targeted.

The second time teachers will likely examine an assessment tool is when learners have completed the assessment. Teachers (individually or as a team) analyze evidence generated by the assessment responses. Besides identifying learners who need additional time and support on essential learning targets or standards, they are looking for items that learners misinterpreted and that need to be revised. If they find an item to be poorly worded or able to be interpreted in multiple ways, they should throw the item out and not use it to determine the overall level of proficiency (or the grade in a traditional system). They will then revise these items for the next administration of the assessment. Sometimes the design of a task or the wording of a rubric needs revision, and so analyzing the assessment evidence is the perfect time to make adjustments based on what the student work is signaling.

No matter when teachers engage in assessment review, each time a teacher gives an assessment for the first time, it is important to ensure that there are no wording issues in the items or tasks, design flaws, biases, or assumed background information that make the results unreliable. When an assessment is a performance task, there are moments along the way to adjust anything that is unclear or contains bias. As learners are engaging in drafts of the performance or product, teachers may revise rubrics, checklists, or directions as the process unfolds. Refining assessment tools can occur anytime it is needed.

**Connected Tenets:** Accurate Interpretation, Assessment Purpose, Communication of Results

**Topics:** Preassessment, Summative Assessment and Grading

# Is there a difference in how I assess products versus how I assess processes?

The answer is both yes and no. The fundamentals of assessment are universal and timeless regardless of whether a process or a product is being assessed. However, the actual assessment procedure is more likely to adjust when focused on assessing a process as opposed to a product.

Whether assessing a product or process, it is imperative that teachers clearly articulate what standards or targets they are assessing, their identified depth of knowledge, and the success criteria that describe the quality of the product or process (proficiency) that learners can or should achieve. Both products and processes require this level of clarity to ensure that the assessment method is an obvious match for the expected level of quality and complexity.

What might be different between products and processes is the assessment procedure teachers use to gather evidence, since teachers can assess a student-produced product asynchronously. Often, but not always, assessing a process will have the teacher and learner simultaneously engaged. This lends itself to performance assessments where the teacher needs to see or hear the demonstration of learning in real time. So, while the fundamental structure of assessment remains the same, the shift happens operationally.

> **Connected Tenets:** Accurate Interpretation, Communication of Results
>
> **Topics:** Authentic Assessment, Criteria

# Assessment Architecture in a Remote Learning Context

In a remote learning context, it may be tempting to assess learners using the most straightforward methods, plucking assignments and tests directly from already-existing unit plans and simply inserting them into an online format. While this approach is certainly practical in some contexts, in others it is not. Remote learning is more complex than simply doing everything done in face-to-face environments on a virtual platform instead. A teacher's ability to monitor learning, to engage learners synchronously, and to adjust in the moment is more challenging in a remote learning context. The assessment architecture may need to shift to address specific needs of both teachers and the learners they serve. In a remote learning context, when ensuring a strong assessment architecture, teachers may want to consider the following.

- Being very clear about the learning goals being assessed, including strong descriptions of the actions learners need to take to demonstrate proficiency as well as the quality of those actions (success criteria); when teachers have made time *in advance of instruction and assessment* to consider these aspects of the learning goals, they are more ready to examine artifacts of student learning and make decisions about what they are seeing.

- Communicating the learning goals to students and families for every learning experience offered in a remote context; building a shared understanding is a great way to structure activities, to offer feedback, and to organize assessment information when making decisions.

- Asking learners for feedback about the assessment processes offered in a remote learning context; this includes making sure assessment experiences are not taking inordinate amounts of time and providing time for learners to ask clarifying questions.

- Being open to flexible assessment methods for learners; this means taking into account limited resources for some learners (time resources, support resources, technology, and materials) and offering asynchronous assessment when possible, followed by a conference when clarification is needed. The concepts of *fair* and *equal* are of importance in a remote learning context. Some learners may be able to navigate a virtual environment with ease, while others may need scaffolds. Ensuring that learners who need supports are not penalized for their skills and understanding in relation to learning goals is paramount. Further, being open to video and photo documentation can help learners communicate their thinking and help teachers interpret those communications.

- Being clear about the connection between formative assessment and summative assessment and communicating this relationship to students and their families; it is important that everyone understands how practice and exploration lead to increased proficiency when combined with targeted instruction and feedback. Teachers need learners to engage in learning experiences and formative assessment that supports growth, so they can intervene and offer support when it makes sense to do so. Learners need to clearly understand and experience the role of formative assessment in summative achievement in order for remote learning contexts to support learning and not just task completion.

# CHAPTER 5

# COMMUNICATION OF RESULTS

It is one thing to assess student skill and understanding, and another thing entirely to make decisions around how to communicate those results back to the students, their families, and other stakeholders. It is this relationship between assessment design and assessment response that can make or break any assessment system. For this reason, questions around the communication of assessment results have preoccupied educational systems for a very long time.

Making these decisions involves a deep understanding of assessment purpose, including understanding how to use the evidence and determining the needs of the people who will be receiving, interpreting, and using the information. In the end, communicating assessment results must generate productive responses from learners and all the stakeholders who support them. This productive response can take the form of feedback or student goal setting. It might manifest itself through data notebooks or through grades on a report card. Behind the scenes, teams of teachers may collaborate to use the assessment results as they design interventions and instructional supports. On a more public front, teachers and learners may work together to lead conferences with parents and caregivers. Deciding how best to communicate assessment information is foundational to many critical aspects of education, and exploring questions in relation to this topic holds great importance to ensure learning and accuracy.

# The Purpose of Communicating Results

## Why is communication of results so important?

Administering assessments will not ultimately benefit learners unless teachers and learners can efficiently and effectively use the results of those assessments. Clear communication is essential so that all stakeholders are able to understand and utilize assessment results.

The purpose of formative assessment is to cause more learning. Communicating the results through effective feedback is a way to help learners close the gap between their own performance and the standard or expectation. This feedback should be descriptive and timely, and build on the learner's current level of understanding. When educators clearly communicate this information to learners, learners are able to take ownership of the steps necessary to meet the standard. This requires teachers to be thoughtful and purposeful when communicating with learners and setting up the context of their learning so they can act on the feedback.

Communicating summative assessment information requires the same levels of preparation and planning. Since the purpose of summative assessment is to determine the levels of learning at a particular point in time, communication about the results should reflect exactly that. The traditional grading systems of the past are constantly being questioned, particularly when they include information outside the learner's achievement related to a standard. Whether or not schools change to standards-based grading systems, most educators are having conversations about how to accurately and concisely communicate achievement.

**Connected Tenets:** Accurate Interpretation, Student Investment
**Topics:** Formative Assessment

## How can I connect today's assessment to future learning?

The connection to future learning is more seamless when an assessment is designed to elicit evidence that makes both strengths and that which needs strengthening clear in relation to every learner. Assessment is used formatively when the results reveal the needs that exist between the learning goal and the learner's current status. In essence, a teacher's ability to leverage assessment to advance learning depends on the effective use of valid and reliable assessment information gathered through careful assessment design and accurate interpretation.

It is critical that the feedback teachers provide learners elicits a productive response and that learners actually use the feedback they receive from their teacher (or their peers or themselves) to advance—or at least attempt to advance—their proficiency. One of the biggest inhibitors to using feedback is grades, scores, or levels. Grades have the potential to inhibit learning if learners find their initial grade satisfactory. If future learning is the desired outcome of an assessment, teachers might be wise to leave grading, scoring, or leveling to assessment processes that fulfill the summative purpose. Formative assessment can be called *informative assessment* since the goal is to inform teachers and learners about what's next.

Another strategy is to create assessment processes focused on readiness. Whether through a preassessment at the beginning of an instructional unit or through a quick check-in at the beginning of a lesson, assessments that determine strengths and needs prior to instruction automatically prioritize future learning by emphasizing what's next instead of just what was.

**Connected Tenets:** Assessment Architecture, Instructional Agility

**Topics:** Differentiation, Feedback, Formative Assessment

# Formative and Summative Assessment Communication

## Is it wrong to put a mark or a score on a formative assessment?

Experts disagree on this point. Internationally recognized assessment consultant Ken O'Connor (2011) believes that formative assessments should receive only feedback and no score, while others such as leading education researcher Robert J. Marzano (2006, 2010) believe that unless learners receive a mark or a score on a formative assessment, they will not be able to ascertain where they are relative to where they need to be— a key factor in the formative assessment process.

But there is common ground: a shared belief between O'Connor, Marzano, and other grading experts such as Douglas Reeves (2016a, 2016b); Thomas R. Guskey (2015, 2020); Tom Schimmer (2014, 2016); and Tom Schimmer, Garnet Hillman, and Mandy Stalets (2018) is that the learner must be able to increase achievement over time. So, formative assessment *can* receive marks or scores *as long as a learner can grow past early marks to show mastery by the end.*

One way to approach this dilemma is to observe how learners respond to whatever decisions are made. If any practice negatively impacts learners, shift the practice. If a score seems to result in a fixed mindset, then opt for feedback only. Alternately, if a score clearly motivates and encourages learners, then this practice is having a positive impact on learners.

For teachers, the greatest dilemma involves the use of online gradebooks that easily prohibit growth over time by (1) documenting scores that are rolled into an averaging algorithm on completion of a course, and (2) revealing to all stakeholders scores that might not lead to mathematically consistent end marks.

There are three potential quick fixes to this dilemma.

1. Turn off averaging in the gradebook. Track standards over time and then look for the mode (most common score generated) in the later samples of work.

2. When entering an assessment result that will be graded, assign it zero value so that the score the learner earns on formative work can be entered without it factoring into the final grade.

3. Use an alternative marking system on formative assessments such as +/−, NY (not yet), P (progressing), or letters instead of numbers that encourage calculation and averaging. Using indicator marks, for example, can help learners monitor for growth leading into the summative assessment that will result in the more traditional score.

Of course, the software will dictate what's feasible, and all grading software systems are different. Educators will need to work together to explore the best possibilities for their learners.

> **Connected Tenets:** Assessment Purpose
>
> **Topics:** Formative Assessment, Summative Assessment and Grading

## Which assessment results are set in stone, and which can I change?

Theoretically, any assessment result can change because assessment captures skills and understanding *at a moment in time*. Learning is continuous; therefore, assessment results will change over time. In particular, formative assessment results are *supposed to change* because, presumably, formative assessment results will be used to increase learning. If a formative assessment result was set in stone, teachers would not have successfully impacted student learning as intended.

When reassessment is designed with forethought and intentionality, educators can directly embed it into a unit of study. When teachers create a pathway that shows where every target fits within their assessments, they can more readily replace old evidence with newer evidence to identify the points at which learners grasp the necessary concepts and skills.

In addition, even though teachers often organize their learning goals into units of study, it is important to remember that most learning goals assigned to grade levels are intended to be learned by the end of the unit, the quarter, the semester, or the year—even if the formal instruction happened in September. Therefore, when instruction progresses to the end of a unit of study, the summative result might feel set in stone, but learners actually have until the end of the year to acquire the necessary skills and understanding. A summative result in September may be replaced with new assessment evidence gathered in May, when teachers reviewed the concepts and learners attained increased proficiency.

Nevertheless, school systems typically have specific times during the year when assessment results become part of reporting decisions and these results are shared with parents and guardians. This is often when teachers verify learning in a more summative way. When teachers communicate these assessment results to families, they may seem more permanent, at least until teachers report something new in the next reporting period.

Ultimately, communicating to students and parents how assessment results will be collected and shared, and how those results might change and under what conditions, can help build readiness for the assessment results teachers choose to share.

**Connected Tenets:** Assessment Architecture

**Topics:** Formative Assessment, Growth Mindset, Summative Assessment and Grading

# Systems of Reporting

## How do I convert a level to a percentage or letter grade?

Converting a level of performance to a percentage-based grade represents an exercise in finding an imperfect solution to some of the dilemmas teachers will face when transitioning from a traditional grading system to one focused more on standards. The solutions are *imperfect* since there will undoubtedly be advantages and drawbacks in each case, but the percentage system itself is imperfect as well.

One strategy is to make the conversion at the source. On a single student sample, a 1–4 scale, for example, could equate to the midpoint of each percentage increment. That is, a 4 would equate to 95 percent, a 3 to 85 percent, a 2 to 75 percent, and a

1 to 65 percent (assuming an A–F or a 60–100 grading scale). Teachers could even use 55 percent to convert a zero (defined as *insufficient evidence*). This way, the scores associated with each learner's demonstration are immediately converted and would be combined to determine students' overall grades, should that process still be the system and routine for the school, district, or division. The conversion occurs immediately, which allows for educators to incorporate the percentage-based gradebook into level-based grading practices. The downside is that no learner could ever earn 96 to 100 percent, an outcome which may have varying degrees of imperfection given the social and school cultural norms of a school or system.

Another method is to level and track demonstrations of learning on the 1–4 scale and then combine achievement on individual standards, with the conversion at the very end. To do this, teachers would need to rethink the way they organize evidence of learning. If 1–4 demonstrations are tracked by traditional task types (such as tests, quizzes, assignments, and so on), then a fairly inaccurate grade could result since the same standard is represented in all of the task types, which are given varying degrees of *weight* when it comes to grade determination. Tracking by standard (even if teachers use task-type labels to communicate the size and scope of the assessment) makes accuracy much more likely.

The second consideration for this approach is how the single demonstrations of learning contribute to the overall level of proficiency. Teachers will have to decide whether the most recent, more recent, or more consistent level of performance is most accurate. The biggest enemy of accuracy is the *averaging over time within the same standard*, especially if the demonstrations are spaced widely apart (averaging across standards or strands is not necessarily problematic).

Here's the key: students' levels of proficiency must accurately reflect their full degree of understanding or skill. If, for example, a teacher determined that a learner was a 2 since she started as a 1 and finished as a 3, and that was repeated across all standards, the combination across standards would produce a level that would be quite inaccurate in terms of reflecting the learner's most current level. The more accurate representation of her proficiency if she started as a 1 and finished as a 3 would be to identify her learning as a 3. How many samples teachers use to make that determination is up to the teachers, but the combination across standards in this case will produce a more accurate picture.

Consider the example in figure 5.1. Assuming that the level of each standard is appropriately determined as described previously, a teacher could simply find the *mean* of the standards (in this case, 2.9) and simply use a percentage equivalent table or grade alignment tool to determine the overall percentage (see "How Do I Bridge Systems of Reporting (Four Levels, Percentages, Letter Grades, and So on)?" for a sample grade-alignment tool).

| Standard 1 | Standard 2 | Standard 3 | Standard 4 | Standard 5 | Standard 6 | Standard 7 | Standard 8 | Standard 9 | Standard 10 |
|---|---|---|---|---|---|---|---|---|---|
| 2 | 3 | 4 | 3 | 3 | 2 | 4 | 3 | 3 | 2 |

**Figure 5.1:** *Example of student achievement on a set of standards.*

If teachers are converting to a letter grade, then 2.9 rounds up to a 3.0, which could equate to a B. Everything in assessment is contextually sensitive and nuanced, so conversations must logically align with the norms and routines of each school. A consistent department-wide or schoolwide approach would be optimal for clarity and transparency.

Whether converting at the source or at the end, translating levels to a percentage will be an imperfect process. That being said, using levels or rubric-based assessment within a percentage-based system can provide learners with critical information for growth and can provide teachers with clarity when verifying quality.

**Connected Tenets:** Assessment Purpose, Accurate Interpretation

**Topics:** Reporting, Summative Assessment and Grading

# How do I bridge systems of reporting (four levels, percentages, letter grades, and so on)?

The simplest way to bridge systems of reporting is to make logical alignments and not try to overthink or overcomplicate the systems, especially when it comes to helping parents understand how the systems overlap. Figure 5.2 offers a clear and streamlined connection between multiple systems (assuming a 60–100, A–F grading scale).

The one assumption with this approach, of course, is that the four levels represent a version of passing or meeting the expectation. The other is that a final percentage-based grade would be determined using the processes outlined previously (see "How Do I Convert a Level to a Percentage or Letter Grade?" page 111).

If schools decided to use only three levels, then they would eliminate a result of D and would set 75 percent for a final grade as the minimal threshold for passing. Single samples would receive nothing lower than a 65 percent

| 4 | 95% | A |
|---|---|---|
| 3 | 85% | B |
| 2 | 75% | C |
| 1 | 65% | D |
| 0 | 55% | F |

**Figure 5.2:** *Grade alignment tool.*

(as a 1 would then become the *not yet* level). This would allow for the combination of 1s (65 percent) and 2s (75 percent).

The key is to find a balance between being number obsessed and number afraid. What's optimal is to *start with the science* (numbers), *but finish with the art* (judgment) of grading (Schimmer, 2016). This would establish both an efficient and effective process for grade determination. Numbers can accelerate the opportunity to see the overall picture, but teachers—not computers—must be the final arbiters of students' grades.

Yet another approach is to skip the bridging work by abandoning the 100-point or percentage-based system altogether. Many districts today have done so, opting for a variety of alternatives that most often align with using *logic rules* instead. In a logic rule system, the learner still graduates with a traditional transcript and a GPA, but the final scores are based on a set of threshold criteria rather than mathematical algorithms. Teachers within a discipline work together to establish their specific threshold criteria (see figure 5.3) based on their essential standards. All tasks used to determine a grade are at the appropriate rigor as determined by the demands of the standard. The body of evidence is then examined to determine the degree to which the qualities of each grade are reflected. An example of a logic rule table can be seen in figure 5.3.

Whichever approach is used, it is critical to share it with students and their families to enhance transparency.

**Connected Tenets:** Accurate Interpretation

**Topics:** Reporting, Summative Assessment and Grading

# Is an open gradebook that students and families can access a good idea?

It certainly can be, but, like most things, it's all in the execution. Let's begin with a potential drawback: an open gradebook can place a disproportionate amount of attention on grades and grading. Grading is not about raising achievement; neither is grading a learning strategy or an intervention. By opening up the gradebook, parents and students can become overly obsessed with grades, scores, and levels and spend less time focused on the quality of what was produced or the type of learning that comes next. A balanced assessment system offsets daily formative assessment strategies with periodic moments of verification; the open gradebook can inadvertently send the opposite message about assessment priorities.

It's not that grades don't matter; they do. As learners age, they begin to focus their attention on higher education and life after the K–12 experience. They know that

| | Threshold Criteria<br>*A sufficient sample size of latest work reveals:* |
|---|---|
| **A** | **Content:**<br>• There are *no* major errors or omissions in content.<br>**Process:**<br>• There is no score below a 3 in any of the student's latest samples of work.<br>• There are at least three scores of 4 for process standards 1–5; and,<br>• At least 50 percent of process standards 6–10 earned 4s. |
| **B** | **Content:**<br>• At least three-quarters of the proficiency scores for content were a 3 or higher; and,<br>• There are no proficiency levels below a 2 in any content measurements.<br>**Process:**<br>• At least three-quarters of the proficiency scores for process standards 1–5 were a 3 or higher; and,<br>• There are no proficiency levels below a 2 in any process standards 1–5.<br>• There are no proficiency levels below a 2 in process standards 6–10. |
| **C** | **Content:**<br>• At least half of the proficiency scores for content were a 3 or higher; and,<br>• There are no proficiency levels below a 2 in any content measurements.<br>**Process:**<br>• At least one-quarter of the proficiency scores for content were a 3 or higher for process standards 1–5; and,<br>• There are no proficiency levels below a 2 in process standards 6–10. |

*Figure 5.3: Example threshold criteria.*

grades and what they (are supposed to) communicate are still the primary currency used to judge whether they have access to certain schools, programs, or opportunities. However, an increase in the frequency or visibility of grades doesn't increase achievement.

At its best, an open gradebook can create a more efficient communication system. While an open gradebook should never be viewed as a replacement for authentic face-to-face (or at least voice-to-voice) communication, it can provide insight as to how the learner is achieving in comparison to the intended learning. It can provide at least an initial verification that more extensive and personalized intervention is or is not necessary.

The one dilemma the open gradebook can never resolve is the need to populate it. Educators can't promise to update parents regularly through the open gradebook but then call everything formative and never update it. In this case, schools would have to be crystal clear with parents that daily updates will not occur. More frequent summative assessment is not the answer—this usually leads schools to populate the gradebook with formative scores, which is clearly a compromise to the bulk of assessment research. That said, most formative scores in open gradebooks are zero-weighted to ensure that formative scores aren't contributing to final grade determination. Tracking the progression of learning can be helpful in more fully understanding both summative results and what comes next. Using that information to also contribute to grade determination is often a step too far.

Supplementing an open gradebook with portfolios or samples of learning is one way to ensure that students and families remain focused on growth and learning. Creating a system of communication that includes but is not solely an open gradebook can communicate a more complex and accurate understanding of what is happening in classrooms each day.

> **Connected Tenets:** Assessment Purpose, Student Investment
> **Topics:** Parent Engagement, Reporting, Summative Assessment and Grading

# Our report card format is determined by the district; I can't change it. What can I do?

If educators cannot change the report card, they should change how they determine grades so that what goes on the report card is accurate and reflective of sound assessment. Many educators work within systems where some of the decision making about report card format, electronic grading programs, and so on are beyond their control or influence. They can achieve long-term adjustments and changes through consistent and clear communication with principals, district staff, and even the board. In the meantime, educators can work to align what is within personal control to move closer to the ideal.

Despite the existence of a traditional system, teachers can change their approach to grading, which remains entirely within their control. Even when percentage grades are required, for example, teachers can change their approach by moving away from averaging old and new evidence and creating a more standards-focused reporting system. First, use the most recent (with straightforward, binary standards) or more recent (with more sophisticated standards) evidence to determine grades. Second, change the way evidence is initially organized. In most cases, teachers have control over how their gradebooks are set up. Moving away from task types to at least curricular strands or categories would bring more alignment between instruction and reporting practices. Rather than tests, quizzes, assignments, labs, and so on, teachers can use the curricular strands (for example, reading, writing, speaking, listening, and language proficiency, in the case of English language arts). Science teachers could organize learning via the eight science and engineering practices of the Next Generation Science Standards (NGSS Lead States, 2013). The point is to organize the evidence of learning in the same manner in which standards are organized.

Task types often produce overlapping evidence in the gradebook since learners could show a growth trajectory toward proficiency with standards through their assignments, quizzes, and tests. When organized this way, the learners who need longer to learn will be disadvantaged in the gradebook since the early evidence will often be combined with later evidence to produce some middle average—this practice does not square with the idea of meeting a standard.

The key is to ensure that the assessment practices that produce report card grades are sound. That way, students, parents, and teachers can trust the information on the report card as an accurate representation of where the students truly are in their learning.

**Connected Tenets:** Assessment Purpose, Accurate Interpretation
**Topics:** Reporting, Standards

# Colleges and universities expect percentage grades. Are we selling our students short by moving away from percentages?

It is a myth that colleges and universities expect percentage-based grades. While they might want a traditional transcript, that doesn't mean the grades must be percentage based. Given that postsecondary institutions already accept learners who come from nontraditional settings, it is also a myth that they will only accept a traditional transcript.

Schools do have an obligation to provide colleges and universities with necessary information while at the same time employing accurate and reliable systems for grading. Both can be accomplished; it is entirely possible to engage in better grading practices and still end with a traditional transcript. Many schools have engaged in proficiency-based grading regarding standards or evidence-based reporting and still had a traditional transcript at the end.

Some would argue that changes in grading practices jeopardize GPAs and college admittance options and that, therefore, change is not possible. However, there are many valid counterarguments.

1. Universities maintain lists comparing the value of the 4.0 GPA in the district to the 4.0 GPA in every other district in the state because they have evidence that not all 4.0 GPAs are equal in value.

2. University expectations have changed over time to include far more than just the traditional intelligence indicators.

3. Universities have established their own additional application and vetting systems to validate and enhance the GPA.

4. Universities want the very best candidates in their schools and find ways to accommodate learners who come from schools that do not do traditional grading.

5. Universities themselves now understand that traditional grading systems are posing problems in their own systems, and several universities are trying alternative things (Schimmer, 2016). For example:

    a. MIT freshmen are only graded with a pass or fail or no record for the first semester, and the very best teachers at MIT work with the freshmen to support their ability to remain in college.

    b. Wellesley College learners earn a pass or fail on their transcript in the freshman year, but they are shown what their actual grades would have been (these are called *shadow grades*).

6. The granular nature of standards-based grading most often provides better information (for example, more clarity on content and process mastery and a separation of other important attributes like attendance, timeliness, responsibility, and so on) than other systems of grading.

Just like any learning organization, colleges and universities do make improvements over time, so before their preferences are assumed, it would be important to ask them what they are currently seeking—and accepting—for admission. In fact, the following list contains potential indicators of success—beyond the GPA—that are frequently part of a college's or university's potential review of postsecondary candidates.

- SAT or ACT scores (or other external test scores)
- Number of higher-level courses taken (Honors, Advanced Placement)

- Recommendation letters from others

- Extra-curricular activities

- Volunteer work

- Essay questions (typically one to six essays) that shed light on personal goals, strengths and weaknesses, and the like:

  - Personal goals

  - Strengths and weaknesses

  - Leadership experiences

  - Evidence of problem-solving skills

  - Evidence of being self-driven

  - Social media footprints

Schools and districts that successfully transform their grading practices often invite colleges and universities to the table so that they can partner with the postsecondary organizations to ensure their learners will eventually meet the criteria for college and scholarship applications.

**Connected Tenets:** Accurate Interpretation

**Topics:** Reporting, Summative Assessment and Grading

## How do we handle honor roll in a standards-based system?

There is much debate about whether traditional practices and structures like honor roll are still relevant. Still, some schools may wish to continue with honor roll; in fact, when those schools employ a standards-based system, they may end up with more accurate and relevant honor roll results.

Traditionally, teachers have determined grades by point accumulation. While the majority of points were accumulated through academic assessment, there were other ways in which learners could acquire points, including by following through with requests (signed permission forms, for example) and demonstrating "proper" behavior. There are likely some common practices that guide honor roll decisions across classes and schools, but it would also be impossible to produce an exhaustive list of all the additional ways learners have historically accumulated points in each of their classes. That said, schools did produce grades and subsequent honor rolls. It would be challenging, however, to confirm that the honor roll designation reflected only academic proficiency in ways that were consistent from school to school.

With a standards-based system, where grades are solely determined by the quality of the evidence produced, the reliability of the achievement levels educators use to make honor roll decisions increases. This is not to suggest that a reductionist process like GPA is a comprehensive way to report learning; it's not. What can be said is that at least the grades in a standards-based system are more closely aligned to learning, which would make grade point determinations more consistent. However, a more nuanced examination of practices and processes would be necessary to ensure reliability. Essentially, schools that choose to continue with honor roll are wise to take the necessary steps to ensure that the scores they are comparing (if this is how they determine honor roll) are as meaningful as possible.

One other aspect worth mentioning is that at least honor roll isn't a competitive process pitting one learner against the other. Unlike class rank, which is more normative in nature, honor roll typically sets a certain threshold, and all learners have the opportunity to reach that level. This can support hope and achievement for far more learners. Additional questions related to equity and inclusivity are fair, but at least the process is a reflection of the learner rather than of the curriculum.

**Connected Tenets:** Accurate Interpretation, Student Investment

**Topics:** Criteria, Summative Assessment and Grading

## How do I identify students who are deserving of scholarships?

Sorting for scholarships, while a reality in many jurisdictions, is antithetical to the core purpose of assessment. Sorting requires competition and norm-referenced decision making, whereas criterion-referenced assessment sets no competition or limits on the number of learners who can reach certain proficiency levels. This means that some compromises are going to be necessary if sorting for scholarships is still a required or desired exercise. Make no mistake, schools can still determine and utilize GPA for scholarship decisions, but more learners may cluster at certain levels if percentage scores are no longer a part of the grading and reporting routines.

Adjusting the requirements for scholarships might be the first place to start. Instead of just deferring to GPA, adjudicators might consider adding more robust components, such as portfolios, to help make scholarship decisions. Additional documentation supports an increasingly holistic view of decision making and encourages learners to focus on multiple aspects of their growth and development. Will this be less efficient? Probably. Will it be more effective? Also, probably. By examining quality and detail at a more in-depth level, schools can provide a more substantive reason for scholarships.

It may be helpful to also withhold becoming too granular in grading distinctions until the end of the semester or year. While fewer levels on a single demonstration of learning is more valid and reliable (as is the case for standards-based assessment, for example), it is possible to make more finite distinctions at the very end. For example, using a plus-and-minus scale to make the distinction between the *consistency* of work produced over time could help make scholarship decisions easier. A learner who almost always produces high-quality work might be an A+, while a learner who mostly produces high-quality work would be an A and a learner who has produced more high-quality work than not could be an A-. Educators could assign each learner competing for scholarships a value in this way and calculate the GPA from there. Figure 5.4 shows how this process could play out, using the aforementioned logic rules.

To be clear, each single sample of work would be judged along four levels, but the final distinctions would be made from the body of evidence, based on consistency of demonstration. Figure 5.4 is an imperfect solution to an already imperfect process. When sorting becomes even a moderately important priority, the question becomes, Which compromises are we willing to live with?

| Levels for Single Sample of Student Work | More Often Than Not | Mostly | Almost Always |
|---|---|---|---|
| Exemplary (4) | A- (3.5) | A (3.75) | A+ (4.0) |
| Proficient (3) | B- (2.75) | B (3.0) | B+ (3.25) |
| Developing (2) | C- (2.0) | C (2.25) | C+ (2.5) |
| Novice (1) | D- (1.25) | D (1.5) | D+ (1.75) |

*Figure 5.4: GPA plus-and-minus scale.*

**Connected Tenets:** Student Investment, Accurate Interpretation

**Topics:** Criteria, Summative Assessment and Grading

# Quality Feedback

## Where do I find time to give timely and specific feedback to every learner?

The first thing to remember is that not every moment of feedback has to be epic. The whole point of feedback is to reinitiate learning, so emphasizing quality over quantity is preferable. Smaller amounts of more targeted feedback that is accessible and applicable is preferable to pages of written feedback that is challenging to interpret. There is unanimous agreement in academia that feedback is what improves learning (Ruiz-Primo & Li, 2013; Wiliam, 2018), so making the time for quality feedback is essential. The prioritization of a formative feedback loop will ensure a learning-focused classroom.

The key is to be timely and specific in proportion to the amount of time learners will have to act on the feedback. Any feedback educators offer, if learners aren't given time to act on it, is useless feedback. Teachers may be guilty, for all the right reasons, of giving learners too much feedback given the amount of response time provided to adjust and make the necessary changes and deepen the required learning. Let the response time guide the volume. Also, while it might be true that some learners have a laundry list of aspects to improve on, focus on what is most pressing and is at or just slightly above the learners' current state. This ensures that the feedback isn't too sophisticated for where they are in the moment. This approach will also ensure that the formative feedback loops are more frequent but smaller in scope.

The strategies themselves can also create efficiency. Instead of thinking about feedback as something that happens after products or performances have been created, consider it as part of the learning process. Feedback in the form of a cue (such as using highlighter), a question, or a prompt can be equally as effective as full sentences or a paragraph. Remember, the whole point is to initiate more learning, and by using cues, questions, or prompts, learners will have to do more of the thinking. Sometimes, again for all the right reasons, teachers do too much thinking for their learners. The more learners think, the more potential they have for long-term growth.

Finally, the goal should be for learners to provide their own feedback through self- and peer assessment. Teacher feedback will always be more expert. However, that doesn't negate the fact that learners have much to tell one another about how to improve the quality of what they are producing. More novice learners may need a more hands-on approach, but as learners gain proficiency, teachers can slowly release this responsibility to learners. Teachers will always be involved with all learners—it is important that they verify self-assessment claims. However, involving learners as assessors does ease the time crunch and creates efficiency. Learners have access to their own thoughts 24/7, which means self-assessment feedback is always available.

**Connected Tenets:** Instructional Agility, Student Investment

**Topics:** Feedback, Self- and Peer Assessment

# What does quality feedback look like?

Quality feedback is any feedback that initiates more learning. While there are a number of considerations around the minutiae of effective feedback, the most important one is that teacher feedback results in learners attempting to advance their levels of proficiency. Feedback is rendered useless if teachers don't provide the time and guidance for learners to act on the feedback and learners don't take subsequent action as a result.

The dichotomy of feedback is that there is unanimous agreement in academia that feedback is what advances student learning, and yet, there is no clear understanding of what absolutely works in feedback (Ruiz-Primo & Li, 2013; Wiliam, 2018). There are practices that lead to more favorable results, but as with most aspects of assessment, what makes feedback work well is nuanced and contextually sensitive. Therefore, teachers would be wise, while implementing what research widely agrees on to be the most favorable practices, to keep a close eye on how their learners respond. Above all else, feedback must elicit a productive response from the recipient (Erkens et al., 2017).

What are some of those favorable practices? The following is a list of qualities most critical to effective feedback.

- **Goal referenced:** When providing feedback, keep the standard or learning target in the forefront of thinking and conversations.

- **Actionable:** Actionable feedback means that the provided feedback gives learners next steps that they can use to improve. Actionable feedback is concrete, is specific, and anticipates future learning.

- **Offers next steps:** While subtle, using language that focuses on *what's next* versus *what was* sends the message that learning is not over and that improvement is the priority.

- **User friendly:** Although learners should be comfortable and familiar with the essential terminology of the learning goals, try not to overwhelm them with too much technical jargon. Learners need to be able to access and understand the feedback in order to apply it.

- **Ongoing:** Learners need to understand that assessment is an ongoing conversation between teacher and learner and not just an event that happens periodically.

- **Manageable:** Feedback must be manageable for learners to act on. Prioritize what is most pressing for them and focus on these "first next steps." Because the feedback loop is ongoing, there will be time to address other misunderstandings in the future.

- **Strength based:** Effective feedback balances both strengths and that which needs strengthening. Maintaining hope and efficacy occurs when teachers seek to identify those skills and understandings learners already possess, instead of simply focusing on deficits.

These favorable qualities can provide teachers with the right starting point. However, it is critical that feedback routines develop organically and allow teachers and learners to find their feedback sweet spot. While there may be no answer to what absolutely works when giving feedback, each class and each learner definitely knows what absolutely works for them.

**Connected Tenets:** Hope, Efficacy, and Achievement; Instructional Agility; Student Investment

**Topics:** Feedback

# What does it mean for feedback to be timely? I don't seem to have time to provide this feedback for all students on all assessments.

Learners should have access to the feedback in a timely fashion so that they can use that feedback to strengthen and improve their own learning to meet the learning standard. The feedback should drive the students' learning forward, and, therefore, teachers must provide it during the learning process so that it supports that learning. It can be very difficult to provide this feedback to learners on a daily basis. Feedback, as a process, engages learners in understanding the intended learning by focusing on qualities, or success criteria. Learners are overwhelmed with the amount of feedback (at times), and teachers tend to be overwhelmed by giving feedback, so targeting one or two areas (focused on the criteria) and building the response learners make into the flow of lesson planning can start to shift feedback from something teachers do outside of class time to a practice that informs instruction and the subsequent actions learners take.

Another way for teachers to manage this challenge is to design specific formative assessment tasks that target specific areas for feedback. For example, when teaching a writing standard, a teacher may provide feedback about different aspects of writing on different formative tasks rather than trying to provide feedback about everything each time. So one formative task may give feedback on the thesis statement, another task will give feedback on organization, and another is on descriptive language. Teachers can offer this feedback during class time as learners engage in the writing process. As learners are working, the teacher moves among them, having brief conversations and providing feedback, and learners act on that feedback in the moment. Educators can target feedback from formative assessments more systematically. This can make it more manageable for both teachers and learners, who can be as overwhelmed with processing feedback on a lot of different things as teachers are with providing it. When teachers are planning instructional units, backward mapping the opportunities to provide this valuable feedback will help both teachers and learners plan ahead to best use the information.

**Connected Tenets:** Culture of Learning, Student Investment
**Topics:** Feedback, Formative Assessment

# Student Involvement in Communication

## Should student self-assessment impact my assessment decisions?

It is the job of the teacher to be the final arbiter of any meaningful determinations of learning. As the experts, teachers' interpretations of student demonstrations must carry the most weight. That said, it isn't at all inappropriate to bring learners inside the assessment process and allow them to make the case for their own interpretations of where their learning ended up.

In fact, not only is student self-assessment not wrong, it is something that should be encouraged. For too long, assessment has been something done *to* learners instead of *with* them. Moving learners from passive to active participants in the assessment process is an effective way to encourage investment in their own learning. The key is to ensure learners are prepared to make such self-judgments through clear learning goals, the clear articulation of success criteria (especially where rubrics are involved), and the understanding of how to infer quality against the criteria. Furthermore, the purpose and use of self-assessment has to be clear to students from the start.

Once that foundation has been laid, the opportunities for authentic and accurate self-assessment are available.

The question of whether the students' self-assessment should impact teacher decisions might depend on the purpose of the exercise. It would be ideal for student self-assessment to influence formative decisions about next steps in learning. Having learners invested in their own learning and making decisions about what comes next and the processes necessary to get there is the epitome of ownership.

Their influence on summative decisions is a little trickier. Students' giving themselves grades has to be safeguarded against potential inaccuracies. Unlike the formative purpose, where the focus is entirely internal and the only thing at stake is next steps in learning, grades carry more weight and influence outside the school walls. This is not to suggest that all student summative judgments will be dishonest, but it is to suggest that the accuracy of those summative judgments has to be filtered through the lens of the expert in the room. Allowing student self-assessment to influence summative judgments is fine if the student has made a solid argument (based on evidence and directly connected to the criteria) for why their self-determined level is justified. Without that grounding, student self-assessment claims may lack substance, and teachers could be swayed by other tangential influences.

So, it's not wrong for student self-assessment to have an impact, but it is something that educators must purposefully organize, intentionally teach, and consistently monitor to ensure that students benefit from the experience itself and not just see it as a means to a grade.

**Connected Tenets:** Assessment Purpose, Student Investment

**Topics:** Formative Assessment, Self- and Peer Assessment, Summative Assessment and Grading

# How can I share responsibility for showcasing learning with my students?

The first step in partnering with learners to showcase learning is to involve them in assessment decisions. This means communicating learning intentions and targets, inviting learners to self-assess and set goals, and helping them to monitor their own growth and celebrate their own strengths. In addition, the minute learners become engaged in learning that is relevant for them, they become interested in sharing their work with others because it matters to them. So, designing assessment processes that are engaging and build confidence makes sharing easier for learners (Dimich, 2015; White, 2017).

Next, teachers can utilize any number of methods for sharing learning with others. They might choose to use portfolios (digital or traditional), classroom blogs or journals, social media sites, newsletters or other publications, photographs, or video. The possibilities are endless, and there are many resources available to support this work.

The important thing is to be clear about the purpose for communication and ensure that the method and processes align with this purpose. Privacy guidelines must be considered, as well as learner comfort with the chosen audience. Showcasing that becomes quite public must focus on strengths and celebrations to protect students' emotional security.

Using artifacts of learning that have been shared with others as a springboard for reflection and future learning is another great benefit of student ownership over this process. Learners might reflect on how their portfolios have changed over time, or they can compare a product they created and shared at the beginning of the year with one they created at the end. This ensures that this process becomes more than just pinning pictures on a wall. Instead, it becomes part of ongoing learning.

**Connected Tenets:** Student Investment

**Topics:** Reporting, Student Engagement and Motivation

# Parental Communication and Transparency

## How can I help my students and families understand the idea of professional judgment?

Unless the entire system of assessment is about right and wrong, teachers will always have to use their professional judgment to determine proficiency. For example, when using a rubric, teachers make what is called a *scoring inference*. There is no straight line between a learner's demonstration and the rubric. Teachers have to examine the demonstration and then match that performance to a particular level of quality— that's professional judgment.

The word *subjective* often comes up in this conversation and is seen as a negative part of assessment, but it isn't. Professional judgment is subjective, but it is informed by the years of experience and practice at analyzing student demonstrations of learning. A teacher who has taught for ten years (with an average of seven classes per year, with an average of thirty students per class, and with an average of thirty-five assignments used for the summative purpose of grade determination) has analyzed

73,500 student samples. That teacher is more than qualified to use their professional judgment without reliance on an algorithm.

Two things are essential when communicating with families. First, performance criteria must be made transparent so parents and students know clearly upon what the teacher's professional judgment is based. This goes a long way to preventing learners from thinking that their grade, score, or level has anything to do with how the teacher feels about them personally. Second, teachers—especially those teaching the same grade-level subjects—must purposefully and regularly calibrate along that performance criteria to ensure that professional judgments are aligned and consistent so a student's grade, level, or score is not dependent on who their teacher is. Proactively explaining how professional judgment is used and why it is valid brings students and parents inside the assessment process.

**Connected Tenets:** Accurate Interpretation, Assessment Architecture
**Topics:** Collaboration, Criteria, Professional Judgment

## What can I do when a parent challenges my grading practices?

The first thing is listen; parents have the right to be heard. The defensive reflex is all too common when parents ask questions or even challenge teacher practices. Keep in mind that parents are really just advocating for their children and trying to understand a complex educational process, and a teacher should never fault a parent for that. Even when a parent's approach may be less than favorable, it is important to keep their overall aims in mind.

Be open to the possibility that parents have a point. Perhaps an aspect of assessment really could be refined or clarified. As difficult as this can be to accept, it is important. However, ensure that the concern or challenge is substantive and not just a dislike for the grade, score, or level their child earned. While it is possible the challenge is simply a projection of their disappointment in their child's performance and representative of a bruised ego, it is also possible that they authentically believe that aspects of quality have been overlooked. In either case—ego or substantive—stay focused on clarifying the specific concern and the criteria that the collaborative team established to determine the single score or the overall grade. Ask parents to substantiate their claims by pinpointing where they believe there was an oversight or error. This will (hopefully) ensure that parents clearly see the decisions weren't personal and that they are based instead on the quality of the work that was produced.

In addition, keep explanations of grading practices grounded in sound assessment practices. Grading is, after all, assessment. Rather than establishing grading practices on idiosyncratic or philosophical bents, utilize sound assessment principles. Basing grading decisions on sound assessment research is defensible, so while the parent might not like or agree with a particular practice, teachers can defend the practice since there is a body of research that guides decisions.

The genesis of challenge is often sourced with a lack of clarity or understanding about practices and processes; a few habits can mitigate this. Be proactive in communicating with students and parents how grades (on either single work samples or the entire body of evidence) are determined. Transparency goes a long way in preventing challenges before they occur. Once everyone knows the rules that guide the game, it becomes easier to play. Opaque or even hidden grading practices can feel like trickery, which almost always produces aversive reactions from parents and students. Also, ensure that assessment evidence is both valid and reliable. This means steering clear of bias and assessment tasks that are overly complex or too simple.

Grading is about verifying that learning has occurred in relation to clear learning goals, and everyone should know how that is done ahead of time and in relation to which goals. Empower learners by bringing them inside the process through co-constructing criteria and inviting self-assessment. Learners will then be able to explain how they are graded to their parents.

**Connected Tenets:** Accurate Interpretation, Student Investment

**Topics:** Criteria, Parent Engagement, Reporting, Summative Assessment and Grading

# Communication in a Remote Learning Context

In remote learning contexts, teachers are increasingly dependent on clear and effective two-way communication with students and families. A strong partnership with homes can have tremendous benefits in the overall academic achievement of students (Henderson & Mapp, 2002; Pushor, 2010), particularly when that partnership focuses on academic goals and supports. It is for this reason that enhancing communication strategies as part of an overall assessment system is critical. In a remote learning context, to enhance communication of assessment results in ways that support authentic partnership and understanding, teachers might consider the following.

- Approaching assessment communication as a *system of strategies* that will build shared understanding, as opposed to depending on a single approach or tool; this may mean frequently sharing the purposes of assessment processes (formative assessment, summative assessment, self-assessment), sharing success criteria, being transparent about summative decision making, sharing samples of student learning, and partnering with learners to co-construct a story of learning that reflects both learning-in-progress and refined products and performances.

- Using formative assessment to analyze strengths and needs, offer timely and specific feedback, adjust instruction, construct student groupings, and select meaningful resources; with this in mind, consider refraining from scoring formative assessment when possible, so learners are more likely to take risks and reveal needs without perceived penalty. Scoring, or grading, student work when the evidence shows mastery can lead to a focus on evidence of learning versus *this is graded and this is not*, or *this is worth this many points and this is only worth a few.*

- Communicating summative assessment results aligned to learning goals and using a system that is transparent, clear, and predictable

- Combining the communication of assessment information with action; for example, virtually confer with learners to share feedback and set goals, or invite learners to work in virtual groups to revise products and select strategies that will increase skills and understanding.

- Opening up two-way communication by inviting learners to share the amount of time an assessment task took, the questions that arose during the assessment, the areas of greater and lesser confidence, and the skills they have learned in terms of approaching assessment processes in a remote learning context

# CHAPTER 6
# ACCURATE INTERPRETATION

Once assessment evidence has been attained through observation, conversation, or any variety of assessment artifacts or products, teachers (and learners) must interpret the results. This interpretation of assessment results must be *accurate* (aligned with learning goals and reflective of the intended degree of complexity of skill or understanding), *accessible* (clearly understood by both teachers and learners), and *reliable* (the interpretation yields the same result on repeated trials and is truly reflective of the skills and understanding a learner holds).

Interpretations of assessment results ultimately lead to any number of actions within a classroom setting. Following interpretations, educators will make decisions about several critical maneuvers: using formative data to acknowledge strengths and address needs; creating interventions, enrichments, and re-engagement strategies; employing planned hinge (reflective) questions, prompts, and cues; and responding to data by skill and by learner. It is vital that teachers feel prepared to make these kinds of decisions with confidence. As a result, exploring ways to enhance the skill of interpreting assessment results is critical to every decision that follows.

## Data Interpretation

### What does it mean to triangulate assessment information?

Accurate interpretation of assessment results requires three criteria: (1) accuracy, (2) accessibility, and (3) reliability. Accurate assessment reflects the student's achievement in relationship to the standard. There is alignment between the expectations of the standard and what learners are asked to do. Accessible design means ensuring the learner is set up to be able to access and demonstrate learning with the method used and accessible results are clear and available to both learner and teacher. Reliable assessment produces stable and consistent results.

Creating assessment experiences that meet all of these criteria can be very difficult for individual teachers, which is why collaboration is so valuable to strengthen the process. Use multiple assessment samples to capture degrees of proficiency in relation to standards. *Triangulation* occurs when teachers use at least three different assessment methods or processes to make decisions about learners' proficiency. For example, an *assessment artifact* may indicate a degree of proficiency, confirmed by *observations* and *conversations* while learners were engaging in the assessment experience. All three sources of evidence provide a clear indication of skill and understanding. This is particularly important when educators are making high-stakes decisions about learners. Individual teachers or collaborative teams may choose to use three different types of data to identify a goal, to make sure that a low set of scores was not simply due to the method of assessment or deficiency in one of the criteria necessary for accurate interpretation of results. The assessment triangulation chart in figure 6.1 can help structure and focus an individual or team of teachers when designing for triangulation of assessment information.

**Connected Tenets:** Assessment Architecture, Assessment Purpose
**Topics:** Collaboration, Summative Assessment and Grading

## How can I know if I'm interpreting data correctly?

One of the major obstacles to interpreting data correctly is how familiar educators are with the assessment they are utilizing. Interpreting the data that they receive from commercially produced, norm-referenced assessments can be challenging. It is important to understand the purpose of any assessment as well as the limitations. Once educators start using assessment for different purposes than intended, they run the risk of misinterpreting data or being inaccurate in their conclusions. Any time educators are using a commercially produced assessment, they must try to learn as much as they can about how the assessment was designed and how it is aligned to the content and skills being taught.

Working collaboratively with colleagues to design assessments is a valuable endeavor. When professional educators with extensive content knowledge and expertise sit down and design assessments or analyze commercially produced assessments

| Learning Goals or Targets to Be Mastered (From Essential Standard) | Criteria or Qualities | Methods or Tasks for Assessment Evidence |
|---|---|---|
| I can cite strong and thorough textual evidence. | ☐ Clearly supports the theme<br>☐ Clearly explains how the text supports the theme | 1. Video Flipgrid<br>2. Constructed response<br>3. Graphic organizer |
| I can determine the central idea of a text, including how to analyze in detail its development over the course of the text (including theme and message). | ☐ Accurately identifies the central idea<br>☐ Clear and important details that support the central idea<br>☐ Clearly articulates multiple pieces of evidence to show how the central idea develops in the beginning, middle, and end | 1. Constructed response<br>2. Interview<br>3. Observation |
| I can critically analyze information found in electronic, print, and mass media and use a variety of these sources. | ☐ Critically articulates the position of the evidence<br>☐ Clearly describes the source of the information<br>☐ Clearly explains any bias the article might represent<br>☐ Convincingly provides the potential counterargument or point | 1. Graphic organizer<br>2. Essay<br>3. Observation of dialogue |

**Figure 6.1:** *Assessment triangulation chart.*

*Visit* **go.SolutionTree.com/assessment** *to download a free blank version of this figure.*

together, the purpose of the assessment is clearer to everyone who is administering it. The group can design that assessment to measure specific learning targets and specific levels of rigor and complexity that meet the group's purpose. Being clear about which standards are addressed by each item and the rigor of each item while designing the assessment will help the group during the interpretation process. It is hard work, but it is also valuable work that is made stronger through collaboration.

**Connected Tenets:** Communication of Results

**Topics:** Common Assessment

# What is the difference between analyzing an assessment and scoring it? How do I use each one?

Scoring an assessment means relating a learner's response to predetermined criteria for proficiency and assigning the response a value that represents that degree of proficiency. This value may be represented in a number of ways—a ratio, a percentage, an alpha code (like P for *proficient* or NY for *not yet*), and so on. To score, a teacher must be crystal clear about both the rigor of the learning goal and the criteria by which that rigor will be measured. Teachers may then collect scores and organize them into data sets, which teachers then use to analyze patterns of strength or challenge and identify any anomalies that may appear within a group of learners. Instructional decisions may follow scoring and data analysis.

Analyzing responses to an assessment requires teachers to critically examine artifacts of student learning (answers to questions, videos, and so on) and determine both strengths the artifact indicates and areas in which improvement or growth is needed. Like scoring, predetermined criteria for proficiency make the analysis of assessment information and subsequent instructional planning more precise and efficient.

Analyzing the assessment itself means looking at learners' results and then deconstructing the parts of the assessment to determine its overall accuracy and sufficiency in measuring the learning expectations that educators targeted. This component is very important if teachers are to ensure that all assessments are quality assessments. Without this component in place, insufficient or inaccurate assessments can lead to both false positives and false negatives in student results.

**Connected Tenets:** Assessment Architecture

**Topics:** Formative Assessment, Summative Assessment and Grading

# How can I ensure my assessment data are truly reliable and representative of what my students know and can do?

Reliability and validity should be the goal of any assessment process in order to collect the most accurate data possible for both teachers and learners. Reliability, or the degree of consistency in an assessment, is more likely when teachers spend time making sure there are consistent results among multiple teachers and across multiple pieces of assessment evidence. This is frequently considered on more subjective tasks, such as the use of a rubric on a writing task, but it is equally important on other types of assessment. Teachers should have conversations about how they will score open-ended items and what concepts are considered the most important. Without these conversations, something that can seem very objective, like a mathematics test, can result in very different scoring procedures and outcomes for learners.

Validity refers to when an assessment accurately measures degrees of learning in relation to goals so that teachers can make accurate decisions about student learning. When teachers spend time on the assessment architecture in advance and have clarity about both the learning goals and the best ways to assess that learning, validity is more likely. Validity also is more likely when there are multiple sources of data, which supports the use of formative assessment tools in the classroom rather than one single summative assessment.

**Connected Tenets:** Communication of Results; Hope, Efficacy, and Achievement

**Topics:** Common Assessment, Formative Assessment, Summative Assessment and Grading

## How can I learn to diagnose error if I was never trained to do so?

Interpreting errors that learners make is an important aspect of helping learners grow and achieve at high levels. The first step in doing this is to clearly articulate the intended learning (the standard or competency) by clarifying the actions teachers hope to see learners engage in and creating a description of what quality evidence looks like. Then, consider all the knowledge and skills needed to achieve that learning (namely, a learning progression). Finally, review the common misconceptions or errors learners make when engaging in that learning. Errors can be observed in what learners say, do, or produce. Intentionally look for and articulate the criteria in advance so that when observing learners and their work, there is focus on what might be present or not present.

This is a process. When engaging with colleagues, it is the way educators come to understand the errors that are most common and to develop innovate instructional moves to help learners grow. In a PLC, collaborative teams identify what's most essential, assess it, and review the assessment data to understand who needs additional time and support to achieve the essential learning. It is not enough to notice that learners need more support. It is essential that educators—individually and in teams—identify *why* learners are making errors. This becomes clearer as colleagues work together and talk about what achieving the standard or proficiency looks like, and clearer again when they review student work in relationship to that intended learning.

Digging into different types of errors specific to the discipline and grade level can be helpful. For example, in mathematics, a team might want to explore computational errors, efficiency errors, strategy errors, or even comprehension errors. Each error requires different supports. Then, intentionally planning how to help learners address the errors that emerge is the way toward new and innovative instruction that will ensure learners develop confidence and grow in their learning.

In essence, being able to accurately diagnose and respond to errors happens individually and in collaboration. This review and interpretation of the errors learners make allows us to become instructional agile (namely, to have the ability to make real-time or close to real-time instructional moves that advance students' learning). (For more information on instructional agility, see chapter 7, page 149.)

> **Connected Tenets:** Communication of Results, Instructional Agility
> **Topics:** Feedback, Professional Learning Communities

# Collaboration

## How should my team prepare to assess together?

The same forethought, planning, and action steps that go into preparing classroom assessments at the individual level remain intact when planning for classroom assessments at the collaborative level. Dimich (2015) recommends five phases that both individual teachers and teams of teachers could follow when preparing to assess together.

- **Phase one:** Choose standards and plan engagement.
- **Phase two:** Sketch out the learning goals.
- **Phase three:** Craft an assessment plan.
- **Phase four:** Create or revise the assessment.
- **Phase five:** Determine the student investment and reporting method.

The difference is that when *teams* are engaged in the work, they must (1) focus on the *most* essential standards; (2) seek clarity and consistency in their interpretation of the standards; (3) find scheduled times or curricular areas where they will all be engaged in assessing the same standards; (4) co-construct an item or items and measurement tools that align in rigor; and (5) generate specific plans regarding how and when they will use the resulting evidence to improve student learning.

It's likely that the most important difference involves the mental mindset required to engage in the work of common assessments. Each teacher on the team must be prepared to release preconceived notions or past practices, compromise in the service of consensus, value evidence over opinion, respect the expertise of peers, and adopt a growth mindset born out of true vulnerability. In sum, the technicalities of designing assessments together remain the same, but the spirit of true collaboration must be inserted into the process.

> **Connected Tenets:** Assessment Architecture, Assessment Purpose
>
> **Topics:** Common Assessment, Professional Learning Communities

## How might I use collaboration to calibrate the effectiveness of my assessment?

Collaboration is key to ensuring that the interpretation of assessment results is both valid and reliable. Reliability, of course, is about the consistency with which teachers are assessing what they claim to be assessing (Heritage, 2010a). Through collaboration, and especially where scoring inferences are required through the use of rubrics, teachers can ensure that their inferences are aligned with their colleagues. For an assessment to be valid, it must first be reliable.

Once an assessment is reliable, colleagues can calibrate their interpretations of the evidence to ensure they are also accurate (or valid). This calibration will align both teachers' determination of quality—whether it is actually assessing what teachers claim to be assessing—and the subsequent interpretation and responses necessary to verify or initiate more learning.

Once assessments are both valid and reliable, then teachers can go about the business of determining the effectiveness of their assessments. For the formative purpose, effectiveness would be about whether the assessment yielded accurate information and whether that information was useable, so as to make the initiation of more learning timely and effective. For the summative purpose, the question of effectiveness would hinge on whether the assessment yielded an accurate reflection of what the learner knows and is able to do.

Through a collaborative process, teachers can share their collective expertise to effectively determine where learners are and what comes next.

> **Connected Tenets:** Assessment Architecture, Communication of Results
>
> **Topics:** Assessment Design, Collaboration

Accurate
Interpretation

## What should my collaborative team do with an assessment once we have given it?

Formative assessment results are the fuel that make a collaborative team in a PLC function and should be treated as such. A high-functioning team will share results freely and openly with the purpose being to improve student learning. At the predetermined time, the team should come together and discuss the results that each member is seeing from learners. There should be some time devoted to analyzing what the results mean in terms of the learning that students have mastered and which learners still need additional instruction to master those learning targets. The majority of the meeting time should be spent on determining how learners will receive additional instruction in a way that is required and not optional, and who will ultimately deliver the instruction.

Some teams have the ability to deliver this instruction at a common time so that learners are redistributed based on their learning needs. For example, different teachers take a learning target—one teacher takes the learners who have mastered the targets for extension, and another teacher takes the learners who need support in multiple targets. This particular model is not the only way to make sure that learners receive that additional opportunity to learn, but the team should discuss it, plan it, and determine each member's responsibility to make sure it occurs.

Collaborative teams within a PLC should be in a constant cycle of planning formative assessments at appropriate points in the instructional unit, collaborating about the results, and making plans based on those results to make sure that all learners are successful.

> **Connected Tenets:** Hope, Efficacy, and Achievement; Instructional Agility
>
> **Topics:** Common Assessment, Professional Learning Communities

# Professional Judgment

## How is professional judgment different from an opinion? Isn't it subjective?

*Subjectivity* includes personal perspectives and biases that can remain unchecked. Such perspectives do not need to be tied to professional standards. *Professional judgment*, on the other hand, is informed by the standards, ethics, laws, or rules that are widely adopted by a given profession. Professional judgment is developed through professional training, required standards, best practices, and the current research that guides decisions and shared agreements across a team of experts. In other words, professional judgment involves expertise.

In education, teachers must come to critical agreements about what their educational standards mean, what the progression of learning will be, what levels of proficiency will look like, and how they will define and evaluate mastery. Any decisions they make in relation to this understanding is professional judgment. (For more information on professional judgment, see "How Can I Help My Students and Families Understand the Idea of Professional Judgment?" on page 127.)

> **Connected Tenets:** Communication of Results
>
> **Topics:** Formative Assessment, Professional Judgment, Summative Assessment and Grading

## What role does professional judgment play in assessment? How can I build my confidence?

Professional judgment is actually required of the assessment process because student mastery cannot be determined simply based on right answers or the accumulation of points. Master teachers notice thinking and must be able to analyze the degrees of proficiency, the caliber of quality, and the specific gaps in knowledge or skill that will require additional instructional support as they move learners to high levels of learning.

The best way to build confidence is to engage in the processes of continued learning based on new research, collaboratively develop assessments and measurement tools, and repeatedly practice the work of calibrating scoring to be more consistent from one teacher to the next within a team, a department, or even an entire school.

> **Connected Tenets:** Communication of Results
>
> **Topics:** Formative Assessment, Professional Judgment, Summative Assessment and Grading

## Observations

## What role do conversation and observation play in the interpretation of assessment information?

Making decisions in order to verify degrees of learning or respond to information that an assessment reveals means that teachers are involved in professional judgment in some way. This professional judgment is increasingly accurate and reliable when teachers gather evidence from multiple sources using a variety of methods. Observation and conversation are two methods that hold tremendous value when making a professional judgment.

There are times, in the course of daily classroom activity, that teachers notice a learner performing a skill or expressing an understanding. The learner may be working in a group, she may be creating a product, or she may be engaging in a performance of some type (for example, playing a game in physical education or giving a speech). In each of these examples, observation of learner behavior and skill will occur, and these observations can serve as assessment information that informs instructional decision making, targeted feedback, or verification of proficiency. Documenting the time, date, and context of the observation can help a teacher track growth and learner need over time, serving as critical assessment information.

Similarly, conversation can serve to uncover evidence of learning or learner need. Through conversation, teachers can turn assessment processes that are often unidirectional (from the student to the teacher) into two-way assessment conversations. When teachers are unsure of the degree of understanding or skill, they can simply ask the learners to share their thinking to clarify their own understanding of what learners know and can do (Davies, 2011).

**Connected Tenets:** Communication of Results

**Topics:** Formative Assessment, Professional Judgment, Summative Assessment and Grading

## How can I know how individual students are performing during cooperative learning?

Observation is the best way to examine individual student performance during cooperative learning. To increase the validity of observations, educators should consider a few things. First, learners need to be independent enough in their cooperative learning that the teacher is not interrupted when making observations. Second, the teacher must be very familiar with the learning goals being assessed through observation. It is helpful to have spent some time exploring learning targets and success criteria within each learning goal being measured, so specific behavior that indicates degrees of proficiency can be observed. For example, if a pair of learners are working together to create patterns, knowing the complexity of patterning that task requires is helpful. Third, having a tool (like a rubric or checklist) can help to focus and document the observations. Lastly, if the observation did not verify individual learning sufficiently, a teacher might consider inviting a follow-up assessment opportunity, like a journal reflection, an explanation video, an exit ticket, or a short follow-up assignment.

Teachers can also intentionally gather and employ student observation data. Imagine, for example, that individual learners within a group are tasked with gathering data regarding important features to the collaborative work. Consider having one learner tally the number of times paraphrases were used, another learner tally the number of times direct quotes were used, another learner tally the number of times questions were asked and answered, another learner tally the number of minutes the group was off task, and so on. Such observational data can be used to correlate with—but not replace—the teacher's observations.

Yet another alternative is to assign a peer coach to each learner in a collaborative venture, so that the coaches on the outside circle are gathering evidence of effectiveness to share with their peer on the inside of the circle during strategic moments in the collaborative process. Another approach might be to have learners fill out reflection forms at the end of each collaborative conversation, in which they answer specific questions like: *Who in your group provided the most meaningful insight in your conversation today? Who in your group offered the best questions in your conversation today? Who in your group emerged as the natural leader today?* and so on. Student observations about what did and did not occur can help teachers validate their own sense of what is happening in collaborative group work.

> **Connected Tenets:** Assessment Architecture
>
> **Topics:** Formative Assessment

# Interpretation Practices

## Why should I share the rubric with students ahead of time? Won't this encourage cheating?

A well-designed rubric should make the criteria for success clear to learners but should still allow learners the opportunity to do the thinking and learning necessary in an effective assessment. These criteria should not be a secret or a surprise. In a standards-based classroom, teachers have to be very clear about what they want learners to know and be able to do. The same should be true about how learners will demonstrate that.

An effective rubric will also help learners determine where they are on those learning targets and what they need to do to move to the next level. There is still learning and work that is required of the learner to demonstrate that understanding to the teacher. The rubric is the map, but the learner still has to follow it and ultimately reach the destination.

> **Connected Tenets:** Assessment Architecture
>
> **Topics:** Self- and Peer Assessment, Student Engagement and Motivation

## Why is it so wrong to reduce scores for late work? Doesn't that teach students to be responsible?

The application of a punitive consequence is *not* teaching. Missing a deadline is a behavioral misstep that is certainly undesirable and unacceptable; however, reducing scores begins to mix achievement and non-achievement factors, which compromises the validity of grades (Brookhart, 2013b). The accuracy of what educators ultimately report—in whatever format—about student learning must be a priority; to mix achievement and non-achievement factors means what teachers report is opaque at best and meaningless at worst.

Teaching learners to be responsible means *teaching* them to be responsible. Punishing irresponsibility does not teach learners *how* to be responsible (Schimmer, 2016). An example in schools is the emphasis on the characteristic of *respect*. Respect is a ubiquitous expectation. As a result, schools, for the most part, outline what it means to be a respectful learner and provide at least some contextualization (such as what respect looks like in the hallway, classroom, or other settings). Whether formal or informal, schools usually make this expectation clear. If learners are disrespectful, adults hold them accountable for their disrespectful behavior. With that said, student academic scores should never be reduced for disrespectful behavior. One thing (how much the learner knows) has nothing to do with the other (how respectful the learner was).

Again, it is not okay for learners to submit late work, but the real question is how teachers and schools respond when learners submit late work. First, when a deadline is missed, responding rapidly and with great intensity is the key; the learner should be required to make up the work in as timely a manner as possible. Waiting several weeks is counterproductive for both teachers and learners. However, *great intensity* does not mean *punitive*. The art of teaching responsibility is to separate being punitive from being tough; the latter is about high expectations and instruction, while the former is about control. Second, if a learner's irresponsibility is chronic, the learner needs specific instruction on how to be more organized in advance of a deadline, how to take a large assignment or project and break it down into manageable pieces, or how to achieve whatever specific skill may be lacking. Teaching learners the skills they do not currently have is how they can be truly prepared for life after high school. Schools would never suspend a learner (behavioral consequence) for not being able to add fractions (academic misstep). Lowering a score (academic consequence) for a late work (behavioral misstep) is equally illogical.

> **Connected Tenets:** Assessment Purpose, Communication of Results
>
> **Topics:** Accountability and Standardized Tests, Assessment Design, Behavior, Summative Assessment and Grading

# Why shouldn't I give a zero for incomplete assignments? What should I use instead?

The practice of using zeros for an incomplete assignment violates the principles of sound assessment by assigning a value to work that the teacher hasn't seen. Missing is missing; so assigning a value to something that doesn't exist is neither valid nor reliable. Of course, some might say that a missing assignment deserves a zero because if it is not submitted, it is worth *nothing*. However, failing to submit something at all—similar to late work—is a behavioral misstep that deserves action. Giving a zero misses the mark in terms of ultimately producing the desirable outcome (learning).

The issue of using zero is exacerbated when used within a percentage-based grading scale. A zero won't carry equal weight to the other scores in the gradebook, especially when most of the scores are much higher along the continuum. The traditional percentage-based grading scale is the only place where *five is greater than twenty-five*, as outlined by the following example. If a learner submitted twenty-five assignments that were all scored as 70 percent, five zeros would result in an average score of 58.3 percent (25 multiplied by 70, divided by 30). In most jurisdictions, that's an F. Obviously this is an oversimplified example, but it does illustrate the mathematics behind why a critical vulnerability to the mean average is extreme scores. If the five zeros were for assignments that carried less weight in the gradebook, that would benefit the learner; if they carried greater weight, it would make it worse.

The point is that annihilating a learner's grade is not the answer and does little to build hope, efficacy, and achievement through assessment and grading. One option to consider is the use of an I or INC (for *incomplete*) instead of a zero. The most accurate way to communicate the result of a marathon for a runner who does not complete the race is *DNF*—did not finish. The most accurate way to communicate achievement levels for learners who have not completed the requisite assignments for determining their achievement is that they are incomplete (INC). Ideally, when an INC is entered in association with a missing assignment, the learner's overall grade would be converted to an INC (instead of A and 93 percent, the student and parents would see INC and INC). The learner also would not have a grade. This is more accurate than leaving an empty space, which disproportionately weights the other assignments and can present a false positive. A zero, on the other hand, produces a false negative.

Educators must reconcile missing work—especially that which is critical to accurate grade determination—in a timely manner, but distorting achievement levels through the use of a zero does little to do that. No matter how philosophically justified one might feel in assigning a zero, philosophical justification does not suspend the principles of validity and reliability when it comes to assessment. If grades don't pass the accuracy test, then they are rendered meaningless and are marginalized into becoming a way for teachers to coerce behavioral compliance.

> **Connected Tenets:** Assessment Purpose, Communication of Results
>
> **Topics:** Accountability and Standardized Tests, Behavior, Summative Assessment and Grading

## I feel like the top tier of proficiency should be hard to achieve. Is this fair?

The top tier of proficiency, regardless of its label, should be the most sophisticated demonstration of learning. However, there is a difference between expecting rigorous, sophisticated demonstrations and simply making the top level of proficiency harder to attain.

Levels of proficiency essentially represent *versions of quality* or *consistency*. Rubrics are developed to make criteria transparent, and the top tier should be the most sophisticated, insightful, or authentic application of the intended learning. In that sense, the top tier will be *hard* to earn, since it does require learners to reach a deep level of understanding or a consistent level of performance; that's rigor and that's fair.

What's not fair is simply making school harder for learners by asking them to perform at a level unreasonable in relation to their developmental levels or the reasonable expectation of proficiency. Expecting third-grade learners to master sixth-grade mathematics in order to *earn* a 4 is unreasonable; that's not rigor and that's not fair. Top-tier proficiency should be hard if *hard* means educators have high, yet reasonable, expectations; have supports in place to ensure that all learners have the opportunity to reach that level; and have taught with the expectation that learners can and will achieve that level from the outset.

> **Connected Tenets:** Assessment Architecture, Communication of Results
>
> **Topics:** Criteria, Summative Assessment and Grading

## Where I am from, we have yearlong learning goals, where students have the whole year to complete the learning. How do I interpret their efforts and report their progress throughout the year?

These types of goals are very typical in several content areas and can be intimidating to teachers who are interested in including formative assessments in their classrooms. This is another reason why collaboration with a colleague can be valuable but is certainly not essential.

The first task will be to unpack those outcomes or standards to understand all components. Typically, there will be a progression of skills that learners require to meet those long-term outcomes. Defining these is an important first step that can then assist with creating an assessment plan for the skills. Determining when and how to assess these skills throughout the year will provide important data for the teacher and the learners about how each learner is progressing toward those outcomes and what reteaching or additional support may be needed. This is sometimes referred to as *benchmarking* because teachers can set shorter-term goals related to those long-term outcomes and check to see if learners are on track to meet those. Benchmark assessments are strategically placed throughout the year to measure those shorter-term goals. They are recorded and analyzed to be sure learners are on track to achieving end-of-year goals or long-term outcomes. Most often collaborative teams (vertical or same grade/course) determine what "on track" means in terms of each benchmark assessment. Using curriculum guides and other district resources will help to determine when these benchmarks can best be placed. On a more formal report card, progress is most often reported using the level of proficiency the most recent benchmark assessment measured and clearly noting the shorter-term goal in the context of the long-term outcome or year-end goal.

It is important to remember that new evidence of learning can always replace old, so when learners master a learning goal at any point during the year, teachers can document this mastery and update gradebooks to reflect this current reality.

## My school uses the term *exceeds* (proficiency), but I am not comfortable with this term. What can I do?

As with all levels of proficiency, it is important that there are clear definitions so that all stakeholders, teachers, students, and parents can accurately interpret the information. This is particularly important for the highest level, often labeled *exceeds* or *advanced*. In simple terms, this level usually means that the student thinking extends beyond what the standard requires. However, some may interpret *advanced* to mean that a learner is proficient in the next grade level's standards. This is an unfair interpretation and encourages a norm-referenced approach to grading. By creating a definition that describes *exceeding* with the ideas of adapting or generalizing content in new and different ways, with deeper levels of creativity and sophistication, educators can provide learners with a target that is reachable and does not depend on mastery of content that they have not had the opportunity to learn. Other terms that may more accurately represent this interpretation are *extends* or *enriches*.

## Accurate Interpretation in a Remote Learning Context

There are factors that may feel particularly challenging when it comes to interpretation of assessment information in a remote learning context. Educators may be concerned that lack of access to and comfort with technology might prevent learners from demonstrating their best learning. They may worry that assessment evidence does not reflect the skills and understanding of their learners but rather that of siblings, friends, or parents. They may strive to differentiate their assessment approaches to support learners in their individual contexts but may be unclear about how to assess and interpret so many different versions of learning. All of these challenges are real and valid. To the best of their ability, educators want to make sure that the decisions they make in relation to assessment information support an accurate, reliable, and accessible interpretation of results. In these shifting contexts, it may be helpful to consider the following.

- Being very clear about the learning goals being assessed, including strong descriptions of the actions learners need to take to demonstrate proficiency as well as the quality of those actions (success criteria); when teachers have made time *in advance of instruction and assessment* to consider these aspects of the learning goals, they are more ready to examine artifacts of student learning and make decisions about what they are seeing. They are also more open to the potential breadth of evidence learners demonstrate.

- Working with one or more colleagues to examine student learning artifacts together; calibrate expectations and develop shared confidence in recognizing work at various degrees of proficiency. This work can be done in collaborative teams, and it serves as a great way to develop shared interpretations, increasing reliability and accuracy.

- Developing assessment tools, such as rubrics and checklists, that can be used to assess learning goals, regardless of the forms and methods used; by aligning these tools to goals as opposed to tasks (namely, by incorporating *task-neutral criteria*), teachers can reduce the number of tools both they and the learners are engaging with, simultaneously increasing understanding of what learning looks and sounds like in a variety of assessment contexts.

- Collecting samples of student work that reflect various degrees of proficiency; these samples can be accessed when interpreting student assessment information and can help to refine understanding of how learning can manifest. These same samples can be used by learners to reflect on the quality of assessment artifacts.

- Developing organizational and process tools that can help align interpretation to subsequent instructional action; these tools can be used to identify specific strengths and needs for each learner and can invite teachers to move to decision making in relation to their interpretation.

- Remaining open to accessing assessment information in a variety of ways to address student accessibility, preferences, and interests; when the assessment is aligned with goals, teachers can become highly flexible in how and when they collect assessment information from learners. The destination remains constant, but the vehicle can shift according to the needs of the learners.

# CHAPTER 7
# INSTRUCTIONAL AGILITY

Instructional agility is an intentional maneuver a teacher makes in response to evidence of learning (for example, formative assessment processes such as observations, dialogue, student questions, student comments, student practice, and quizzes). Teachers respond to and engage learners in a fluid instructional cycle that combines the recursive collection of daily evidence with responsive decision making. In this iterative process, teaching and assessment should happen simultaneously. When gathering evidence, a teacher makes flexible and precise decisions about which maneuver to use and where to spend more instructional time—for example, immediately during the lesson or the next day.

Instructional agility requires three components: (1) *learning targets* with surface understanding as well as great depth (a description of what students are expected to learn) for each learning experience, (2) formal or informal *assessment information* to explore what learners understand and what they have yet to learn, and (3) *instructional strategies* to target misconceptions and deepen understanding of the learning goal.

Instructional agility impacts the everyday work of teachers and students. It addresses the intersection between advance planning and the reality that exists in each classroom—what learners bring to the learning experience. Through ongoing, formative assessment that educators can analyze efficiently for strengths and needs and create a targeted response based on that analysis, student learning and engagement is vastly enhanced. This is why instructional agility is so important to the teaching and learning cycle.

Instructional
Agility

# Instructional Agility and Learning

## How exactly does assessment help learning?

The assessment process helps educators advance the learning. Formative assessment *is* quality instruction. While teachers are in the midst of teaching, they are gathering emerging evidence in order to make strategic, precise maneuvers that advance the learning for all learners in the room.

Assessment is defined as the intentional gathering of *clean data* with which to make informed decisions. Clean data suggests the evaluative component is suspended for a period of time and the information gathered takes the form of facts and evidence regarding accuracies and errors or misconceptions. Evaluative information arrives in the form of marks, grades, scores, or value-laden feedback such as, "This is excellent!" This kind of information is often unhelpful in guiding next steps. Clean data, on the other hand, sounds like, "You have mastered three of four targets. When you are engaged in *assessing evidence* (target 3), you are identifying the appropriate evidence, but you are not yet assessing, or evaluating, the *quality* of the evidence you find. You will want to work on using a set of criteria to determine whether the evidence provided is quality evidence, and then form your responses around your conclusion."

Done well, the assessment process helps learners focus and drive their own learning. Assessment guides learning when students can use the feedback or the evaluation results to answer the following three questions in the learning process.

1. Where am I going?

2. Where am I now?

3. How do I reduce the discrepancy between where I am and where I need to be? (Chappuis, 2015)

Though they typically happen at the conclusion of a unit of study, even summative assessments can support the continued learning process. When teachers use a consistent set of measurement tools over time (like a rubric on writing or the scientific and engineering processes, for example), when learners can use feedback to set goals to improve on the next summative assessment, and when teachers find the mode (most common score) in the later samples of work, then learners can use summative data to improve performance over many units of study.

**Connected Tenets:** Assessment Purpose, Student Investment
**Topics:** Student Engagement and Motivation

# What is the teacher's role in responding to assessment, and what is the role of the student?

The teacher's role in responding to assessment information is to observe students' words, actions, and work to make inferences about their strengths and next steps based on those observations. From the inferences teachers make, they take action and facilitate student action. A teacher might respond in any of the following ways.

- Designing an instructional lesson that addresses what the teacher or team noticed individual or groups of learners needed to move forward (addressing misconceptions, errors, or deepening)

- Setting up and implementing instructional activities and time to address each next step identified throughout observations

- Grouping learners according to strengths, needs, or preferences

- Individually talking with a learner to provide feedback on strengths and next steps and guide a student's actions

- Setting up instruction to make learners explicitly aware of their strengths and next steps; the teacher ensures learners uncover their strengths and understands how to lead them to acting on their next steps. Sometimes for a learner to act, they must receive direct instruction on a concept or see a model of how to revise or fix something.

- Noticing what helps individual and groups of learners thrive and what shuts them down

The learner's role in responding to assessment is critical. Ensuring learners reflect on what their assessment evidence means in terms of learning creates a sense of hope and focus. This reflection should lead to identifying strengths and next steps. So, a teacher would guide the learner to act in any of the following ways.

- **Acting on feedback:** As teachers provide verbal and written feedback, learners take actions.

- **Self-assessing:** Learners should identify strengths in terms of qualities of the learning goals and next steps.

- **Goal setting:** Learners should identify short-term goals that will serve as the focus of practice, exploration, and refinement.

**Connected Tenets:** Communication of Results, Accurate Interpretation, Student Investment

**Topics:** Differentiation, Feedback, Self- and Peer Assessment

Instructional
Agility

## How does deeply understanding my learning goals improve my agility?

During the assessment design process, one of the critical steps educators must take is focusing on the learning goals and articulating smaller targets that will lead to proficiency on these goals over time. Once teachers understand the learning goals, they can begin to isolate the specific knowledge, skills, progressions of learning, criteria for quality, levels of rigor, and common errors or misconceptions to avoid. Armed with such information, teachers can then make informed maneuvers during instruction so they can ensure all students advance in the learning. By understanding how learning goals may be developed over time, teachers are far more prepared to adjust instruction in the moment when they see that what they are doing is not resulting in the desired learning. A teacher's deep understanding of the learning goals ensures that this instructional agility is targeted to student needs and that it is well informed by the evidence they are gathering moment by moment.

> **Connected Tenets:** Assessment Architecture
>
> **Topics:** Formative Assessment, Unpacking and Learning Progressions

## How does questioning connect to instructional agility?

Effective questions are a valuable tool for both teachers and learners. Purposefully designed questions help teachers make informed decisions during instruction, particularly at those *hinge points* in the learning when a teacher must determine if learners are ready to move on to more complex content and skill development (Wiliam, 2011).

Questions can serve many different instructional purposes. Teachers can design questions in advance of instruction to provide evidence of student learning. By planning and identifying the criteria for success, teachers can purposefully design questions to determine which learning targets have been mastered and which still may need support. Questions can also help teachers identify any misconceptions or errors learners have. The questions that learners ask during instruction can also provide helpful information. This is particularly true when teachers have spent time anticipating and planning for common errors or challenges learners might encounter during learning. Teachers can also use questions to nurture engagement. These kinds of questions can cause learners to think deeply about new information or apply it in a new or different way. They can create connections to the learning and to the learners themselves. They can also create a strong classroom culture where other questions are encouraged. Questions can promote dialogue and probe students' understanding, encouraging them to think critically about their learning. Questions also promote discussion and debate about ideas, providing learners with the skills and opportunity to question each other's ideas.

Questioning is a central component of instructional agility, but it has its foundations in other tenets as well. Effective questions are part of the assessment architecture where the learning goals and the criteria for success are clear to both teacher and learner. Questions are also important to the accurate interpretation of results once that assessment architecture is in place, as they can provide evidence to determine if learners are learning as expected.

**Connected Tenets:** Assessment Architecture, Student Investment

**Topics:** Formative Assessment, Questioning

## How might my lesson and unit plans shift to reflect a more refined understanding of assessment?

Assessment forms the basis of unit and lesson plans. Teachers will often engage in backward planning, as Wiggins and McTighe (2005) describe in *Understanding by Design*. The first step is to analyze and unpack the standards to get a full and complete understanding of what learners should know and be able to do. This includes conversations about how to recognize proficiency and what to expect for a particular grade level since some standards are repeated across grade levels with more complex understanding using more complex texts, data, and information.

Once teachers have thoroughly explored the standards or outcomes and created learning progressions, then they must determine the best way to gather evidence on student progress and achievement of the standards or competencies. An end-of-unit assessment (intended to be used summatively) is best created before the instructional unit begins. An assessment plan also establishes the priorities for common formative assessments (prioritized around those essential learning targets that are challenging for teachers to teach, challenging for students to learn, and often in need of more instructional time), the assessment methods, the timing of those assessments, and when the results will be analyzed and responded to. This ensures the collaborative team knows when and how they will utilize the data to plan instruction, or Tier 1 prevention. Lesson and unit plans should include references to both the administration of these assessments and the utilization of that data so that instructional adjustments can be made based on that data.

While learners are exploring the unit and lessons, the pacing and time needed for practice and learning may shift according to formative assessment evidence. Assessment informs instructional planning—the relationship between the two cannot be separated.

**Connected Tenets:** Assessment Architecture, Assessment Purpose

**Topics:** Collaboration

## Doesn't instructional agility jeopardize a guaranteed and viable curriculum?

Instructional agility is what leads to a guaranteed and viable curriculum. Instructional agility is based on shared knowledge of significant, agreed-on expectations; a clear shared set of criteria for success; and a commitment to constantly improve the instructional pathway—all the ingredients of a guaranteed and viable curriculum.

For each grade level or course, individual and teams of teachers identify essential standards or competencies. These are the standards or learning that schools guarantee learners will learn. All students do not learn at the same pace and in the same way. To guarantee that students learn these essential standards, individual and collaborative teams of teachers must respond when they recognize learners do not understand or have not achieved the essential standard. This is the type of agility needed to ensure all learners achieve the essential standards. When teachers and collaborative teams are instructionally agile, this agility ensures the guaranteed curriculum becomes the achieved curriculum.

There is no such thing as one-size-fits-all instruction. What works for one teacher might not work as well for another, just as one strategy might not connect with all learners. The learning journey is indeed a personal one. Instructional agility is required, but agility does not mean *at my own pace* and *only in my way*. Agility requires precision yet flexibility. Precision is based on using *best instruction* to meet the demands of the guaranteed and viable curriculum. Flexibility involves using masterful maneuvers to adjust instruction with prowess so that a learner who might be three steps behind in the progression of learning can make up those three steps in a single, targeted move.

**Connected Tenets:** Assessment Architecture, Communication of Results

**Topics:** Differentiation, Feedback, Intervention and Instruction, Unpacking and Learning Progressions

# How can administrators support a culture of agility?

One of the main ways administrators can support a culture of instructional agility is to de-emphasize grading, especially through policies that require a certain number of grades in the gradebook each week. There is no doubt that as learners get older, grades play an increasingly important role in a learner's life. This culminates, of course, with the transcript and the application to college (if this is what learners decide to do). However, this doesn't mean that grades should always dominate the assessment narrative.

Administrators who sponsor the notion of using assessment primarily for *instructional decision making* will begin to change the conversation to one that values action over quantification in response to assessment evidence. Assessment *of* learning strategies, and even more formal formative assessment (whether common or not), can distract teachers and learners from the assessment's original intent—to inform instructional decision making. Being instructionally agile is about making real-time maneuvers to emerging assessment evidence—something that becomes increasingly difficult when the flow of instruction is lost through the start-stop mechanics of grading.

Also, administrators can begin to ask different questions of classroom teachers and, even more importantly, create opportunities for teachers to work collaboratively to elicit more moments of agility. Working together to craft questions that target *how* teachers might know, mid-lesson, that students are still learning or what strategies they might use to remediate or accelerate learning within a lesson sequence can send a clear signal that assessment is a verb and that acting as a result of the assessment is far more important than simply gathering the information to have data. By working together, teachers can build their ability to be as agile as possible and meet the needs of all learners.

Finally, administrators can lead conversations with parents about a shift in assessment practices that has likely occurred since they were in school; that assessment is primarily used as an instructional strategy rather than exclusively an evaluative one. In this way, they are helping parents understand how they can support their child's own agility at home and helping build the relationship between the learners' experience at school and at home.

**Connected Tenets:** Accurate Interpretation, Assessment Architecture

**Topics:** Feedback, Formative Assessment, Leadership

# Instructional Adjustments

## How will assessment impact my instruction?

Assessment provides essential information to teachers and students in a timely and precise manner, so that both parties can make instructional decisions to optimize learning. Effective assessment processes identify when learners have developed desired skills and understanding and when learners have not yet achieved the desired degree of proficiency. Assessment is essential for letting teachers know when and how to provide additional instruction, practice, and guided reflection. Assessment is the foundation of instructional agility because it gives teachers the information they need to adjust instruction in real time in order to advance learning for every learner. For example, an assessment may inform a teacher that a small group of students needs additional instruction on a particular concept. In this case, the teacher may adjust their instructional plan to include ten minutes of small-group instruction while the other learners are practicing problems that are more difficult. Assessment may also let a teacher know that learners have become proficient ahead of schedule and it is time to move onto new learning, even though the original plan was to have learners complete another practice assignment.

> **Connected Tenets:** Assessment Purpose
> **Topics:** Formative Assessment, Summative Assessment and Grading

## How do I know what the right adjustment is? How do I know when to adjust?

Using assessment information to make instructional adjustments requires some preplanning on the part of the teacher. The teacher should be very clear about the learning targets he or she will teach and should also spend some time analyzing the typical errors and misconceptions associated with those learning targets. The teacher should intentionally plan assessments at points in the learning when gathering the information about student learning allows the teacher to make instructional adjustments as quickly as possible and before those misconceptions can become errors that are harder for learners to overcome.

The adjustments that a teacher makes based on these data include how to deliver the content and what types of learning opportunities would help those learners who have not mastered the learning targets to have another chance to learn them. The teacher should be analyzing the data to determine what aspects learners still have not mastered and also thinking about other ways that learners can learn that information. The adjustments to instruction should be intentional and purposeful and maintain the high expectations from the initial learning experiences. Additional formative data can help the teacher know if the additional learning experiences were more successful.

There may be times when a teacher discovers, after examining formative assessment data, that the majority or more of learners have not mastered the learning targets. It is important that the teacher uses the data to plan additional learning experiences for learners. These formative data revealed that the instruction had not been successful, and learners deserve another chance to learn that information. When this happens, teachers often find value in collaboration with colleagues through the PLC process to identify different and more successful ways to teach that content.

**Connected Tenets:** Assessment Architecture, Assessment Purpose
**Topics:** Collaboration

## How do I make instructional adjustments when I have so much to cover?

The feeling that there is too much content and not enough time is a common experience for many educators. Add district curriculum guides, pacing guides, and other tools, and this feeling compounds and can make teachers feel like they have little autonomy or time to make the adjustments necessary to ensure that students are learning essential standards or competencies. The simple answer is individual teachers (and teams) need to do the critical work of reviewing all that is intended for learners to learn and identifying a smaller portion of what is essential for students to learn to be successful in the next grade level or course, or what will be important for learners to know and be able to do beyond a single assessment. Once they have identified this smaller subset of standards or outcomes, individual teachers (ideally teams) work to ensure that they protect time and that when they make instructional adjustments, they are focused on the learning that is most essential. If teachers cover everything but learners have only a surface-level understanding (if that), they will do no better and, in some cases, worse than if they have a deeper mastery of some of the most essential learning.

This is another place where collaborative conversations can be valuable. Teams can and should identify what is most essential in terms of learning, map out that learning across units or time frames, and use a calendar to ensure that there is some flexibility (even if it is part of a day or a day or two) to respond to students' learning needs on those most essential learnings. Teams will also engage with school and district tools as well as standards and other documents to create a plan that reflects what will be taught, when, and how. Gaining a better understanding of how concepts are connected and ultimately learned by students will help teachers identify those points during the instructional calendar when instructional adjustments are most valuable.

Teams will intentionally plan space to adjust, and when they identify the most essential learning, individual teachers will know when to respond in the moment and on the fly and when to let things go. If educators build that time into unit plans, then they can make sure learners are able to learn all the essential standards for the course or grade level.

**Connected Tenets:** Assessment Architecture, Student Investment
**Topics:** Formative Assessment

## How am I supposed to manage a class of learners who all need different supports after I assess them?

Using assessment to guide instruction is a valuable tool, but it can also be overwhelming when teachers are faced with results that indicate the many different things learners need. Using other assessment tenets will clarify purpose and establish an assessment architecture to focus and provide clarity around the learning to be assessed, how it will be assessed, and how the results will be used (and how they will not). Making time during planning to identify potential areas of misconception, error, or challenge for learners in the context of what is expected to be learned will help to create a system of response after educators have gathered the assessment evidence.

Delivering targeted instruction to individual or smaller groups of learners can be challenging within the context of a larger class. To meet this challenge, create clear procedures and routines. For example, when learners enter the classroom, the first twenty to thirty minutes could be devoted to a warm-up activity, which may be different for individual learners based on assessment results.

When learners are working collaboratively in groups to deepen their learning based on assessment results, co-create a list of what is expected with learners. This may include ensuring that each group has an agenda and a learning target on which they are focused. One learner helps keep the group on track while another makes sure everyone gets a chance to talk. A clear idea of what to do when the group has a question is also essential. With clearly established and implemented procedures, small-group instruction can lead to effective learning by the youngest to the oldest learners.

One way to think about the role of a teacher in this setting is as an emergency room doctor who must assess the needs of several patients who arrive at the same time. This triage system will help group learners of like needs and help determine who needs the most significant help with direct instruction from the teacher and who may be able to do something independently or with a group of peers (practice to increase confidence, quality, and automaticity). Using this type of differentiated instruction does not need to happen all day, every day. Planning for it at key points in the learning will help to build capacity for students and teachers.

**Connected Tenets:** Assessment Purpose, Student Investment

**Topics:** Collaboration, Differentiation

## What can I do about students who achieve a standard earlier than the rest of the class?

While educators may spend much time planning for learners who need additional instruction and support to learn essential standards, individual teachers and teams also design intentional learning and instruction when learners either come possessing the skills and knowledge in the standards or may learn it at a faster pace. When teams of teachers have unpacked standards and created learning progressions by sequencing the instructional unit from the simplest to the most sophisticated learning targets, the road map includes what it looks like when learners have mastered the standards. Teachers create unit plans that include opportunities for assessing learners both formally and informally throughout instruction. Those learners who are demonstrating mastery before other learners need additional challenges and support to deepen their learning. When the learning progression articulates how to deepen and push them to their next step, the analysis of the assessment results leads to instruction for learners along the learning continuum.

During the planning process, it is helpful to anticipate this need, determining which enrichment or extension opportunities will help students take their knowledge to deeper levels or apply it in unique ways. Grounded in a learning progression, instructional adjustments will be more intentional and natural for individual and teams of teachers and students.

**Connected Tenets:** Assessment Architecture, Student Investment

**Topics:** Differentiation

## Can I add assessments to my unit plan after I start teaching?

Yes. While engaging in assessment design before instructional planning leads to a focused approach to teaching and learning, it is important to remain flexible and responsive in day-to-day interactions with learners. Educators must design the summative assessment in advance of instruction. Once it is designed, it remains stationary (short of discovering significant errors in the original design) for neither teachers nor learners can hit an invisible moving target. The formative assessments can be backward mapped at this point to ensure a scaffold to success exists. However, once in the throes of instruction, teachers might realize the learners do not require some of the planned formative assessments, while they may also benefit from some other additional formative assessments. In that case, those assessments can and *must* be altered to better prepare students for the summative task at hand.

**Connected Tenets:** Assessment Architecture

**Topics:** Formative Assessment, Reassessment

# Is it okay to use different assessment tools for different students? Will this make my assessment less reliable?

If assessment prompts and tools are carefully aligned with what is being measured (learning goals or targets), educators can vary the tool itself. The questions to ask oneself are as follows.

- Does each tool measure the learning goal or target within that learning goal as intended?

- Does each tool measure the intended learning to the same degree of rigor?

- Will each tool capture the best kinds of learning from my students?

- Will each tool tell me what I need to know to move learning forward?

If the answer is *yes* to each of these questions, then using more than one tool to measure the same learning goal with the same criteria for proficiency not only is okay but, depending on the preferences of the learners, may even be optimal.

**Connected Tenets:** Assessment Architecture, Student Investment

**Topics:** Student Engagement and Motivation, Unpacking and Learning Progressions

# How can I make sure the questions I ask during instruction provide me with good information about what my students know and can do?

Asking quality questions is an important part of instructional agility. Generations of teachers have used questioning as part of their instructional strategy toolbox.

Research has shown that the majority of questioning falls under the Initiate-Response-Evaluate method, which typically involves the instructor and one learner and is typically ineffective (see https://knilt.arcc.albany.edu/Why_the_IRE_Model_of_Questioning_is_Ineffective for an example of this method). To move away from this method, teachers must spend time planning strong questions, determining when they will be asked, exploring how they might be asked, and deciding what types of information they hope to learn from these questions in advance of instruction, so they can respond to what they hear from learners in the moment. The planning template in the reproducible "Questions to Elicit Evidence of Student Learning" (page 176) illustrates how a teacher or team might design questions and engineer conversations to ensure questioning leads to learning. This reproducible could be used as an assessment method.

As teachers plan their instruction, the inclusion of a *hinge-point question* (Wiliam, 2011) at strategic moments during instruction can provide valuable information about the learners' understanding and skill at that point in time. Open and closed questions should be purposely written to elicit the type of information that the teacher needs to make the best instructional decisions. Teachers can also establish classroom practices where learners generate questions. Simply asking learners, "Do you have any questions?" is less likely to generate actionable information for the teacher. Creating opportunities for learners to engage in reciprocal instructional approaches through a combination of direct instruction, reading, reflection, and collaboration is far more likely to elicit thoughtful and insightful responses from learners. Intentionally and purposefully planning both the questions and the opportunities for learners to generate their own questions creates a framework within which the teacher can operate and demonstrate instructional agility.

**Connected Tenets:** Assessment Architecture, Student Investment

**Topics:** Questioning, Relationships

# How can I use data to inform instruction when my instructional plans are due before I even have a chance to analyze the data?

While pacing guides and other instructional planning documents are valuable documents for assuring that a guaranteed and viable curriculum is delivered throughout a system, it can feel like the instructional decision-making power of teachers is limited. It is possible to create a balance between the needs of a system and the needs of individual teachers.

Individual teachers should build their instructional plans by including both formative and summative assessment opportunities for learners. Often this starts with the summative assessment and can build backwards to include opportunities for learners to receive feedback throughout the instructional process. For example, if teachers know that a unit of instruction will take six weeks, culminating with a summative task, then they will want to include some formative assessment throughout that time. This may include quizzes or tests, or even homework assignments. As described in *Collaborative Common Assessments* (Erkens, 2016), mapping out how and when the learning targets will be assessed is an important task for a collaborative team. Once this map is created, then the instructional plans can include opportunities for either a team or an individual teacher to utilize the information from those formative tasks to help learners address the learning gaps that have been identified. While the team or teacher may not know exactly which learners may need reteaching at these points in the unit, the learning targets a teacher will address would be known. The collaborative team could make plans for reteaching and extension related to those targets and then identify the learners who need them through the formative task.

> **Connected Tenets:** Assessment Architecture, Assessment Purpose
>
> **Topics:** Formative Assessment

## What if my students need more time before they're ready for a summative assessment?

One of the values of an effective system of formative assessments is that teachers can know not only that learners need more instruction before they are ready for a summative assessment but also the specifics of what those students need to learn. When planning assessment as part of an instructional unit, it is important to include time to respond to what teachers learn from formative assessment. Planning this time into the unit from the beginning saves teachers the stress of feeling they must create time in an already-packed instructional calendar. During units when learners do not require the additional time for reteaching or relearning, teachers can use that time for extension and enrichment that strengthen learners' understanding of the concepts. It also helps to make sure that students and teachers alike move through the curriculum at an appropriate pace to meet all the learning goals for the year.

> **Connected Tenets:** Assessment Purpose
>
> **Topics:** Differentiation, Formative Assessment, Response to Intervention

# Not every learner can or will perform well on the paper-and-pencil test, but I know they know the content. Doesn't that matter?

It's imperative to certify proficiency of a standard or set of standards for each learner. While teachers generally have a keen sense of where their learners might be on the continuum of learning, it is insufficient and unprofessional to leave such important decisions to hunches. There is more than one way to assess, and typically constructed-response assessments (essays, performance tasks, or authentic tasks) can provide learners with choice *and* offer teachers a more thorough opportunity to examine each learner's depth of proficiency with more accuracy.

*If* a learner requires accommodations or modifications, then educators must appropriately address those in the assessment design and delivery systems. If one of the accommodations or modifications requires teacher involvement during the assessment process (for example, reading to the learner, writing the learner's answers for him or her, and so on), then it's important that the teacher withhold additional scaffolds that provide unfair advantages to the learner (for example, using nonverbal cues to hint that a learner might be headed on the wrong path with one of their answers).

**Connected Tenets:** Assessment Architecture

**Topics:** Assessment Design

# How can I get my students to pay attention to my feedback?

For learners to pay attention to feedback, the following conditions must be met.

- The feedback must meet a perceived need by the learner. In other words, they need to see the purpose for the feedback.

- The feedback must be understood by the learner. This means the language is clear and connected to a goal the learner clearly understands.

- The learner must be ready to receive the feedback. This means they have a relationship with their teacher that they perceive as supportive, and they have the time to really take in what the teacher is saying. This also means that they are familiar enough with proficiency to reflect on their own work in relation to this goal.

- The learner feels as though they have both the time and the capacity to apply the feedback.

- The learner believes that their attention to feedback will result in increased success on whatever goal they are pursuing.

Learners, like most adults, apply feedback when it matters to them to do so. This means that meaning and purpose are foundational for creating the investment required to ensure feedback is productive. Furthermore, feedback hinges on the teacher-student relationship, and so devoting time to developing strong relationships will support the feedback process. Lastly, feedback must be strong, which means it is timely, clear, focused on both what learners need to do and how they might do it, and embedded within a true formative assessment process.

> **Connected Tenets:** Communication of Results
> **Topics:** Feedback, Growth Mindset

# Differentiation and Interventions

## How does assessment connect to differentiation?

Assessment is the process by which teachers decide when and how to differentiate instruction. It is through analyzing assessment information (student artifacts and proficiency data) that student strengths and needs are identified. Learners who possess similar needs (for example, clarity about regrouping during multiplication, support with enhancing dialogue in writing, practice with self-monitoring and self-correcting) can be grouped together for instructional support, feedback, goal setting, and practice. In these cases, educators can tailor resources and instructional supports to meet specific student needs, and different groups of learners may engage in different resources at the same time—from those who need additional time and attention to those who are ready for stretching and a challenge. In a single class period, because learners may require several different kinds of supports as indicated by their assessment results, learners will work in small groups to address their specific, shared need. This differentiates the strategies learners are applying, the work they are engaged in, and the time they may need to spend on developing further skill and understanding.

Assessment itself can be differentiated for process and product if (1) the assessment options comprehensively and accurately assess the scope of the standards, (2) the design incorporates the required level of rigor, and (3) the criteria and levels of proficiency remain consistent. Student choice is an important feature in the assessment process, and assessing learners from their place of strength will increase learners' sense of efficacy and hope about their potential for success.

It is through engagement in all aspects of the assessment processes that teachers can design differentiated approaches to instruction. One cannot exist effectively without the other.

**Connected Tenets:** Assessment Purpose

**Topics:** Differentiation, Formative Assessment

## How will assessment help me with differentiation for my learners?

Assessment evidence at its best is designed with standards, learning targets, and criteria as the foundation. If there are multiple items on an assessment related to the same learning target or standard, ideally they are grouped. If the assessment is a more complex performance task, a set of criteria—either a checklist or a rubric—guides the scoring and feedback. As a result, when assessment evidence is broken down by learning target or criteria, it is much simpler to identify each learner's strengths and their next steps, moving learning forward. Consider figure 7.1 (page 166) as an example of how learning targets might lead to identifying students' learning needs and then differentiating instruction by readiness for that particular skill.

Collaborative teams in a PLC context can use this type of assessment design and analysis to target areas in which learners need intervention or additional instruction. Asking the question, "Why did students not meet these criteria?" can lead to the kind of instruction or strategy needed for learners to take their next steps in achieving the essential standard. Identifying where learners need support and why they made the errors they did allows teachers to get at the root cause of challenges and design instruction to meet these needs. When more than one student needs the same kind of support, teams can leverage flexible groupings to respond to needs. Identification of specific student needs and flexible responses are the foundation of differentiated instruction.

Assessment can also help teachers differentiate by interest. As in figure 7.1 (page 166), the learning progression and the criteria remain the same, but the topics learners read about and the research they engage in can change based on learners' interests and propensities. Remaining focused on the *learning* allows teachers to differentiate the ways in which learners demonstrate that learning since the task is merely a means to an end; it's the way in which learners demonstrate that they've met the learning goals.

**Connected Tenets:** Communication of Results, Assessment Architecture

**Topics:** Differentiation, Feedback, Professional Learning Communities

Name: _____ Date: _____

| Learning Targets | Criteria | Scoring |
|---|---|---|
| • I can describe and explain how the similarities and differences increase my understanding. | □ Draws unique connections between two articles<br>□ Draws clear and precise connection between physical characteristics and adaptations | 4 |
| • I can use new information from two texts in order to create comparisons. This means I can explain what key details are the same and different from the text (not my opinion). | □ Accurately describes 2 similarities from the text in the articles<br>□ Accurately describes 2 differences from the text in the articles | 3 |
| • I can use a graphic feature to find facts and details to help me support my comparisons. | □ Accurately describes 2 similarities from the tables (graphic and text features) in the articles<br>□ Accurately describes 2 differences from the tables in the articles | 2 |
| • I can identify key details in a text. | □ Accurately lists details from the articles | 1 |

To be completed by the teacher.

| Check level of independence | Descriptions |
|---|---|
| | Students read and respond to questions independently.<br>**Goal by the end of the year |
| | Teacher reads text, and students independently respond to questions. |
| | Teacher reads text and questions; prompts students through discussion to lead them to their answers. |

***Figure 7.1: Example use of learning targets to identify learners'
strengths and needs.***

# How can we make sure that differentiation isn't just lowering expectations for some students?

One of the challenges of differentiation is how to make sure that a different path still leads learners to the same ultimate destination and keeps the expectations high. According to Carol Ann Tomlinson and Tonya R. Moon (2013), "Differentiating assessment means that 'the learning outcomes remain the same . . . while the format of assessment, time allowance, and scaffolding may vary' (p. 417)" (as cited in Erkens et al., 2018, pp. 22–23). The first aspect of ensuring differentiation is being responsive to student learning needs but not trapping learners where they are. Educators should create learning progressions so both teachers and learners clearly see the pathway to achieving the standard, or competency, and the steps along the way. Then they administer an assessment (most often at grade level or at the level of expectation). When looking at the results or the student work from the assessment evidence, teachers determine where a learner is along that pathway. Learners will inevitably be at different places, but they are all on the same path. Individuals and groups of learners engage in instruction based on what the assessment indicated. Teachers plan instruction for the different needs that emerge from the assessment evidence. Then, they assess again to see their progress. Learners and the teacher are clear about the pathway to proficiency, and the learners and the teacher are clear where they are on that pathway and what their next step is.

This is where the work of a collaborative team can be valuable. It is difficult for individual teachers to plan for multiple pathways to a given learning goal. Collaboratively, a team of teachers may find this task slightly less daunting. Collaboration also provides additional perspectives to make sure that the expectations for all learners stay at the same rigor while allowing for variation of time, support, instructional strategies, and practice opportunities based on the needs of learners. When the collaborative team works together to create common formative and summative assessments, the team can be assured that learners are making progress toward the same learning goals even if they are accomplishing this growth in different ways.

**Connected Tenets:** Assessment Architecture, Assessment Purpose

**Topics:** Differentiation, Rigor and Cognitive Complexity

# How do I know when my response requires more than Tier 1 prevention?

Tier 1 prevention is informed by formative (individual or common) assessment that provides evidence of what learners understand and can do, or don't understand

and are struggling to do in relation to an essential standard or learning target. When educators administer a formative assessment, they analyze its results and build time into core instruction for responding to students' learning needs based on the information provided within the assessment.

If learners don't achieve the intended learning during core instruction, they may need another chance to learn what the first instructional response didn't help them get. It is essential that the instructional response be different than how the learning target was originally taught. If it is a simple misconception or a need to build automaticity, learners may just need a one-on-one with the teacher or more time, which can be built into the instruction before the end of the unit.

If the end of the unit comes and learners still haven't mastered that same essential learning target, a school builds in Tier 2 systems (more targeted, predictable, and often group based) so that learners get additional time and support on that essential standard without missing the next unit's core instruction. Tier 2 intervention is for learners who need additional time and support to master grade-level essential standards.

Finally, if there is a pattern of the learner not achieving essential standards or learning targets over time and with support, the teaching team may need to take a deeper look at the student's strengths and challenges and find additional time and support for foundational skills that may be contributing to not achieving essential standards at Tier 1. In essence, if there are patterns of a learner struggling over time with various concepts, and if multiple attempts to help the learner learn in multiple different ways are unsuccessful, then more intense and personalized support may be needed; this is Tier 3 remediation.

By definition, essential standards often recur across units, so it is important to look at the skill in various contexts to see if learners are struggling not with the skill but with the context or background information. This is not a foundational skill issue and can sometimes be a trap that learners fall into, which sends them into low achievement cycles that are hard to get out of.

**Connected Tenets:** Assessment Architecture, Assessment Purpose
**Topics:** Differentiation, Formative Assessment, Response to Intervention

## Can't Tier 2 interventions just address what students don't know?

It is essential that teams of teachers identify essential standards or outcomes. Tier 2 intervention occurs when learners have not met an initial level of proficiency (quality of products and performances) for essential standards. Standards require demonstrated skills, so when learners struggle, it usually indicates a need for additional knowledge and skill development; this often occurs in a small, group-based setting where similar skill development is necessary amongst the learners.

While teachers often feel the need to pause and reteach everything learners do not understand, this level of response is often unmanageable; there is just simply not enough time. So, when teams of teachers prioritize their standards or outcomes, they identify what they will ensure students learn. While teachers will share or cover all standards and outcomes, the essential goals are where they focus their feedback and intervention efforts. In this way, Tier 2 interventions address both skills and knowledge articulated within the essential or priority learning goals.

> **Connected Tenets:** Assessment Architecture, Assessment Purpose
> **Topics:** Differentiation, Formative Assessment, Response to Intervention

# Reassessment

## Why is reassessment important? When should I reassess?

Reassessment is a process that educators employ when the learner did not meet the desired state or goal in an earlier assessment. If all learners must achieve the required expectations and a learner has failed to do so in the allotted time frame, then teachers must extend learning opportunities. In the classroom, time is the variable and learning must remain the constant. Teachers must apply additional and *different* instruction if a learner has not yet met the standards. Following any instruction aimed at improving achievement levels, teachers must employ a *new* assessment—a reassessment—to know where the learner stands after the intervention.

Just as with all good teaching, decisions to assess are based in teacher perceptions of student readiness. Good decision making is dependent on the professional judgment of teachers, who have the most precise and current assessment information available to them. For this reason, the following three circumstances may necessitate reassessment.

1. Conflicting information is preventing a teacher from making professional judgment about degrees of proficiency and actions needed. For example, a learner may have been showing signs of proficiency during formative assessment processes and yet a summative assessment indicates difficulty. In this case, the teacher may need to seek more evidence in order to be certain about how proficient a learner is and what they need.

2. External circumstances are interfering with the validity of the assessment (for example, a poorly constructed prompt that confused the learners, or a family trauma that supersedes a learner's ability to concentrate). Again, the teacher may choose to reassess to gain valid and reliable results.

3. A learner has truly grown his or her learning (through additional instruction, further practice, targeted feedback, personal goal setting) and is willing and able to demonstrate this growth. In this case, the old evidence is no longer accurate, so new evidence must be collected.

It is important to note that reassessment will not occur after every single assessment experience. The importance of the learning being measured, the learning plans (which may address relearning and reassessment naturally and recursively), and the age of the learners may all influence the decision to reassess. When the purpose of assessment guides their decision making, teachers can feel more confident in their reassessment decisions.

> **Connected Tenets:** Accurate Interpretation, Student Investment
>
> **Topics:** Professional Judgment, Reassessment

## What changes in my mindset must occur before I consider the topic of reassessment?

The first shift in mindset is to decide whether it is important that every learner learns what is being taught. On the surface, that sounds obvious and oversimplistic. However, the processes and practices of reassessment hinge on the mindset that every learner can and should learn what is being taught.

The second shift is to accept that some learners will need more time, support, feedback, and opportunities to reach proficiency within any given set of learning goals or standards. If what's being taught matters, and teachers know that some learners need longer to learn, then reassessment emerges as a natural part of the learning process.

A third mindset shift is to view assessment through the lens of standards instead of task types. The concept of reassessment through the task-type lens can conjure up images of duplicating every assessment that is conducted. Teachers are already busy, and the idea that every assessment must now be duplicated is both unnecessary and unsustainable. To *re*test, *re*quiz, *re*lab, and so on is daunting. However, when examined through the lens of standards, teachers can see that the reassessment process is a natural part of the instructional progression since teachers already assess most, if not all, standards at least twice. Whether one assessment is labelled *test* or *quiz* is irrelevant.

The fourth change in mindset is to recognize that assessment can occur at a variety of times, in a variety of ways. Observation, conversation, and artifacts all inform decision making and professional judgment, and it is possible to assess learners in more than one way at different times from their peers. This is especially the case when assessment information is organized by standard as opposed to task type or time period. Learners do not have to be assessed in batches.

> **Connected Tenets:** Assessment Architecture, Communication of Results
>
> **Topics:** Criteria, Reassessment, Summative Assessment and Grading

## Does reassessment really prepare students for the real world?

Reassessment *is* replicating the real world when considering how many real-world assessments allow for multiple attempts. Whether it's the SAT, driving tests, or the bar exam, reassessment is afforded if participants are unsuccessful the first time. The United States Medical Licensing Examination (n.d.) can be taken three times in a twelve-month period. The fourth attempt must be twelve months after the first, and all subsequent attempts must be at least six months after the previous attempt. Notice, no limit. The suggestion that reassessment isn't part of the real world is absurd.

But, there are two more important and larger issues at play with reassessment. The first is that learners are not adults. No matter how mature they might seem, the adult brain does not function and rationalize as an adult brain until the early to mid-twenties. There's a lot of space between being an adolescent and being an adult in a chosen profession. Children go through several stages of development before becoming adults, and that process can't really be rushed; it's physiological. Any attempt to replicate the real world (usually in reference to the world of adults) would at best be premature and at worst would be completely misguided.

The second important and larger issue is the suggestion that learners don't live in the real world already. Of course, it's not the world of an adult, but the suggestion that learners' worlds aren't real downplays (and maybe even disrespects) the complexities of being a young person. Their worlds are real, and educators need to decide whether preparation is about replicating tomorrow's experience or ensuring success today through skill development and an attentiveness to what students need in the present moment.

> **Connected Tenets:** Assessment Architecture, Communication of Results
>
> **Topics:** Criteria, Reassessment

# Sometimes I feel like I am working harder than my students. How can I fix this?

Feedback and learning should lead to action and work for the learner so that the teacher is not doing more work on a learner's progress than the learner. Far too often, teachers spend vast amounts of time offering detailed and specific feedback to learners and then inviting, but not requiring, learners to do something with that feedback. Teachers should provide feedback and instruction that facilitate further learning, not simply rehash what was done in the past. The purpose of feedback and responsive instruction should be to propel learners to the next level of proficiency. Focus feedback on a few essential qualities (not everything) of the learning and require action on the feedback, or revision. Build the required revision into lesson time, knowing that revision is a powerful tool for learners in propelling their learning forward. It is that action that will lead to results. This means teachers reduce the amount of feedback and commenting they are doing on student work that is invitational or done without the learner present.

Educators should take the same approach with reassessment. Learners need to take additional responsibility to engage in and document further learning before reassessment takes place. They must teach learners what it means to review their assessments for strengths and next steps and take responsibility for their learning. This doesn't mean that educators invite learners to reassess and leave it up to them to come or not. If the learning is essential, teachers should intentionally guide learners who did not demonstrate mastery to reflect on what they still need to work on based on the assessment, give additional instruction to address those areas of need, and then require learners to reassess. Too often learners who most need additional support will not voluntarily show up to reassess or get the help they may need. They may not have the confidence or, even more so, the belief that it will matter. Thus, the process of reassessment isn't about just doing something over and over again, which leads to endless time on the teacher's part chasing learners to get work done or to come in for help. Reassessment is about learners reflecting on what they know and what they still need to work on. It is focused on the most essential learning. Intervention or additional instruction is focused on the essential learning targets or goals that still need to be mastered. Teachers structure this into the day—either as part of the flow of the unit or during protected time for intervention, if schools have it.

**Connected Tenets:** Communication of Results, Student Investment
**Topics:** Feedback, Student Engagement and Motivation

# Time Management

## It seems like all I ever do is test; I never get to teach. How can I regain my ability to teach?

Testing and teaching can, when engineered correctly, have a reciprocal relationship. *Testing* involves measuring (directly or through inference) the current status of achievement; *teaching* is what educators do to positively impact achievement. When balanced, teaching can influence testing while testing can equally inform teaching, but balance is the key. While each informs the other, one—*teaching*—is what positively impacts learning. Testing positively impacts learning no more than a scale helps one lose weight.

When assessment is viewed as a noun, then the paradigm is one where the teacher must stop teaching to conduct an assessment. Within the *assessment as noun* paradigm, assessment (testing) interferes with instructional flow. In this case, never getting to teach would be a predictable result since testing and teaching serve different purposes.

If *testing* were replaced with the word *assessment*, then a different paradigm emerges. Using assessment to guide instructional maneuvers is exactly where the true power of formative assessment lies. Teachers who can elicit valid and reliable information about student learning can use that information to make the subsequent instructional decisions; this is the *assessment as verb* paradigm. In this case, continual assessment is necessary because teachers will be informed as to whether learning is occurring, to what degree it is occurring, and which next steps are necessary.

When assessment holds the primary purpose of informing instructional next steps, teachers can't effectively or efficiently teach without assessment since there would be no way of confirming (until much later) that the students are learning what they are expected to learn and no way of determining how to address student needs. If all a teacher is doing is testing, then that must change. However, if the teacher is assessing to determine the next instructional steps, then constant assessment is necessary.

**Connected Tenets:** Accurate Interpretation, Communication of Results

**Topics:** Feedback, Formative Assessment

## I don't have time for best practices in assessment; I already don't have time to cover all of the curriculum. How can I manage everything?

Effective assessment practices can save teachers valuable time and can lead to increased learning, which is far more important than coverage of curriculum. Certainly, the expectations set forth by many curricular and state or provincial documents can seem overwhelming, which is why one of the most important steps teachers can make in their assessment design is to articulate the guaranteed and viable curriculum (the non-negotiables) through the identification of essential learnings. These are the curricular expectations teachers deem critical for each learner in their subject area at their grade level. This step allows teachers to curate their focus to that which is most important, and it allows learners to spend the most time on the most important aspects of a course or grade level. When teachers provide interventions, they are in relation to the essential learnings. When learners are reassessed, it is connected to the non-negotiable skills and understanding within a subject area. This, in turn, allows teachers to use the best assessment practices available to address learner needs.

**Connected Tenets:** Assessment Purpose

**Topics:** Essential Standards, Reassessment, Response to Intervention

# Instructional Agility in a Remote Learning Context

It is easy to imagine how instructional agility might be essential in a remote learning context. Learners in varied home circumstances may have vastly different needs on any given day, and teachers have to be agile in determining those needs and responding effectively and efficiently. Like in a classroom context, each learner arrives each day with their own background knowledge, learning preferences, and interests. Added to this, learners must navigate what may well be new technology (although likely not new for everyone), all under a backdrop of very individual learning contexts. This makes formative assessment and the responsive instructional agility important to determine.

To be instructionally agile in this context, teachers must design ways to collect evidence of the current state of learning so that they can make decisions. Next, educators will have to develop processes for recording the information they gather, so they can manage flexible groupings and differentiated responses. Thirdly, teachers will likely spend additional time investigating ways to invite questions from learners, build strong questions into their lessons, encourage conversation, and develop observational tools that can provide additional information. Lastly, teachers may consider ways to include learners in decision making, so the likelihood of learners responding appropriately is increased.

In a remote learning context, teachers might consider the following.

- Align evidence collection with essential learning goals so that decisions focus on the most important things and educators can easily identify patterns, strengths, and needs.

- Design ways to collect evidence that offer the most flexibility possible. This can include establishing success criteria that they can apply across different tasks and collecting evidence at different times for different learners.

- Be open to the idea that formative assessment does not have to be in the form of a written quiz (although it can be). Evidence can be collected from concept maps, infographics, video clips, audio recordings, photographs, oral explanations, and any number of other methods. If teachers and learners are clear about the specific goals and targets being explored, how evidence is gathered is very flexible.

- Develop a method for record keeping that allows teachers (and learners) to readily identify needs and organized differentiated responses. Some gradebooks allow teachers to record formative evidence without it being part of a grade calculation, which is important. If a gradebook does not have this option, teachers can develop additional spreadsheets organized around learning goals and targets to help them make instructionally agile decisions.

- Investigate ways to respond immediately to student needs. Finding digital tools that allow immediate feedback on student work, tools that ask learners to offer quick responses to mid-lesson learning, ways for learners to ask questions right when they need to, and tools that allow teachers to listen to student conversations and watch learners as they are learning will be important. Furthermore, methods for grouping learners at times and communication tools so learners can connect with teachers and each other will be helpful. The more familiar learners become with these processes, the more effective they will become.

- Leverage student strengths and connect learners with each other based on these strengths. Teachers do not have to be the only people who can respond to student needs. Finding ways for learners to work with each other on advancing learning will be critical.

- Include learners in investigating ways to grow learning. Many learners are incredibly knowledgeable about technology and what they need to get better at the skills teachers are working to develop. Letting learners explore their own learning processes and reflect on their own decisions will help them not only advance their learning but become better learners overall. This also nurtures student investment, which is very important in a remote learning context.

Instructional
Agility

# Questions to Elicit Evidence of Student Learning

| Learning Target | Questions | Purpose |
|---|---|---|
| I can describe weathering and how it affects the earth.<br>I can describe erosion and how it is measured. | What is the difference between weathering and erosion? | Teachers use this as an exit ticket to check for understanding on the concept of erosion. All students must understand this concept in order to interpret and make predictions. Teachers talk to individual students who do not master the concept. |
| I can interpret data from maps to describe patterns and changes in the earth. | Compare the interpretation statements you made with those of your partner's. How are they the same and different? | Teachers can use this activity to find out if students understand interpretation and can read a map. Through student dialogue and interpretation, teachers see who can identify what the maps actually say, who can make statements that show relationships (clear evidence they can interpret), and who can draw conclusions or think like a scientist. |
| I can use data interpreted from maps of the earth to describe changes over time. | How do interpretation statements help us understand how the earth has changed over time? | Students work in collaborative groups to discuss this question. To make predictions, teachers check whether students can see the changes and patterns that emerged over time. They may even generate a model to represent the changes. |

page 1 of 2

*Concise Answers to Frequently Asked Questions About Assessment and Grading* © 2022 Solution Tree Press
*SolutionTree.com* • Visit *go.SolutionTree.com/assessment* to download this free reproducible.

| I can use what I know about the earth's features and how they change to identify problems, make predictions, and pose solutions. | Why are erosion and weathering a threat to the earth? Back up your thinking with evidence from our readings and investigations. | In groups of three, students explore this question and identify evidence. The teacher collects the questions that arise and uses them to encourage further thinking as students engage in small-group dialogue. |
|---|---|---|
| I can use what I know about the earth's features and how they change to identify problems, make predictions, and pose solutions. | What questions might a scientist ask to try to predict the impact of erosion on the earth over the next two hundred years? | Teachers use these questions to determine the level of understanding students have about how the earth is changing. Teachers use surface-level questions to show students how to trace the data. They use deeper-level questions to generate dialogue in the classroom. |

*Source: Erkens, C., Schimmer, T., & Dimich, N. (2018).* Instructional agility: Responding to assessment with real-time decisions. *Bloomington, IN: Solution Tree Press.*

# CHAPTER 8
# STUDENT
# INVESTMENT

As established previously in this book, assessment must create a culture of learning and hope. This can only happen when the assessment architecture is tightly designed and effectively employed and when learners are engaged in their learning and are able to describe where they are and how they can grow. This is when student investment emerges as a critical feature of effective assessment systems.

This type of self-regulation is only possible when learners clearly understand what they are trying to achieve, have a sense of what quality work looks like, and can adapt and revise in order to get closer to the learning goal. When deep student investment exists, the culture of the school and classroom is focused on meaningful learning, and learners use instruction and assessment experiences to understand where they are in their own learning. This information leads to action where learners strive to thrive—they are taking steps forward in their learning and seeing value, relevance, and meaning in their daily work. Learners gain confidence and efficacy in these spaces because they are seeing results (Dimich, 2015).

Student investment happens by design. When teachers intentionally consider ways to empower learners to reflect on their experiences, set meaningful goals, and make decisions that address their needs, everyone benefits. Educators can plan for student investment in daily lessons and unit plans, enhance student investment through instructionally agile choices that embrace student efficacy, and nurture student investment during decision making before, during, and after assessment experiences. When teachers enhance student investment, improved learning out-comes will follow.

# The Basics of Student Investment

## How can I involve students in the assessment process? What can they do?

Educators can involve learners in all aspects of the assessment process. Rather than being passive recipients to the assessment experience, learners can be actively involved in shaping how assessment is carried out, what responses to the assessment are most appropriate, and what new targets will comprise the next set of short-term goals.

Prior to any assessment experience, it is crucial that learners be aware of (and poten-tially involved in the creation of) both the learning targets and the success criteria. While it isn't necessary to always co-create targets and criteria, it is vital that learners have clarity on what success looks like. Using exemplars is often beneficial to show, not just tell, what a quality product or performance could look like. In addition, learners can use the targets and criteria to set specific goals and gauge their level of efficacy with the task at hand. Barry J. Zimmerman (2011b) calls this the *forethought* phase.

During the assessment process, learners have the opportunity to monitor the qual-ity of what they are doing or producing. By clarifying the criteria prior to the pro-cess, learners can compare the quality of their performance or product to the quality of what their teachers expect at several points throughout the learning cycle. This comparison can be challenging, since often it requires learners to make an inference when the assessment is not anchored on right-or-wrong responses. For this reason, modeling and explicit instruction are key when asking learners to compare their own efforts to success criteria.

Teachers can also utilize a peer assessment structure, where learners are assessing and reflecting on one another's work, to increase involvement. By using feedback from peers combined with their own reflections, learners can monitor themselves as learners, paying close attention to what habits, skills, and dispositions lead to suc-cess, how they overcome initial challenges, and what they might do differently next time. In both cases—either monitoring the learning or assessing their habits and dispositions—the goal is for learners to provide themselves or others with *what's next* feedback that continues to advance their learning.

After an assessment experience, student involvement can include reflection on both performance and learning dispositions. For their performance, learners could reflect on whether they were satisfied with the outcome, what overall progress they made toward a larger learning goal, and potentially what they would do next time. When it comes to dispositional reflection, learners could articulate whether they noticed their approach to the task waver at any point, what strategies they used to stay (or get back) on track, and how affected they were by any challenges they faced. Essentially, reflecting on what they learned and how they learned it can feed the forethought phase of their next learning cycle.

> **Connected Tenets:** Accurate Interpretation, Assessment Purpose
>
> **Topics:** Criteria, Self- and Peer Assessment

## What does a school look like when student investment is high?

Indicators of high student investment within a school setting may look like the following.

- Higher rates of completion of practice work (because it is seen as meaningful)
- A balance of teacher and student voices heard when decisions are being made and when topics are being explored
- Greater evidence of feedback and time to respond
- Frequent self-assessment and goal setting, and time to attend to this work
- Higher degrees of risk taking, curiosity, and question generation
- Fewer discipline issues; greater evidence of self-regulation
- Higher attendance and on-task behavior
- Evidence of students expressing their understanding in personally meaningful ways

> **Connected Tenets:** Culture of Learning
>
> **Topics:** Student Engagement and Motivation

## How do assessment and student confidence intersect?

Assessment is not just a clinical exercise in gathering information; it's also a human one. Every learner will have an emotional reaction to the prospect of being assessed, which means a student's disposition will play a role in how they perform during any assessment. Learning cannot be separated from its social context, so the emotional side of the assessment experience must always be taken into consideration.

Confidence is *grounded optimism* (Kanter, 2004) and should not be mistaken for arrogance or a sense of entitlement. Real confidence is authentic optimism about the potential for success, which can be built through the strategic use of assessment strategies, especially when assessment is used formatively to lead learners to proficiency. Unpacking standards, creating learning progressions, strategically infusing assessment strategies throughout the learning, and providing continual feedback on *what's next* reveal the pathway to success, from the simple to sophisticated. At each step along the progression, teachers and learners will see the path forward and know what it will take to remain on the trajectory. As the saying goes, nothing succeeds like success, so being purposeful about making the learning goals and criteria transparent will create a *success trajectory* where confidence builds as learning deepens.

Grading practices can also impact student confidence. Grading practices that have the potential to erode student confidence are counterproductive, even if those practices are long-standing and traditional (Schimmer, 2016). So many traditional grading practices serve to distort achievement levels by including non-learning factors (for example, late penalties) that make precision in grading more unlikely. This, in turn, gives learners an opaque view of where they are in their learning. Learners should never be able to behave their way up or down the grading scale, which is why teachers must take care in how they determine and report learning. Building and maintaining confidence through grading is not about being dishonest to learners about where they are in their learning. Instead, it's about ensuring the pathway to proficiency is never closed through a continual process of reassessment and allowing flexible methods of demonstration.

The fact that nothing can derail student confidence like a poorly designed and executed assessment system tells us that assessment is a deeply personal experience. Recognizing the residual emotional impact assessment can have is important for teachers to keep in mind; how teachers *handle* assessment will either *contribute to* or *take something away* from the relationships teachers are trying to build with every learner and the confidence those learners hold in the long term.

**Connected Tenets:** Assessment Purpose, Accurate Interpretation
**Topics:** Formative Assessment, Summative Assessment and Grading

## How do assessment and teacher confidence intersect?

The more confident teachers are in their assessment practices and the results their assessments are yielding, the better they can continue to reflect on and search for the best possible ways to both measure learning and respond to student needs. Confidence breeds enjoyment, creativity, collaboration, and effective communication.

This means teachers are able to design assessment tools and processes that precisely capture the learning intended within the learning goals. It means teachers are crystal clear about their standards and the ways these standards develop over time for learners. It also means they are confident in their ability to design assessment architecture that brings out the best in their learners and measures those things that need to be measured. Knowing which prompts to use, which texts to offer, and which conditions to ensure learning allows teachers to be confident in their assessment decisions.

Knowing what their assessment information tells them about their learners—their strengths and challenges—means teachers can also feel confident in their ability to offer learners the kinds of flexible grouping, feedback, and additional learning opportunities that will help them to move their learning forward. This is confidence, and it will yield strong learning.

**Connected Tenets:** Assessment Purpose, Culture of Learning

**Topics:** Feedback, Formative Assessment

## What makes an assessment experience positive for students?

An assessment experience is positive for learners if it leads to increased confidence, clear and meaningful action, verification of strength, clarity about next steps, and enhanced efficacy. When learners feel that hope remains, regardless of the assessment outcome, the assessment has served a positive purpose.

Sometimes, assessment results indicate the need for supports, the need to re-engage in the content, or the need to continue to practice and reflect. When this happens, learners can still have a positive experience *if* they receive clear feedback, reteaching and support when necessary, and time to practice and address specific criteria. With rich, supportive scaffolds in place and an eye to the likelihood of ultimate success, the assessment experience can sustain and even inspire student investment. Assessment results can reveal both strength and challenge, but the experience itself can remain positive when hope is nurtured.

**Connected Tenets:** Assessment Purpose

**Topics:** Formative Assessment, Student Engagement and Motivation

Student Investment

# Isn't student investment the same as caring about a grade?

Student investment is indicated by a number of behaviors, and caring about a grade may be one of those behaviors. However, this particular indicator is not the only way learners may demonstrate investment, and in many cases, caring about the grade alone can even reduce true investment for some learners. When educators see investment, they see highly motivated learners who make decisions based on personally meaningful engagement in the learning context.

Investment is the extent to which learners are engaged in their learning and are able to describe where they are in the process of moving toward goals and how they can make strong next steps. When deep student investment exists, the culture of the school and classroom is focused on learning and all of the experiences and opportunities that are part of this learning. Certainly, a grade may be part of the end goal, but true investment extends more deeply into the process of learning—the questions being posed, the exploration being encouraged, and the successes along the way. At times, the drive for a good grade can undermine these things. Learners may, for example, be hesitant to take risks and ask their own questions when their perception of getting a high grade means focusing on what matters most to the teacher as opposed to what matters to them.

This is why strong student investment is closely linked to learners who are engaged in assessment processes like self-assessment and goal setting, co-construction of success criteria, and feedback. Further, when learners care deeply about the contexts for their learning, they are invested, and good grades are simply a byproduct of this personal meaning-making.

> **Connected Tenets:** Accurate Interpretation, Assessment Purpose
> **Topics:** Student Engagement and Motivation, Summative Assessment and Grading

# How can I take my students' focus off grades?

The answer is both simple and complex. The *simple* answer is to stop assigning grades so often. Teachers don't need grades to teach, and learners don't need grades to learn. Through many bodies of research, it is understood that grades and scores can interfere with learners' willingness to keep learning (Schimmer, 2014, 2016; Schimmer et al., 2018; Vatterott, 2015; Wiliam, 2011, 2013a, 2018). Sure, grades are the currency learners currently use to apply to colleges and universities, but *grades* are not necessary to assign to every product or performance learners generate.

Instead, shift the assessment focus away from grades and toward feedback, practice, or other productive responses.

The *complex* answer requires a broader shift away from the pervasive paradigm around grades. Most kindergarten learners don't know what grades are until the adults in their lives—both teachers and parents—introduce them to grades. Kindergarten learners don't ever ask, "Are you grading this?" Learners don't enter the education system with a focus on grades. That said, once grades become part of the school experience, the way teachers talk about and utilize grades will make a difference in how learners think about them. What adults pay attention to is what learners eventually believe is important, so an obsession about grades by the adults will create an obsession about grades within students.

A first step would be to only utilize grades for the summative purpose when assessing—to verify that learning has occurred. Through the formative assessment process, remove any grade, score, or level and provide learners with only feedback that serves to validate strengths and identify areas in need of strengthening. Another step would be to ensure grades only reflect learners' abilities to meet the standards or the quality of the evidence learners produce. As long as the expectation of performance is at the appropriate cognitive complexity and all non-achievement factors are handled separately, teachers can ensure that getting a higher grade means doing more learning.

Teachers may not be able to completely eradicate a grade-focus for all learners, but if they can turn grades (when they decide to offer them) into a reflection of quality rather than a commodity that's acquired, then when grades are assigned, learners can be more confident their grades are actually meaningful.

**Connected Tenets:** Assessment Purpose, Communication of Results

**Topics:** Feedback, Summative Assessment and Grading

# Assessment Practices

## How do I plan for investment before even giving an assessment? Is it possible to increase investment through assessment?

When learners are invested in an experience (learning or assessment), they will often access and demonstrate the best of what they know and can do. These conditions are perfect in assessment contexts because it means that teachers can really examine what a learner is doing and thinking during the assessment process and remain confident that any difficulty they are observing is not due to a lack of engagement.

So teachers must consider the number of times and ways they will actively strive to engage learners throughout the learning while they are immersed in designing assessment tools and processes. Assessment design begins with teachers making time to consider the meaning behind the learning goals they will be teaching and assessing. Why, out of all the things that could be explored with learners, was this particular goal chosen? Exploring this question can help teachers get at the heart of each learning goal. Is the purpose to encourage the exploration of worldview? It is important because it invited critical thinking? Creative expression of ideas? Once teachers are clear about the deep intent of learning goals, they can begin to imagine how the answer to this question might shift a little when examined from the learner's point of view. Why should this matter to them? And how might teachers invite their learners to explore this goal in a personally meaningful or compelling way?

In effect, student investment is built through a strong understanding of both the learning goals and the students who will be engaging in the learning and assessment experiences. A commitment to assessment architecture that leverages student investment will yield more valid and reliable assessment data, while also helping students maintain focus on the bigger picture of education.

**Connected Tenets:** Assessment Architecture

**Topics:** Critical Competencies, Student Engagement and Motivation

## How do I help learners understand the different purposes of assessment and encourage them to buy in?

Sometimes educators overshare. Just as a driver doesn't need to understand the mechanics of the engine, a learner doesn't need to understand the technicalities of a teacher's craft and tools. What they *do* need to understand is that they will have many opportunities to practice before they are evaluated. With that context in mind, the question becomes twofold: (1) how do teachers get their learners to value practice, and (2) how do they ensure that they use practice to improve achievement between assessments so they can ensure student mastery on the final assessments?

The following are tips for helping learners value practice work.

- Design amazing summative tasks and performances—experiences that learners can't wait to do.

- Reveal the breakdown of skills and knowledge required to be successful on the summative assessment.

- Create resources that enable learners to monitor growth over time and track readiness for the summative assessment on the identified set of required knowledge and skills—for example, consistent rubrics that are employed multiple times and data tracking forms.

- Provide diagnostic feedback that highlights strengths and analyzes the gaps in a manner that empowers learners to make the necessary adjustments required for improvement. Make feedback invaluable, so learners couldn't stand to miss getting it.

- Empower learners to use evidence generated from their practice work to qualify themselves for future opportunities or next steps, or to disqualify themselves from having to continue practicing mastered concepts and skills.

The following are tips for ensuring practice work leads to success on the summative assessments.

- Maintain the option for learners to achieve mastery at the point of the summative assessment. Ensure early errors and mistakes during practice work do not prohibit success at the conclusion of the learning.

- Create a road map that ensures *each* practice opportunity (1) is aligned to the summative expectations, (2) will provide results that offer both teacher and learner alike degrees of proficiency on the necessary skills, and (3) provides multiple opportunities for improvement per each learning target. See figure 8.1 (page 188) for an example.

**Connected Tenets:** Assessment Architecture, Assessment Purpose

**Topics:** Formative Assessment, Summative Assessment and Grading

# How might schools lower the current anxiety around assessment to nurture confident and empowered learners?

When connecting teacher assessment practices to learner confidence and empowerment, the details matter. How schools explain assessment (including the language they use) as well as how they use assessment and how they respond to results can increase or decrease anxiety. Anxiety often involves unpleasant feelings or dread and can

---

Common Core State Standards, Reading Informational Texts

**Target 1:** **RI.3.1** Ask and answer questions to demonstrate understanding of a text, referring explicitly to the text as the basis for the answers.

**Target 2:** **RI.3.2** Determine the main idea of a text.

**Target 3:** **RI.3.2** Recount the key details and explain how they support the main idea.

**Target 4:** **RI.3.3** Describe the relationship between a series of historical events, scientific ideas or concepts, or steps in technical procedures in a text, using language that pertains to time, sequence, and cause/effect.

Assessments: (H) homework, (CP) checkpoint, (Project) projects, and (Final) final assessments

|  | H1 | H2 | H3 | CP1 | H4 | H5 | CP2 | H6 | H7 | Project | Final |
|---|---|---|---|---|---|---|---|---|---|---|---|
| **Target 1:** | X | X |  | X |  |  |  |  | X | X | X |
| **Target 2:** |  | X | X | X |  | X | X |  |  | X | X |
| **Target 3:** |  |  | X |  | X | X | X | X | X | X | X |
| **Target 4:** |  |  |  |  | X |  | X | X | X | X | X |

---

*Source for standards: National Governors Association Center for Best Practices & Council of Chief State School Officers, 2010.*

**Figure 8.1:** *A road map of formative assessments that lead to success on the summative assessments.*

be accelerated by a lack of predictability over future events. When assessment reduces agency, minimizes voice, and offers no ability to prepare for success, anxiety increases. All assessment processes within a school should be examined through the following lenses.

- Do assessment practices make learners feel like they have much or little control or agency? Do learners feel represented and reflected in assessment, or do they feel tricked?

- Are learners prepared for assessment? Do they understand how it will be used? Do they have the chance to increase their learning and refine their efforts over time, or is assessment one-and-done?

- Do assessment decisions and responses cause emotional or social pain for learners, or do they support and encourage learners through challenge?

- Do assessment practices accentuate or ignore strength and capacity?

- Do assessment practices increase or decrease optimism?

- Do assessment practices support flexibility, choice, and responsiveness, or do they diminish them?

- Do families and learners understand assessment decisions? Assessment language? Do they share an understanding of assessment and how it will be used to advance learning?

The school culture and the role assessment plays in learning make all the difference. These questions can help schools examine any and all assessment practices that occur every day within a school and ensure that assessment nurtures confidence and empowerment and eliminates anxiety.

**Connected Tenets:** Accurate Interpretation

**Topics:** Growth Mindset, Homework, Parent Engagement, School and Classroom Culture and Climate

## How should I respond when learners aren't using my feedback?

When learners aren't using feedback, a response is definitely needed. Feedback and action go hand in hand, and, therefore, a lack of response to feedback is worth examining. However, before jumping to a response, it may be helpful to consider the root cause or reason why the feedback is being ignored. The following are some questions to reflect on.

- Did the learner receive the feedback at a time when it made sense to respond? If feedback comes too early, creativity and ownership might be stifled. If it comes too late, there may not be adequate time to respond.

- Was the feedback specific? Did it refer to specific criteria for success or attributes of quality work? Without this level of specificity, learners may have been unclear about precisely which aspects of their learning to attend to. Engaging learners in work samples can help learners make sense of success criteria.

- Did the feedback also offer suggestions as to how learners might achieve a different outcome? Even when learners are made aware of what needs attention, this information may need to be paired with how to achieve successful revision and relearning.

- Did the learner receive time and resources to respond? Were there external pulls on learners' time that may have prevented a response? Building in time for revision and reflection can make a response more likely.

- Did the feedback invite thinking and decision making? Some learners may not respond to feedback that is too directive because they don't see the point—all the decisions were already made for them. Strong feedback communicates a belief in the person receiving it to resolve challenges. Sometimes it is helpful for learners to receive feedback from more than one source so decisions stay in the hands of the person to whom the learning belongs.

- Did learners feel encouraged and recognized for their strengths? Strength-based feedback leverages optimism, skill, and knowledge to build up areas needing support. A learner might feel defeated if the negative feedback was too large to feel manageable and encouraged.

- Are learners receiving feedback on authentic tasks by people who matter to them? It might be easy to think that feedback should always matter, but sometimes learners may not be invested in the task itself, and sometimes feedback may be received more productively when given by someone other than the teacher. Mentors, peers, family members, leaders, or artists are all individuals from whom feedback can emerge.

**Connected Tenets:** Communication of Results
**Topics:** Feedback, Growth Mindset

## How can I encourage learners to pursue extension rather than just settling for proficiency?

Learners of all ages—even teachers as learners—engage in experiences when those experiences tap into intrinsic motivations, when they provide just enough challenge to stretch a little, and when they occur in an environment that is safe for intellectual risk taking. Inviting learners to engage in extended learning has to follow the same principles. With that in mind, the following are some things to consider when offering extended learning.

- Notice and acknowledge proficiency when it is visible. This might mean noticing it when it happens before predicted. Some learners demonstrate proficiency before the official assessment event, and, if teachers are sure that what learners say and do reflects clear proficiency, they need to acknowledge it. This may be as simple as saying something like, "I can see that you already know how to multiply fractions and reduce the product to simplest form. I would like to offer you a couple of problems with more challenge."

- Anticipate the need to extend and consider ways this might occur when the need arises. When teachers think about how to invite deeper thinking and more complex application of skills ahead of time, they more carefully consider and design the extended learning to be offered.

- Recognize that extension requires instruction, feedback, and support, like any other kind of learning. Extension is not about "blowing the teacher's socks off" or "impressing the teacher." Rather, it is about exploring learning goals with increased complexity or in new ways to enrich learning and appropriately challenge the learner.

- Ensure that there is no grading downside to extension. Sometimes learners need reassuring that when they engage in extended learning, they will maintain their high grades. Extension should not be punitive.

- Give learners enough time to explore extended learning. This means time for practice, time for exploration, time for feedback, and time for revision.

- Work to ensure that extended learning is compelling, and rich in content and context. Learners will gravitate toward extension if it seems engaging and worth their while.

- Honor learners' need for belonging by ensuring that extension does not carry social risk. Learners need to continue to interact with their friends, to make meaning with peers, and to share their learning with others.

**Connected Tenets:** Assessment Architecture
**Topics:** Enrichment and Extension, Growth Mindset

## How do I talk about data with my students? Should I?

It is helpful for learners to learn that data are a way of representing complex ideas and variables in a manner that is more easily digested. Further, data facilitate analysis of these ideas and variables so that patterns, anomalies, and relationships can be explored. Data invite questions about cause and effect, strategies and future possibilities, and strengths and challenges. For these reasons, talking with learners about assessment data can be beneficial.

If educators are going to talk with learners about data, the learners have to understand not only the data but also the reason for the conversation and the actions teachers hope their learners will take as a result. In order to increase the likelihood of positive learner outcomes as a result of talking about data, teachers might consider the following.

- Have learners construct their own graphs and charts from their personal assessment data. This ensures their own assessment results are seen by no one else, and it invites learners to take ownership of their assessment information.

- Make sure the assessment data are organized in a way that is easily digestible. The process of examining and working with data should not be cumbersome for anyone, least of all learners.

- When working with formative data, make sure learners can set goals and plan how they might address their learning needs. This illustrates that data are only as important as the degree to which they nurture learning.

- Work with learners to ensure data are reflecting continuous improvement. Nobody wants to work with data sets when all they reflect are failure.

- Explicitly model how data analysis leads to learning experiences that are tailored to the learner. Assessment data are a great way to help learners understand the importance of flexible grouping and differentiated instruction.

**Connected Tenets:** Communication of Results, Accurate Interpretation
**Topics:** Growth Mindset, Student Engagement and Motivation

## How should I group learners in heterogeneous classrooms with a wide range of mixed abilities?

Grouping learners in heterogeneous classrooms, at its best, should be fluid, flexible, and varied for purpose and impact. Groupings that are effective are grounded in purpose and focused on learning. Learners should be grouped with multiple people in many different ways.

Learners can form groups to learn or explore a concept. There are options here. This is a great time to identify a few topics and have learners choose based on interest. Another option and opportunity is to have learners with like understandings work together. If those with more sophisticated understandings of the concept are paired with those with beginning understanding, the learners with more sophisticated understandings often answer and do more of the work because it usually comes quicker. In this situation, learners at the beginning of understanding don't have the opportunity to explore and wonder and struggle to dig into those concepts at a deeper level, which would be needed to set them up to be able to learn those concepts deeply. However, teachers making observations about how learners interact and who works well together in that give-and-take exchange can influence all of these potential groupings. The key is to watch the impact of groupings, and if they show evidence of working, then keep doing them. If it doesn't work, try a new grouping or structure.

It is beneficial to group learners based on like misconceptions. For example, all of the learners who need to work on *explaining their textual evidence* might work together to explore how to do this. Then, they would return to their drafts and revise their writing based on what they learned in the group. It is also best to group learners who have like understanding in this case as well, because if learners at the beginning of understanding their learning are grouped with those further along, learners who understand deeply may take over and do the work for learners who are still learning. In this case, those at the beginning of understanding don't get time or support to learn and grow. If learners feel the purpose is just about getting the work done, then often other students will do it for them.

When grouping learners, keep everyone focused on their next step in their learning and not on the grade they received. Grouping by learning goal and next step keeps the focus of any instruction and intervention focused on everyone learning more versus getting more points.

Finally, when grouping, be transparent about the learning focus of each group. This means that learners review their assessment information that led to where they are grouped. With a focus on learning and evidence from their assessments, the pathway and reasoning is much clearer for learners, leading them to be able to take that next step in their learning.

It is paramount to the teachers' and the learners' success at the grouping juncture that the focus remains on *what* is to be learned and not what the categories of groupings mean. Eric M. Anderman and Adriana I. Martinez Calvit (2021) note, "Research indicates that when teachers publicly point out which students are doing well on a task, or when teachers make it obvious that some students are experiencing challenges, students become focused on how they are perceived by their peers, *rather than on mastering the task*." Teachers can virtually eradicate student embarrassment or hurt if they (1) constantly mix groups, (2) remain focused on the learning needs by standard or target and not the students personally, (3) establish a classroom culture in which mistake making is a natural and welcome part of the learning journey for everyone, and (4) maintain a growth mindset with a heavy dose of optimism that all learners will be successful with the learning expectations.

**Connected Tenets:** Communication of Results, Accurate Interpretation

**Topics:** Feedback, Response to Intervention

## How can I help learners develop perseverance and persistence through my assessment practices?

In truth, three conditions—all teacher owned—must be in place for a learner to persist and attend to precision: (1) all feedback must feed forward so learners can apply it to future assessments, (2) major assessments must revisit task-neutral skills so learners can attempt to improve, and (3) grading practices must empower learners to achieve through the mode found in later samples of work. If those teacher systems are not embedded—if feedback is disjointed and does not span multiple assessments, and if early mistakes dictate final results—then learners have no reason to persevere or attend to precision.

> **Connected Tenets:** Communication of Results
>
> **Topics:** Feedback, Growth Mindset, Summative Assessment and Grading

## How do I prepare learners to engage in self-assessment?

Self-assessment involves a complex set of interdependent skills that educators must exclusively teach, but not in isolation. Self-assessment is best taught step by step and while embedded in the expected learning, using actual student artifacts and evidence of learning to guide the efforts.

To prepare their learners for successful self-assessment, teachers might try the following practices.

- Embed self-assessment into daily learning experiences—don't save it until the end. Self-assessment is most successful when it is *part* of learning and, in fact, leads to greater proficiency by learners. Plan to make time to pause, observe, and reflect on the current state of affairs and set small, manageable goals for the next stage of learning.

- Make sure that the first time learners engage in self-assessment is to advance learning in an area or skill that matters to the learner. The more invested learners are in the learning, the more naturally self-assessment occurs (think about how naturally self-assessment flows out of a video game, a sport, or a game).

- Offer learners prompts that will help them self-assess (for example, What are you really proud of? What gave you some trouble? How did you approach this challenge? Was your approach successful? Why or why not? What might you try next?). This can help learners to really focus their reflection.

- Give learners tangible, real-time artifacts to use as a catalyst for self-assessment. Having their work (paragraphs, videos, photographs, images) in front of them alongside criteria for success makes self-assessment much easier for learners.

- Make sure to embed time for learners to respond to their self-assessment and action planning. A self-assessment will seem pointless pretty quickly when it does not serve a purpose.

- Avoid praise whenever possible. Praise invites learners to see the purpose of self-assessment as a way to meet the teachers' goals. Instead, ask learners to explain their own thinking and decision making. In this way, the learner continues to own the learning.

**Connected Tenets:** Communication of Results, Accurate Interpretation
**Topics:** Self- and Peer Assessment

## How can I help younger learners be more invested in assessments?

The first step in building student investment in assessment is to make sure that the story of assessment communicated to the students focuses on learning. When learners experience, from a very young age, that assessment is part of exploration and learning, learners will see it as a process that helps them maneuver through challenges all the way to success and celebration.

Learners can engage in assessment when a teacher or a peer takes video of them making patterns in mathematics class so they can *show what they know*. They may also experience assessment when they talk about a story they wrote the previous day and set a goal to work on during today's class. They may experience assessment when they keep track of the number of sight words they have learned in a bar graph and celebrate milestones. All these examples give learners the chance to see their learning as it develops, reflect on decisions and choices they will be making in the future, and celebrate growth. Teachers can help learners understand that this is the important role assessment plays in the classroom. Using assessment helps teachers plan great learning experiences, and it helps learners become learners who care about their learning.

**Connected Tenets:** Assessment Purpose
**Topics:** Formative Assessment, Self- and Peer Assessment

# Support and Motivation

## How should I react when a learner does not respond well to an assessment experience?

When a learner does not respond well to an assessment experience (for example, they appear discouraged, angry, defeated, competitive, combative), it indicates to teachers a need to explore the reasons for this response. Assessment is a process that intentionally leads learners to develop strength, confidence, and deep learning, and when it is not accomplishing these things, teachers may need to adjust either their assessment design and practices, classroom culture, or conversations about assessment itself.

Some things teachers may check when learners do not respond well are as follows.

- Were learners adequately prepared for the assessment? Did they know how they would be assessed, and did they have time to practice and adjust?

- Did the learners understand the purpose of the assessment? Were they clear about how the assessment information would be used?

- Did learners have the resources they needed during the assessment? (Resources include materials, time, and appropriate supports.)

- Do learners think assessment results indicate their value as a learner? Are they clear about assessment in relation to success criteria as opposed to assessment in relation to each other?

- Were the questions, prompts, or tasks clear, precise, and aligned with targets and standards?

- Was there time to reflect on and discuss the assessment and future steps? Do learners still have hope?

- Are the events following an assessment connected to the assessment itself? Do learners see how instruction is adjusted according to assessment results?

Once teachers narrow down the specific challenge learners are having in relation to assessment, they can take action to adjust this experience in the future. Learners may need to relearn why assessment occurs and how to respond in a positive manner. Like any skill, educators may need to explicitly model, teach, and reinforce how learners can respond to an assessment in a prosocial way.

**Connected Tenets:** Assessment Architecture, Assessment Purpose
**Topics:** Growth Mindset, Student Engagement and Motivation

## Is it realistic for learners to love everything I do? Don't learners have to learn how to work, even when they don't like it?

No, it's not realistic for learners to love everything a teacher does. Everyone, including learners, has a range of things they love to do, things they don't enjoy doing, and all points in between. That said, especially at the elementary and middle school levels, learners may not be clear on what they actually love to do if they have never been exposed to it. So, both points can be true: learners will not love everything educators do, and learners still need to learn to work even when they don't like it.

One way to mitigate this is to work toward teaching transferable skills and processes. Where possible, teachers can strive to create opportunities to learn skills that are at least somewhat transferable to other subject areas. For example, critical thinking, while not seamlessly transferable since aspects of it are discipline specific (critical thinking involves thinking about *something*), can be developed across subject areas—the strengths acquired within one discipline apply to other curricular domains. Aspects of *analysis*, for example, are applicable across subject areas (the close examination of aspects or components to find associative patterns is potentially transferable). This connection from one area to another can help learners see the benefits of what they are learning, regardless of their enjoyment.

Another way to build resilience would be to focus on the dispositional side of work learners deem to be less than favorable. In other words, it is through the work learners find less than favorable that dispositions and habits such as work ethic, self-directedness, integrity, and follow-through (just to name a few) are learned and even tested.

Teachers should not be shy about admitting to learners that they aren't going to love everything they'll be asked to do. Instead, it's through the discovery of that which they find less than favorable that they'll discover what they love to do, and that contrast is necessary. So while the work may be less than favorable, learners can authentically learn about *how they learn* and *who they are* through everything they do.

**Connected Tenets:** Assessment Architecture, Instructional Agility
**Topics:** Critical Competencies

## How do I help learners overcome the mindset that "I'm just bad at this subject"?

If this mindset seems challenging for the teacher to overcome, imagine what it must be for the learners. Fixing such a mindset likely requires reframing a lot of prior experiences and feedback that initiated the learner's point of view. To begin, focus on the learner's DNA (Erkens, 2016): desires, needs, and assets. Address what's *right* about what the learner is bringing to the task at hand, emphasizing his or her strengths, interests, talents, and skills. Second, create the space for possibilities by giving bite-sized challenges with laser-focused feedback. Do not give feedback about everything that needs to be fixed; rather, give feedback that focuses on the most significant areas for improvement and use the feedback to continue the learning (do not do the thinking for the learner). Then, celebrate each small victory along the way. Finally, provide the opportunity for the learner to achieve mastery, even though it may come later in the process than it did for other learners, and there may have been initial failures to overcome.

Teachers can interrupt this cycle with quick wins and confidence-building approaches to both learning and assessment. Smaller formative assessment opportunities followed by celebrations of strength and attainable feedback will show learners that growth is non-negotiable. Providing time to recover from errors and designing environments that support risk taking can reverse a fixed mindset. Learning experiences that are unique and invite wonder and curiosity can wrestle learners away from a lack of belief in themselves and the subject matter they are exploring. When learners sustain hope, there is no room for apathy or defeat.

**Connected Tenets:** Culture of Learning; Hope, Efficacy, and Achievement

**Topics:** Feedback, Growth Mindset

# How can I support learners who do not do well on an assessment?

When learners do not perform well on an assessment, teachers will look to the assessment evidence (whatever the learners have written, spoken, or represented in some way) and determine exactly where and why learners struggled so they can provide them with supports targeted directly at their learning needs. For example, teachers may notice that a learner needs support with writing using sensory details, so they design an instructional response that addresses this need. Or maybe a learner needs support with factoring numbers, so this is what an educator plans to address through additional instruction, reflection, and practice. Assessment is at its most powerful when it helps teachers design responses that address the root cause of misconceptions or errors.

Teachers may also need to support learners in ways that address their social or emotional needs. When a learner is upset or discouraged by an assessment outcome, teachers can help learners frame the assessment in a way that helps learners understand assessment as a process used to decide next steps. Teachers can work with learners to foster continuous hope for enhanced learning and design the steps needed to create this outcome.

**Connected Tenets:** Accurate Interpretation

**Topics:** Formative Assessment, Student Engagement and Motivation

# How can I motivate intentional non-learners through my assessment practices?

An intentional non-learner is a learner who opts to avoid intellectual risk taking. Most often, intentional non-learners are considered to be those who are seldom in school, rarely ready with assignments, often missing the necessary resources, and sometimes causing discipline problems when in school. In truth, though, a high-performing learner who gets good grades but opts to avoid an intellectual risk for the fear that it might compromise the grade is also an intentional non-learner. The high-performing learner who refuses to engage in intellectual risk taking is compliant and academically successful but is still opting out of stretch opportunities and deeper learning.

No matter whether the learner is low performing or high performing, there are several assessment guidelines educators can implement to re-engage all learners in the robust process of intentional, intellectual risk taking.

- Engage learners in monitoring their personal progress over time. Employ a few key rubrics that learners see repeatedly so that assessments can change but the criteria for quality on similar assessments remain consistent (for example, writing rubrics).

- Provide diagnostic feedback that helps learners isolate the specific errors so they can improve *between* assessments.

- Offer learners constant opportunities to reflect on their personal strengths and areas of growth.

- Make feedback to learners invaluable, so they couldn't stand to miss it. For example, offer more success feedback than growth feedback, and make growth feedback focused and actionable.

- Turn mistakes into productive failure. Teach learners how to navigate difficult or challenging concepts. Expand their toolkit of strategies.

- Allow learners to use their assessment data to make decisions. If they have proven they have mastered a concept, they can direct their practice work toward the concepts they do not yet have.

- Keep mastery on the table. As soon as the option to attain the top score disappears, motivation takes flight.

**Connected Tenets:** Hope, Efficacy, and Achievement

**Topics:** Formative Assessment, Response to Intervention

# Goal Setting

## What role does goal setting play in learner investment?

Learner investment is focused on ensuring learners know where they are going (the learning targets or progressions), where they are now (using assessment evidence to identify strengths and next steps), and what to do next to grow (action based on assessment evidence). This process promotes and cultivates self-regulation in learners, and assessment sits at the center of this process.

Teachers help learners utilize assessment information to reflect on their learning and connect the assessments to the learning targets and then determine which learning targets are strengths and what is next in their growth. A goal-setting process helps put structure and organization around this progression. It assists learners in identifying the target so they can reflect on how the actions they take help them or don't help them make progress toward the learning destination. The teacher engages learners in ensuring there is a clear understanding of proficiency definitions and expectations. Teacher feedback, along with guidance in reflecting on their assessment evidence, supports learners in understanding how their current progress compares to that goal and what steps are necessary to be successful. There should be opportunities for monitoring progress for both teachers and learners. Reflection before, during, and after the process provides valuable information about next steps for both the learner and the teacher, regardless of whether the goal was met.

A goal-setting process can and should be implemented with the youngest of learners as they learn to describe their learning and begin to understand how they learn. Goal setting can be a valuable tool for teachers to create a growth mindset in learners. As learners set a goal and monitor their progress, reflecting on what is helping them and what is getting in the way, they start to uncover that what they do makes a difference in their learning and achievement. It is a scaffolded process where teachers are ultimately teaching learners the steps for self-regulation and self-assessment, which they can continue for the rest of their lives as learners.

**Connected Tenets:** Communication of Results

**Topics:** Self- and Peer Assessment, Student Engagement and Motivation

## How can I encourage learners to set more ambitious goals?

People set ambitious goals when they are invested in something and when they possess confidence in their ability to achieve the goals they set. A truly meaningful goal is set by individuals who have a personal interest in achieving it. With these factors in mind, the path to ambitious goal setting becomes clearer.

First, teachers need to work with learners to build investment. Learning experiences that matter in the context of relationships that also matter will create a necessary foundation for goal setting. Teachers and learners need to create meaningful and purposeful learning contexts so that authentic goals can emerge. When learners buy into the reason for the work, they will see the purpose of setting goals that matter.

Second, learners will need a base of understanding for the concepts and skills at hand as well as baseline evidence of current proficiency levels before setting goals. It is common to ask learners to set goals long before they have a deep understanding of the content or a realistic image of their own strengths and gaps in that content.

Third, learners will set more ambitious goals when they believe they can achieve them. When assessment supports growth and instruction builds hope, learners will see that goals lead to success. Teachers can increase confidence by ensuring learners experience frequent wins, achieved through attention to goal setting. The connection between goals and learning has to be absolutely clear to each and every learner.

Finally, whenever possible, learners need to be responsible for setting their own goals. When the majority of goal setting is done by teachers (for example, "I want you to . . ." or "I need you to . . ."), learners become passive recipients of other people's goals. Learners have to experience the decision making, risk taking, and challenges associated with ambitious goal setting. They also have to experience recovery, revision, and success. As learners become increasingly familiar with goals that drive learning in school, they will become more proficient at setting goals that matter.

**Connected Tenets:** Assessment Purpose

**Topics:** Self- and Peer Assessment

## Can I set goals with younger learners?

Young learners (ages three to six), like their older counterparts, make decisions every day based on personal goals. The difference is in their ability to articulate those goals within a school setting; although, to be clear, older learners (anyone above age six) can find this challenging as well. Younger learners will need time to adjust to new rules and guidelines for existing within a classroom setting. In a classroom setting, their goals often no longer serve just their physical or emotional needs. Instead, attending school means learning to set different goals that will serve intellectual and social outcomes.

Student
Investment

With this idea in mind, and considering the developmental nature of young learners, part of nurturing learners who can self-assess is helping them learn and practice more specific skills or sub-skills that lead to the broader and more complex skill of self-assessment. For example, educators may spend time finding ways to help young learners notice and describe their environment. Or they may focus on teaching how to compare two things, analyzing similarities and differences. Learners also need time to practice seeing events from the perspective of people other than themselves and imagining different possibilities when embarking on discovery and practice. These kinds of skills enhance the larger skill of self-assessment (White, 2017).

A great approach, when trying to develop strong self-assessors and goal setters, is to focus on capturing or documenting learning as it is happening. This may mean taking photographs or video, or saving drafts and brainstorming. By making learning visible through documentation, as it is developing for young learners, teachers can help them notice decisions they are making and think about adjusting their actions if goals are not being met. This helps learners understand how learning is often about thinking about how things are going and deciding whether decisions are supporting goals.

> **Connected Tenets:** Accurate Interpretation
>
> **Topics:** Early Learning, Self- and Peer Assessment

# Self-Regulation

## What is self-regulation, and how can I recognize it?

Self-regulation involves the set of processes, mindsets, and skills that learners use to control for their own learning. When learners self-regulate, they engage in the actions that empower them to address three questions: (1) Where am I now? (2) Where am I going? and (3) What can I begin to do to bridge the gap between where I am and where I need to be?

While a self-regulated classroom seems highly desirable, it's important for teachers to anticipate that empowering learners can lead to organized chaos, challenges to the status quo, and a learner's desire to control for his or her own choices along the learning journey. It is the *right* work, but—at its highest and most comprehensive level of implementation—it will require educators to relinquish some control and compliance issues.

> **Connected Tenets:** Hope, Efficacy, and Achievement
>
> **Topics:** Growth Mindset, Student Engagement and Motivation

## How do I teach self-regulation?

Fortunately, the process of being self-regulated is naturally tied to both the brain's instinctive compulsion to learn and a learner's innate drive to control for personal goals and aspirations. Unfortunately, while the underpinning premise of self-regulation is intuitive, the skills involved with bringing the desires to fruition are not, so they must be taught.

Many things have been tried for teaching self-regulation: using goal-setting sheets, creating data trackers, activating peer and self-assessment and feedback, incorporating self-reflection, and teaching about growth mindset. While each of those components is a contributing factor to teaching self-regulation, they are insufficient by themselves. First, they are tools and require instruction, not a mere application following an assessment. Teachers would need to teach learners (1) how best to use each tool, (2) how it fits with the overall system of self-regulation tools, and (3) what the end goal looks like when it is successfully applied. Second, and maybe even more importantly, it is the *system* and the *culture* into which these things are operationalized that will determine whether or not the tools work as desired. For example, asking learners to set academic goals without an initial foundation of data or the unfettered opportunity to achieve mastery in the gradebook, even with early failures while learning, will just seem like requiring extra work without a purpose.

> **Connected Tenets:** Hope, Efficacy, and Achievement
> **Topics:** Growth Mindset, Student Engagement and Motivation

## How can I help learners know when they have met the standard?

Assessment evidence is best when it is incredibly clear what standards are being assessed and the level of proficiency achieved on the standard being measured. There are multiple ways to guide learners in monitoring and reflecting on when they have met the standard.

1. Provide learners a list of standards, outcomes, or competencies. Be sure to include the qualities or criteria that are met when learners have achieved the targeted learning. Have learners record their assignments and assessments by this list so they can see how much evidence shows they have proficiency on that standard. Learners can record and track their progress on standards by evidence of learning.

2. Ensure that each assessment has the standards and learning targets visible on the assessment. This may mean there is a cover page or a back page that

indicates which items are assessing which standards or learning targets. If there are rubrics, they should clearly describe the qualities of the work at each level so learners understand where they are in achieving proficiency.

3. Guide learners to reflect on their assessment results using these tools. Each and every assessment should include some sort of reflection so learners understand where they are in achieving the standard. Learners can then set goals and make decisions based on the information they gather from their assessment evidence. It is the processes of reflection and decision making that lead to investment of learning and not just compliance or completion.

**Connected Tenets:** Assessment Architecture

**Topics:** Assessment Design, Self- and Peer Assessment

# Student Investment in a Remote Learning Context

To say that educators are dependent on their students' investment to make remote learning work is an understatement. Without student investment in the learning goals, in the processes and technologies they are introducing, and in the relationship with teachers, remote learning will fall flat very quickly. This is why it is essential to consider how educators might nurture student investment as soon as planning begins.

Strong assessment systems are designed to invite learners to make decisions, to reflect on progress, to select products and performances that will be personally significant, to give and receive feedback, and to be a true partner in learning. When working to enhance student investment in a remote learning context, it may be helpful to consider the following.

- Working with families and learners to ensure that assessment systems are transparent, growth focused, and centered around clear goals and success criteria; partnership is key.

- Inviting learners to co-construct criteria and set personally meaningful, short-term goals; making exemplars available can help learners visualize products and performances. Offering samples of learning that are less than proficient can also serve as an entry point into online conversations about the features of quality work.

- Engaging learners in monitoring their personal progress over time; it might be helpful to use fewer, consistent assessment tools (rubrics, criteria checklists) that capture key skills to be learned and introduce them more than once, so learners can clearly see their growth over time.

- Providing feedback using a few key digital processes (such as embedded written assessment, verbal assessment, conferencing); it is also important to provide learners designated time in which to work on improving their products and performances. Make sure feedback is both strength-focused and actionable.

- Storing several iterations of work over time and inviting learners to reflect on decisions made and the connection to progress on goals; portfolios are a great way to make this progress visible and accessible.

- Inviting learners to frequently self-assess, using transparent and co-constructed success criteria, to set goals, and to reflect on decision making in relation to strengths and needs; it may be helpful to use a few familiar processes and templates so learners can begin to quickly build self-confidence.

- Turning mistakes into productive failure; by designing formative assessment processes that identify not only *that* a learner has made a mistake but *why* they may have made that mistake is key. In this way, learners can learn how to navigate difficult or challenging concepts. Through targeted instruction, expand learners' toolkits of strategies.

- Ensuring proficiency is always available; as soon as the option to demonstrate mastery disappears, motivation disappears with it. Remote learning contexts offer the advantage of seeking additional evidence in flexible ways. Learners can be part of the decision-making process, and teachers can work with them to set deadlines, monitor success, and address needs.

- Building in two-way communication; this may mean asking learners for feedback about how long an assessment took and which aspects were particularly challenging or too easy. It could also mean seeking insight into how well learning and assessment are integrating with expectations at home. When learners are not directly in front of teachers, intentional methods for seeking information that may be important to student success must be built into daily expectations.

# TABLE OF CONTENTS BY TOPIC

The Table of Contents that opens this book lays out the questions by key tenets, which creates a holistic and important view of assessment as a practice. This Table of Contents is organized by topic so readers can quickly find responses to questions based on common topics.

## Accountability and Standardized Tests

## Assessment Design

# Authentic Assessment

# Behavior

# Collaboration

# Common Assessment

# Criteria

# Early Learning

# English Learners

# Enrichment and Extension

# Essential Standards

# Feedback

# Formative Assessment

# Growth Mindset

# Homework

# Intervention and Instruction

# Leadership

# Pacing Guides

# Parent Engagement

# Preassessment

# Professional Judgment

# Professional Learning Communities (PLCs)

# Questioning

# Reassessment

# Relationships

# Reporting

# Response to Intervention (RTI)

# Rigor and Cognitive Complexity

# School and Classroom Culture and Climate

# Self- and Peer Assessment

# Standards

# Student Efficacy

# Student Engagement and Motivation

# Summative Assessment and Grading

# Unpacking and Learning Progressions

# GLOSSARY OF TERMS

**Alignment.** The degree to which assessment matches the learning expectations as outlined in the academic standards. When alignment is in place, assessors can draw accurate inferences from the assessment results regarding the student's current level of knowledge and skills relative to the learning expectations. Total alignment involves five criteria:

1. Categorical Concurrence—the degree to which the same or consistent categories of content appear in the standards and assessments.

2. Depth-of-Knowledge Consistency—the extent to which the levels of cognitive complexity of the task(s) match the levels required by the standards.

3. Range-of-Knowledge Correspondence—the degree to which the assessment elicits the span of knowledge students need in order to correctly respond to the questions, prompts, or tasks intended to measure the learning outcomes.

4. Balance of Representation—the measure of balanced emphasis on all parts of the standard(s) or appropriate emphasis on most important parts of the standard(s) being assessed.

5. Source of Challenge—the match between a student's level of readiness in content knowledge and skill and the level of difficulty of the assessment items as aligned to standard expectations.

**Assessment.** The process of collecting information about a student to aid in decision making about the student's progress and development.

**Assessment literacy.** The knowledge and understanding of the principles of sound assessment practices and their effective and efficient application in a classroom, school, or school district.

**Assessment map.** A plan for the strategic timing and use of both formal and informal assessments through an instructional progression; a plan for both formative and summative uses of assessment evidence.

**Authentic assessment.** Any assessment that attempts to emulate the real-world context within which the intended learning is meant to be applied.

**Balanced assessment system.** The strategic use of assessment evidence for both the formative and summative purposes. Balance doesn't mean equal; rather, balance means both purposes of assessment are strategically deployed to improve and prove learning.

**Bell curve.** A frequency distribution statistic. Normal distribution is shaped like a bell.

**Benchmarking.** The use of established criteria for comparative purposes at increasingly more complex intervals through a unit, grading period, semester, or school year or across educational settings.

**Central tendency.** These measures indicate the middle or center of a distribution (namely, mean, median, and mode).

**Common assessment.** An assessment developed by more than one teacher (typically a team) designed to assess all students within a particular cohort; an assessment that assesses the same content, skills, or competencies found to be *common* amongst the subject(s) at hand.

**Credibility.** A researcher's ability to demonstrate that the object of a study is accurately identified and described, based on the way in which the study was conducted.

**Criterion-referenced interpretations.** When the interpretations of students' assessment performance are in reference to a pre-established set of criteria rather than their relative standing within the group.

**Data.** Recorded assessment information, usually in numeric or textual form (quantitative or qualitative).

**Deviation.** The distance between the mean and a particular data point in each distribution.

**Distribution.** The range of values of a particular variable.

**Essential learning.** Learning goals, standards, or outcomes that are determined by a team of teachers to be non-negotiable if students are to reach proficiency.

**Evaluation.** The systematic investigation and determination of the worth or merit of student learning. Using information from an assessment to make judgments about student skill or understanding.

**Evaluation standard.** A principle mutually agreed to by people engaged in the professional practice of evaluation that, if met, will enhance the quality and fairness of an evaluation.

**External validity.** The extent to which the results of a study are generalizable or transferable. See also *validity*.

**Formative assessment (evaluation).** Assessments conducted while a learning process is under way; designed to and used to promote growth and improvement in a student's performance or in a program's improvement (including instructional practice) through the use of descriptive feedback.

**GVC (guaranteed and viable curriculum).** A curriculum that is fully accessible to all learners, rigorous in expectation, and standards based. The curriculum often includes prioritized standards that are important for student proficiency in that grade level or course.

**Instructional agility.** The ability to make real-time instructional adjustments based on emerging assessment evidence.

**Internal consistency.** The extent to which all questions or items assess the same characteristic, skill, or quality.

**Inter-rater reliability.** The extent to which two or more individuals agree. It addresses the consistency of the implementation of a rating system.

**Learning progression.** A learning progression describes a student's pathway to proficiency in relation to a standard or cluster of standards. It is used to inform instruction and potential feedback as students move from the simplest of concepts to the most sophisticated (namely, the standards).

**Mean.** The average score within a distribution.

**Measurement.** The process of assigning numbers or categories to performance according to specified rules.

**Median.** The middle score in a distribution.

**Meta-evaluation.** An overall evaluation of your evaluation practices. An evaluation of an evaluation.

**Mode.** The most frequent score in a distribution.

**Norm-referenced interpretations.** When the interpretations of students' assessment performance are based on a comparison to the performance of a well-defined group of other students (the norm-group).

**Preassessment.** Any assessment utilized in advance of any intentional instruction; assessments that typically reveal current student strengths and areas in need of strengthening, but can also be used to pique curiosity for the upcoming learning or elicit the experiences or preconceived notions learners might bring into a new unit of study.

**Proficiency scale.** A formal scale used to rate the level of student performance along a learning progression.

**Qualitative information.** Information presented or summarized in narrative form; for example, written expressions descriptive of a behavior or product.

**Quantitative information.** Information presented or summarized in numerical form; for example, scores on a paper-and-pencil test or on a five-point analytical scale.

**Range.** The difference between the highest and lowest scores in a distribution.

**Reassessment.** An assessment that assesses the same learning goal; the learning goals and assessment methods remain constant, though the assessment items or format can change.

**Reliability.** The extent to which a measure, procedure, or instrument yields the same result on repeated trials.

**Response to intervention (RTI).** A multitiered, proactively driven system of support where students' academic needs are addressed with progressively more intense interventions, should initial interventions produce little to no impact.

**Rigor.** The degree to which a task, prompt, or assignment challenges student thinking in new and complex ways.

**Rubric.** A rubric describes degrees of quality related to specific criteria for a student's performance or product, which reflects the appropriate level of rigor and comprehensiveness of the standards involved to inform feedback and grades.

**Sample.** The population researched in a particular study. Usually, attempts are made to select a "sample population" that is considered representative of groups of people to whom results will be generalized or transferred. In studies that use inferential statistics to analyze results, or which are designed to be generalizable, sample size is critical—generally the larger the number in the sample, the higher the likelihood of a representative distribution of the population. A sample can also mean a representation of student thinking through a specific product. For example, "this sample of student thinking demonstrates proficiency in relation to the standard."

**Scaffold.** The process used as students move through the learning progression where teachers build on prior knowledge to begin layering new, more complex learning.

**Stability reliability.** The agreement of measuring instruments over time.

**Standard.** A learning goal for what students should know, understand, or be able to do at a particular grade level or within a particular subject discipline.

**Standard deviation.** A term used in statistical analysis. A measure of variation that indicates the typical distance between the scores of a distribution and the mean; it is determined by taking the square root of the average of the squared deviations in a given distribution. It can be used to indicate the proportion of data within certain ranges of scale values when the distribution conforms closely to the normal curve.

**Standards-based grading.** Grades based solely on the quality of evidence that students produce as it is assessed against the identified curricular standards.

**Summative assessment (evaluation).** Evaluation designed to present conclusions about the merit or worth of a student's performance.

**Target.** An underpinning of a curricular standard that can serve both as daily learning and as a step within the scaffold of a learning progression.

**Traditional assessment.** Assessments that are typically pen-and-paper assessments (such as tests and quizzes) to be completed by individual students within a designated time period.

**Transferability.** The ability to apply the results of research in one context to another similar context. Also, the extent to which a study invites readers to make connections between elements of the study and their own experiences.

**Triangulation.** The use of a combination of research methods in a study or the use of a combination of assessment methods to determine degrees of proficiency. An example of triangulation would be a study that incorporated surveys, interviews, and observations. A classroom example would be assessment of student proficiency based on observations, conversations, and artifacts.

**Validity.** The degree to which a study accurately reflects or assesses the specific concept that the researcher is attempting to measure. A method can be reliable, consistently measuring the same thing, but not valid.

**Variance.** A measure of variation within a distribution, determined by averaging the squared deviations from the mean of a distribution.

**Variation.** The dispersion of data points around the mean of a distribution.

# A COMPREHENSIVE RESOURCE LIST FROM THE SOLUTION TREE ASSESSMENT CENTER (STAC)

The following resources contain deep explorations of any number of topics related to assessment.

Bailey, K., & Jakicic, C. (2017). *Simplifying common assessment: A guide for Professional Learning Communities at Work*. Bloomington, IN: Solution Tree Press.

Bailey, K., & Jakicic, C. (2022). *Formative tools for leaders in a PLC at Work®: Assessing, analyzing, and acting to support collaborative teams*. Bloomington, IN: Solution Tree Press.

Brown, T., & Ferriter, W. M. (2021). *You can learn! Building student ownership, motivation, and efficacy with the PLC at Work process*. Bloomington, IN: Solution Tree Press.

Burke, K., & Depka, E. (2011). *Using formative assessment in the RTI framework*. Bloomington, IN: Solution Tree Press.

Cooper, D. (2011). *Redefining fair: How to plan, assess, and grade for excellence in mixed-ability classrooms*. Bloomington, IN: Solution Tree Press.

Cooper, D. (2022). *Rebooting assessment: A practical guide for balancing conversations, performances, and products*. Bloomington, IN: Solution Tree Press.

Depka, E. (2015). *Bringing homework into focus: Tools and tips to enhance practices, design, and feedback*. Bloomington, IN: Solution Tree Press.

Depka, E. (2017). *Raising the rigor: Effective questioning strategies and techniques for the classroom.* Bloomington, IN: Solution Tree Press.

Depka, E. (2019). *Letting data lead: How to design, analyze, and respond to classroom assessment.* Bloomington, IN: Solution Tree Press.

Dimich, N. (2015). *Design in five: Essential phases to create engaging assessment practice.* Bloomington, IN: Solution Tree Press.

Erkens, C. (2016). *Collaborative common assessments: Teamwork. Instruction. Results.* Bloomington, IN: Solution Tree Press.

Erkens, C. (2019). *The handbook for collaborative common assessments: Tools for design, delivery, and data analysis.* Bloomington, IN: Solution Tree Press.

Erkens, C., Schimmer, T., & Dimich, N. (2017). *Essential assessment: Six tenets for bringing hope, efficacy, and achievement to the classroom.* Bloomington, IN: Solution Tree Press.

Erkens, C., Schimmer, T., & Dimich, N. (2018). *Instructional agility: Responding to assessment with real-time decisions.* Bloomington, IN: Solution Tree Press.

Erkens, C., Schimmer, T., & Dimich, N. (2019). *Growing tomorrow's citizens in today's classrooms: Assessing 7 critical competencies.* Bloomington, IN: Solution Tree Press.

Gobble, T., Onuscheck, M., Reibel, A. R., & Twadell, E. (2016). *Proficiency-based assessment: Process, not product.* Bloomington, IN: Solution Tree Press.

Gobble, T., Onuscheck, M., Reibel, A. R., & Twadell, E. (2017). *Pathways to proficiency: Implementing evidence-based grading.* Bloomington, IN: Solution Tree Press.

Hierck, T., & Freese, A. (2018). *Assessing unstoppable learning.* Bloomington, IN: Solution Tree Press.

Hillman, G., & Stalets, M. (2019). *Coaching your classroom: How to deliver actionable feedback to students.* Bloomington, IN: Solution Tree Press.

Hillman, G., & Stalets, M. (2021). *Assessment as a catalyst for learning: Creating a responsive and fluid process to inspire all students.* Bloomington, IN: Solution Tree Press.

Reibel, A. R., & Twadell, E. (Eds). (2019). *Proficiency-based grading in the content areas: Insights and key questions for secondary schools.* Bloomington, IN: Solution Tree Press.

Schimmer, T. (2016). *Grading from the inside out: Bringing accuracy to student assessment through a standards-based mindset.* Bloomington, IN: Solution Tree Press.

Schimmer, T., Hillman, G., & Stalets, M. (2018). *Standards-based learning in action: Moving from theory to practice.* Bloomington, IN: Solution Tree Press.

Twadell, E., Onuscheck, M., Reibel, A. R., & Gobble, T. (2019). *Proficiency-based instruction: Rethinking lesson design and delivery.* Bloomington, IN: Solution Tree Press.

White, K. (2017). *Softening the edges: Assessment practices that honor K–12 teachers and learners.* Bloomington, IN: Solution Tree Press.

White, K. (2019). *Unlocked: Assessment as the key to everyday creativity in the classroom.* Bloomington, IN: Solution Tree Press.

White, K. (2022). *Student self-assessment: Data notebooks, portfolios, and other tools to advance learning.* Bloomington, IN: Solution Tree Press.

# REFERENCES AND RESOURCES

Abdul-Alim, J. (2016). *Poll: About half U. S. students identify as "hopeful" and "engaged."* Accessed at http://diverseeducation.com/article/82431 on May 11, 2016.

Allen, J. D., & Dai, Y. (2016, April). *A comparative analysis using reciprocal questioning with college students in China and the United States.* Paper presented at the annual meeting of the American Educational Research Association, Washington, DC.

Allensworth, E., Correa, M., & Ponisciak, S. (2008, May). *From high school to the future: ACT preparation—too much, too late. Why ACT scores are low in Chicago and what it means for schools.* Chicago: Consortium on Chicago School Research. Accessed at https://consortium.uchicago.edu/sites/default/files/2018-10/ACTReport08.pdf on January 24, 2022.

Anderman, E. M., & Martinez Calvit, A. I. (2021). *Is your deeper learning instruction boring students? Educational Leadership*, *79*(4), 32–37. Accessed at https://www.ascd.org/el/articles/is-your-deeper-learning-instruction-boring-students on January 24, 2022.

Andrade, H. L. (2010). Students as the definitive source of formative assessment: Academic self-assessment and the self-regulation of learning. In H. L. Andrade & G. J. Cizek (Eds.), *Handbook of formative assessment* (pp. 90–105). New York: Routledge.

Andrade, H. L. (2013). Classroom assessment in the context of learning theory and research. In J. H. McMillan (Ed.), *SAGE handbook of research on classroom assessment* (pp. 17–34). Thousand Oaks, CA: SAGE.

Andrade, H. L., & Du, Y. (2005). Student perspectives on rubric-referenced assessment. *Practical Assessment, Research and Evaluation*, *10*(3), 1–11.

Andrade, H. L., Du, Y., & Mycek, K. (2010). Rubric-referenced self-assessment and middle school students' writing. *Assessment in Education: Principles, Policy, & Practice*, *17*(2), 199–214.

Andrade, H. L., Du, Y., & Wang, X. (2008). Putting rubrics to the test: The effect of a model, criteria generation, and rubric-referenced self-assessment on elementary school students' writing. *Educational Measurement: Issues and Practice*, *27*(2), 3–13.

Applebee, A. N., Langer, J. A., Nystrand, M., & Gamoran, A. (2003). Discussion-based approaches to developing understanding: Classroom instruction and student performance in middle and high school English. *American Educational Research Journal, 40*(3), 685–730.

Atkinson, P. (2003). *Assessment 5–14: What do pupils and parents think?* Accessed at https://files.eric.ed.gov/fulltext/ED480897.pdf on March 3, 2022.

Bailey, K., & Jakicic, C. (2012). *Common formative assessment: A toolkit for Professional Learning Communities at Work.* Bloomington, IN: Solution Tree Press.

Bailey, K., & Jakicic, C. (2017). *Simplifying common assessment: A guide for Professional Learning Communities at Work.* Bloomington, IN: Solution Tree Press.

Bailey, K., Jakicic, C., & Spiller, J. (2014). *Collaborating for success with the common core: A toolkit for Professional Learning Communities at Work.* Bloomington, IN: Solution Tree Press.

Barron, B., & Darling-Hammond, L. (2008). *Book excerpt: Teaching for meaningful learning—A review of research on inquiry-based and cooperative learning.* Accessed at https://files.eric.ed.gov/fulltext/ED539399.pdf on January 24, 2022.

Bennett, S., & Kalish, N. (2006). *The case against homework: How homework is hurting our children and what we can do about it.* New York: Crown.

Berger, W. (2014). *A more beautiful question: The power of inquiry to spark breakthrough ideas.* New York: Bloomsbury.

Black, P. (2013). Formative and summative aspects of assessment: Theoretical and research foundations in the context of pedagogy. In J. H. McMillan (Ed.), *SAGE handbook of research on classroom assessment* (pp. 167–178). Thousand Oaks, CA: SAGE.

Black, P., Broadfoot, P., Daugherty, R., Gardner, J., Harlen, W., James, M., et al. (2002). *Testing, motivation and learning* [Pamphlet]. Cambridge, England: University of Cambridge Faculty of Education.

Black, P., & Wiliam, D. (1998a). Assessment and classroom learning. *Assessment in Education: Principles, Policy and Practice, 5*(1), 7–74.

Black, P., & Wiliam, D. (1998b). Inside the black box: Raising standards through classroom assessment. *Phi Delta Kappan, 80*(2), 139–144, 146–148.

Black, P., & Wiliam, D. (2005). Changing teaching through formative assessment: Research and practice—the King's-Medway-Oxfordshire formative assessment project. In *Formative assessment: Improving learning in secondary classrooms* (pp. 223–240). Paris: Organisation for Economic Co-operation and Development.

Bloom, B. (1956). Taxonomy of educational objectives, handbook I: The cognitive domain. New York: David McKay Co Inc.

Bonner, S. M. (2013). Validity in classroom assessment: Purposes, properties, and principles. In J. H. McMillan (Ed.), *SAGE handbook of research on classroom assessment* (pp. 87–106). Thousand Oaks, CA: SAGE.

Bowers, A. J. (2019). Report card grades and educational outcomes. In T. R. Guskey & S. M. Brookhart (Eds.), *What we know about grading: What works, what doesn't, and what's next* (pp. 32–56). Alexandria, VA: Association for Supervision and Curriculum Development.

Brimi, H. M. (2011). Reliability of grading high school work in English. *Practical Assessment, Research and Evaluation, 16*(17). Accessed at https://scholarworks.umass.edu/cgi/viewcontent.cgi?article=1287&context=pare on January 24, 2022.

Brookhart, S. (2007). Expanding views about formative classroom assessment: A review of the literature. In J. H. McMillan (Ed.), *Formative classroom assessment: Theory into practice* (pp. 43–62). New York: Teachers College Press.

Brookhart, S. M. (2001). Successful students' formative and summative uses of assessment information. *Assessment in Education: Principles, Policy & Practice, 8*(2), 153–169.

Brookhart, S. M. (2013a). Classroom assessment in the context of motivation theory and research. In J. H. McMillan (Ed.), *SAGE handbook of research on classroom assessment* (pp. 35–54). Thousand Oaks, CA: SAGE.

Brookhart, S. M. (2013b). Grading. In J. H. McMillan (Ed.), *SAGE handbook of research on classroom assessment* (pp. 257–271). Thousand Oaks, CA: SAGE.

Brookhart, S. M., Andolina, M., Zuza, M., & Furman, R. (2004). Minute math: An action research study of student self-assessment. *Educational Studies in Mathematics, 57*(2), 213–227.

Brookhart, S. M., Guskey, T. R., Bowers, A. J., McMillan, J. H., Smith, J. K., Smith, L. F., Stevens, M. T., & Welsh, M. E. (2016). A century of grading research: Meaning and value in the most common educational measure. *Review of Educational Research, 86*(4), 803–848.

Brown, G. T. L., & Harris, L. R. (2013). Student self-assessment. In J. H. McMillan (Ed.), *SAGE handbook of research on classroom assessment* (pp. 367–394). Thousand Oaks, CA: SAGE.

Brown, N. J. S., & Wilson, M. (2011). A model of cognition: The missing cornerstone of assessment. *Educational Psychology Review, 23*(2), 221–234.

Bryant, D. A., & Carless, D. (2010). Peer assessment in a test-dominated setting: Empowering, boring or facilitating examination preparation? *Educational Research for Policy and Practice, 9*(1), 3–15.

Buffum, A., Mattos, M., & Malone, J. (2018). *Taking action: A handbook for RTI at Work.* Bloomington, IN: Solution Tree Press.

Butler, D. L., & Winne, P. H. (1995). Feedback and self-regulated learning: A theoretical synthesis. *Review of Educational Research, 65*(3), 245–281.

Butler, R. (1987). Task-involving and ego-involving properties of evaluation: Effects of different feedback conditions on motivational perceptions, interest, and performance. *Journal of Educational Psychology, 79*(4), 474–482.

Butler, R. (1988). Enhancing and undermining intrinsic motivation: The effects of task-involving and ego-involving evaluation on interest and performance. *British Journal of Educational Psychology, 58*(1), 1–14.

Calderón, M. (2007). *Teaching reading to English language learners, grades 6–12: A framework for improvement achievement in the content areas.* Thousand Oaks, CA: Corwin Press.

Calderón, M. (2012). Why we need a new way of schooling language-minority children. In Calderón, M. (Ed.), *Breaking through: Effective instruction and assessment for reaching English learners* (pp. 7–26). Bloomington, IN: Solution Tree Press.

Calderon, V. J. (2015). *Americans say there is more to school success than test results.* Accessed at www.gallup.com/opinion/gallup/184793/americans-say-school-success-test-results.aspx on September 16, 2016.

Campbell, C. (2013). Research on teacher competency in classroom assessment. In J. H. McMillan (Ed.), *SAGE handbook of research on classroom assessment* (pp. 71–84). Thousand Oaks, CA: SAGE.

Campbell, C., & Collins, V. L. (2007). Identifying essential topics in general and special education introductory assessment textbooks. *Educational Measurement: Issues and Practice, 26*(1), 9–18.

Canadian Council on Learning. (2009). *Homework helps, but not always.* Accessed at http://en.copian.ca/library/research/ccl/lessons_learning/homework_helps/homework_helps.pdf on October 4, 2021.

Cazden, C. B. (2001). *Classroom discourse: The language of teaching and learning* (2nd ed.). Portsmouth, NH: Heinemann.

Chappuis, J. (2015). *Seven strategies of assessment for learning* (2nd ed.). Boston: Pearson.

Chappuis, J., Stiggins, R. J., Chappuis, S., & Arter, J. A. (2012). *Classroom assessment for student learning: Doing it right—using it well* (2nd ed.). Boston: Pearson.

Chappuis, S., Chappuis, J., & Stiggins, R. (2009). Supporting teacher learning teams. *Educational Leadership, 66*(5), 56–60.

Charteris, J., & Smardon, D. (2015). Teacher agency and dialogic feedback: Using classroom data for practitioner inquiry. *Teaching and Teacher Education, 50*, 114–123.

Chenoweth, K. (2007). *It's being done: Academic success in unexpected schools.* Cambridge, MA: Harvard Education Press.

Chenoweth, K. (2009a). *How it's being done: Urgent lessons from unexpected schools.* Cambridge, MA: Harvard Education Press.

Chenoweth, K. (2009b). It can be done, it's being done, and here's how. *Phi Delta Kappan, 91*(1), 38–43.

Chin, C. (2007). Teacher questioning in science classrooms: Approaches that stimulate productive thinking. *Journal of Research in Science Teaching, 44*(6), 815–843.

Clark, I. (2011). Formative assessment: Policy, perspectives and practice. *Florida Journal of Educational Administration and Policy, 4*(2), 158–180.

Clarke, S. (2005). *Formative assessment in action: Weaving the elements together.* London: Hodder Education.

Clarke, S. (2008). *Active learning through formative assessment.* London: Hodder Education.

Cooper, H., Robinson, J. C., & Patall, E. A. (2006). Does homework improve academic achievement? A synthesis of research, 1987–2003. *Review of Educational Research, 76*(1), 1–62.

Corcoran, T., Mosher, F. A., & Rogat, A. (2009). *Learning progressions in science: An evidence-based approach to reform.* Philadelphia: Consortium for Policy Research in Education.

Corley, M. A., & Rauscher, W. C. (2013). *TEAL Center fact sheet no. 12: Deeper learning through questioning.* Accessed at https://lincs.ed.gov/sites/default/files/12_TEAL_Deeper_Learning_Qs_complete_5_1_0.pdf on May 16, 2016.

Daft, M. (2009). *Artists as education consultants.* Accessed at https://www.movingthroughmath.com/news-awards/artists-as-education-consultants/ on March 8, 2022.

Darling-Hammond, L. (2010). *The flat world and education: How America's commitment to equity will determine our future.* New York: Teachers College Press.

Daro, P., Mosher, F. A., & Corcoran, T. (2011). *Learning trajectories in mathematics: A foundation for standards, curriculum, assessment, and instruction* [Research report]. Philadelphia: Consortium for Policy Research in Education.

Davies, A. (2007). Involving students in the classroom assessment process. In D. Reeves (Ed.), *Ahead of the curve: The power of assessment to transform teaching and learning* (pp. 31–57). Bloomington, IN: Solution Tree Press.

Davies, A. (2011). *Making classroom assessment work* (3rd ed.). Bloomington, IN: Solution Tree Press.

Depka, E. (2015). *Bringing homework into focus: Tools and tips to enhance practices, design, and feedback.* Bloomington, IN: Solution Tree Press.

Depka, E. (2017). *Raising the rigor: Effective questioning strategies and techniques for the classroom.* Bloomington, IN: Solution Tree Press.

Dimich, N. (2009). Inspiring and requiring action. In T. Guskey (Ed.), *The teacher as assessment leader* (pp. 203–226). Bloomington, IN: Solution Tree Press.

Dimich, N. (2015). *Design in five: Essential phases to create engaging assessment practice.* Bloomington, IN: Solution Tree Press.

Dörnyei, Z. (2001). *Teaching and researching motivation.* New York: Longman.

Dougherty, E. (2012). *Assignments matter: Making the connections that help students meet standards.* Alexandria, VA: Association for Supervision and Curriculum Development.

DuFour, R. (2015). *In praise of American educators: And how they can become even better.* Bloomington, IN: Solution Tree Press.

DuFour, R., & DuFour, R. (2015). Deeper learning for students requires deeper learning for educators. In J. Bellanca (Ed.), *Deeper learning: Beyond 21st century skills* (pp. 21–52). Bloomington, IN: Solution Tree Press.

DuFour, R., DuFour, R., & Eaker, R. (2008). *Revisiting Professional Learning Communities at Work: New insights for improving schools.* Bloomington, IN: Solution Tree Press.

DuFour, R., DuFour, R., Eaker, R., Many, T. W., & Mattos, M. (2016). *Learning by doing: A handbook for Professional Learning Communities at Work* (3rd ed.). Bloomington, IN: Solution Tree Press.

DuFour, R., Reeves, D., & DuFour, R. (2018). *Responding to the Every Student Succeeds Act with the PLC at Work process.* Bloomington, IN: Solution Tree Press.

Dunning, D., Heath, C., & Suls, J. M. (2004). Flawed self-assessment: Implications for health, education, and the workplace. *Psychological Science in the Public Interest, 5*(3), 69–106.

Dweck, C. (2006). *Mindset: The new psychology of success.* New York: Random House.

Dysarz, K. (2016). *Assignments matter.* Accessed at https://edtrust.org/the-equity-line/assignments-matter on September 9, 2020.

Educational Testing Service. (2012). *The CBAL English language arts (ELA) competency model and provisional learning progressions.* Accessed at www.ets.org/cbal/ela on July 14, 2016.

Eren, O., & Henderson, D. J. (2008). The impact of homework on student achievement. *The Econometrics Journal, 11*(2), 326–348.

Ericsson, K. A., Krampe, R. T., & Tesch-Römer, C. (1993). The role of deliberate practice in the acquisition of expert performance. *Psychological Review, 100*(3), 363–406.

Erkens, C. (2013a, September 25). Becoming assessment architects [Blog post]. *Deep Within.* Accessed at http://anamcaraconsulting.com/wordpress/2013/09/25/237 on July 6, 2016.

Erkens, C. (2013b, October 21). Data notebooks [Blog post]. *Deep Within.* Accessed at http:// anamcaraconsulting.com/wordpress/2013/10/21/data-notebooks on October 21, 2013.

Erkens, C. (2014, May 30). The power of homework as a formative tool [Blog post]. *Deep Within.* Accessed at http://anamcaraconsulting.com/wordpress/2014/05/30/the-power-of-homework-as-a-formative-tool on May 30, 2014.

Erkens, C. (2015, April 21).Groupings for collaborative learning [Blog post]. *Solution Tree Blog.* Accessed at https://www.solutiontree.com/blog/groupings-for-collaborative-learning/ on October 4, 2021.

Erkens, C. (2016). *Collaborative common assessments: Teamwork. Instruction. Results.* Bloomington, IN: Solution Tree Press.

Erkens, C. (2019). *The handbook for collaborative common assessments: Tools for design, delivery, and data analysis.* Bloomington, IN: Solution Tree Press.

Erkens, C., Schimmer, T., & Dimich, N. (2017). *Essential assessment: Six tenets for bringing hope, efficacy, and achievement to the classroom.* Bloomington, IN: Solution Tree Press.

Erkens, C., Schimmer, T., & Dimich, N. (2018). *Instructional agility: Responding to assessment with real-time decisions.* Bloomington, IN: Solution Tree Press.

Erkens, C., Schimmer, T., & Dimich, N. (2019). *Growing tomorrow's citizens in today's classrooms: Assessing 7 critical competencies.* Bloomington, IN: Solution Tree Press.

Erkens, C., & Twadell, E. (2012). *Leading by design: An action framework for PLC at Work leaders.* Bloomington, IN: Solution Tree Press.

Every Student Succeeds Act of 2015, Pub. L. No. 114-95, 20 U.S.C. § 1177 (2015).

Finn, J. D., & Zimmer, K. S. (2012). Student engagement: What is it? Why does it matter? In S. L. Christenson, A. L. Reschly, & C. Wylie (Eds.), *Handbook of research on student engagement* (pp. 97–131). New York: Springer.

Fisher, D., & Frey, N. (2007). *Checking for understanding: Formative assessment techniques for your classroom.* Alexandria, VA: Association for Supervision and Curriculum Development.

Fisher, D., & Frey, N. (2010). *Guided instruction: How to develop confident and successful learners.* Alexandria, VA: Association for Supervision and Curriculum Development.

Fisher, D., & Frey, N. (2012). Making time for feedback. *Educational Leadership, 70*(1), 42–47.

Fisher, D., & Frey, N. (2015). *Unstoppable learning: Seven essential elements to unleash student potential.* Bloomington, IN: Solution Tree Press.

Fisher, D., Frey, N., & Pumpian, I. (2012). *How to create a culture of achievement in your school and classroom.* Alexandria, VA: Association for Supervision and Curriculum Development.

Francis, E. M. (2022). *Deconstructing depth of knowledge: A method and model for deeper teaching and learning.* Bloomington, IN: Solution Tree Press.

Fuchs, L. S., & Fuchs, D. (1986). Effects of systematic formative evaluation: A meta-analysis. *Exceptional Children, 53*(3), 199–208.

Gallup. (2015). *Gallup student poll: Engaged today—ready for tomorrow.* Accessed at https://kidsathope.org/wp-content/uploads/2015/05/2015-Gallup-Student-Poll-Overall-Report.pdf on October 4, 2021.

Gawande, A. (2010). *The checklist manifesto: How to get things right.* New York: Metropolitan Books.

Gay, G. (2002). Preparing for culturally responsive teaching. *Journal of Teacher Education, 53*(2), 106–116.

Gay, G. (2010). *Culturally responsive teaching: Theory, research, and practice* (2nd ed.). New York: Teachers College Press.

Gill, B. P., & Schlossman, S. (2004). Villain or savior? The American discourse on homework, 1850–2003. *Theory Into Practice, 43*(3), 174–181.

Ginsburg, H. P. (2009). The challenge of formative assessment in mathematics education: Children's minds, teachers' minds. *Human Development, 52*(2), 109–128.

Gladwell, M. (2008). *Outliers: The story of success.* New York: Little, Brown.

Gobble, T., Onuscheck, M., Reibel, A. R., & Twadell, E. (2016). *Proficiency-based assessment: Process, not product.* Bloomington, IN: Solution Tree Press.

Gobble, T., Onuscheck, M., Reibel, A. R., & Twadell, E. (2017). *Pathways to proficiency: Implementing evidence-based grading.* Bloomington, IN: Solution Tree Press.

The Gordon Commission on the Future of Assessment in Education. (2013). *To assess, to teach, to learn: A vision for the future of assessment* [Technical report]. Princeton, NJ: Author.

Gordon, E. (2008). The transformation of key beliefs that have guided a century of assessment. In C. A. Dwyer (Ed.), *The future of assessment: Shaping teaching and learning* (pp. 3–6). New York: Erlbaum.

Gregory, K., Cameron, C., & Davies, A. (2011). *Setting and using criteria* (2nd ed.). Bloomington, IN: Solution Tree Press.

Guskey, T. (2005, April). *Formative classroom assessment and Benjamin S. Bloom: Theory, research, and implications.* Paper presented at the annual meeting of the American Educational Research Association, Montreal, Canada.

Guskey, T. R. (2007). Using assessments to improve teaching and learning. In D. Reeves (Ed.), *Ahead of the curve: The power of assessment to transform teaching and learning* (pp. 15–30). Bloomington, IN: Solution Tree Press.

Guskey, T. R. (2011). Five obstacles to grading reform. *Educational Leadership, 69*(3), 16–21.

Guskey, T. R. (2015). *On your mark: Challenging the conventions of grading and reporting.* Bloomington, IN: Solution Tree Press.

Guskey, T. R. (2020). *Get set, go! Creating successful grading and reporting systems.* Bloomington, IN: Solution Tree Press.

Guskey, T. R., & Bailey, J. M. (2010). *Developing standards-based report cards.* Thousand Oaks, CA: Corwin.

Hambrick, D. Z., Oswald, F. L., Altmann, E. M., Meinz, E. J., Gobet, F., & Campitelli, G. (2014). Deliberate practice: Is that all it takes to become an expert? *Intelligence, 45,* 34–45.

Hargreaves, A., & Fullan, M. (2012). *Professional capital: Transforming teaching in every school.* New York: Teachers College Press.

Harward, S. V., Allred, R. A., & Sudweeks, R. R. (1994). The effectiveness of four self-corrected spelling test methods. *Reading Psychology, 15*(4), 245–271.

Hattie, J. (2009). *Visible learning: A synthesis of over 800 meta-analyses relating to achievement.* New York: Routledge.

Hattie, J. (2012). *Visible learning for teachers: Maximizing impact on learning.* New York: Routledge.

Hattie, J., & Donoghue, G. M. (2016). Learning strategies: A synthesis and conceptual model. *Science of Learning, 1*(16013). Accessed at www.nature.com/articles/npjscilearn201613 on June 21, 2018.

Hattie, J., & Timperley, H. (2007). The power of feedback. *Review of Educational Research, 77*(1), 81–112.

Hattie, J., & Yates, G. C. R. (2014). *Visible learning and the science of how we learn.* New York: Routledge.

Heemsoth, T., & Heinze, A. (2014). The impact of incorrect examples on learning fractions: A field experiment with 6th grade students. *Instructional Science, 42*(4), 639–657.

Heflebower, T., Hoegh, J. K., & Warrick, P. B. (2014). *A school leader's guide to standards-based grading.* Bloomington, IN: Marzano Resources.

Henderson, A., & Mapp, K. (2002). *A new wave of evidence: The impact of school, family, and community connections on student achievement.* Austin, TX: Southwest Educational Development Laboratory.

Herbst, S., & Davies, A. (2014). *A fresh look at grading and reporting in high schools.* Bloomington, IN: Solution Tree Press.

Heritage, M. (2007). Formative assessment: What do teachers need to know and do? *Phi Delta Kappan, 89*(2), 140–145.

Heritage, M. (2008). *Learning progressions: Supporting instruction and formative assessment.* Washington, DC: Council of Chief State School Officers.

Heritage, M. (2010a). *Formative assessment: Making it happen in the classroom.* Thousand Oaks, CA: Corwin Press.

Heritage, M. (2010b). *Formative assessment and next-generation assessment systems: Are we losing an opportunity?* Washington, DC: Council of Chief State School Officers.

Heritage, M. (2013). Gathering evidence of student understanding. In J. H. McMillan (Ed.), *SAGE handbook of research on classroom assessment* (pp. 179–196). Thousand Oaks, CA: SAGE.

Heritage, M. (2016, April). *The use of formative assessment results to educate all in diverse democracies: Research results from four different countries.* Paper presented at the annual meeting of the American Educational Research Association, Washington, DC.

Hierck, T., & Freese, A. (2018). *Assessing unstoppable learning.* Bloomington, IN: Solution Tree Press.

Hogan, T. (2013). Constructed-response approaches for classroom assessment. In J. H. McMillan (Ed.), *SAGE handbook of research on classroom assessment* (pp. 275–292). Thousand Oaks, CA: SAGE.

Holme, J. J., Richards, M. P., Jimerson, J. B., & Cohen, R. W. (2010). Assessing the effects of high school exit examinations. *Review of Educational Research, 80*(4), 476–526.

Horn, M. B., & Staker, H. (2015). *Blended: Using disruptive innovation to improve schools.* San Francisco: Jossey-Bass.

Jerald, C. D. (2009). *Defining a 21st century education.* Alexandria, VA: Center for Public Education. Accessed at www.mifras.org/know/wp-content/uploads/2014/06 /Defininga21stCenturyEducation_Jerald_2009.pdf on May 12, 2016.

Jones, S., & Vagle, M. D. (2013). Living contradictions and working for change: Toward a theory of social class-sensitive pedagogy. *Educational Researcher, 42*(3), 129–141.

Jung, L. A., & Guskey, T. R. (2010). Grading exceptional learners. *Educational Leadership, 67*(5), 31–35.

Kane, M. T. (2006). Validation. In R. L. Brennan (Ed.), *Educational measurement* (4th ed., pp. 17–64). Westport, CT: Praeger.

Kanter, R. M. (2004). *Confidence: How winning streaks and losing streaks begin and end.* New York: Crown Business.

Kay, K., & Greenhill, V. (2013). *The leader's guide to 21st century education: 7 steps for schools and districts.* Boston: Pearson.

Keller, B. (2007). No easy project. *Education Week, 27*(4), 21–23.

Kelly, S., & Price, H. (2014). Changing patterns of engagement in the transition to high school. In D. J. Shernoff & J. Bempechat (Eds.), *Engaging youth in schools: Evidence-based models to guide future innovations* (pp. 15–36). New York: NSSE Yearbooks by Teachers College Record.

King, A. (1990). Enhancing peer interaction and learning in the classroom through reciprocal questioning. *American Educational Research Journal, 27*(4), 664–687.

King, A. (2002). Structuring peer interaction to promote high-level cognitive processing. *Theory Into Practice, 41*(1), 33–39.

Klem, A. M., & Connell, J. P. (2004). Relationships matter: Linking teacher support to student engagement and achievement. *Journal of School Health, 74*(7), 262–273.

Kluger, A., & DeNisi, A. (1996). The effects of feedback interventions on performance: A historical review, a meta-analysis, and a preliminary feedback intervention theory. *Psychological Bulletin, 119*(2), 254–284.

Knight, J. (2014). *Focus on teaching: Using video for high-impact instruction.* Thousand Oaks, CA: Corwin Press.

Kohn, A. (2006). *The homework myth: Why our kids get too much of a bad thing*. Cambridge, MA: Da Capo Life Long.

Kulhavy, R. W. (1977). Feedback in written instruction. *Review of Educational Research*, *47*(2), 211–232.

Kulik, J. A., & Kulik, C. C. (1988). Timing of feedback and verbal learning. *Review of Educational Research*, *58*(1), 79–97.

Ladson-Billings, G. (2009). *The dreamkeepers: Successful teachers of African American children* (2nd ed.). San Francisco: Jossey-Bass.

Ladson-Billings, G., & Gomez, M. L. (2001). Just showing up: Supporting early literacy through teachers' professional communities. *Phi Delta Kappan*, *82*(9), 675–680.

Lane, S. (2013). Performance assessment. In J. H. McMillan (Ed.), *SAGE handbook of research on classroom assessment* (pp. 313–329). Thousand Oaks, CA: SAGE.

Lemov, D. (2010). *Teach like a champion: 49 techniques that put students on the path to college*. San Francisco: Jossey-Bass.

Lemov, D., Woolway, E., & Yezzi, K. (2012). *Practice perfect: 42 rules for getting better at getting better*. San Francisco: Jossey-Bass.

Levin, B. (2008). *How to change 5000 schools: A practical and positive approach for leading change at every level*. Cambridge, MA: Harvard Education Press.

Marso, R. N., & Pigge, F. L. (1993). Teachers' testing knowledge, skills, and practices. In S. L. Wise (Ed.), *Teacher training in measurement and assessment skills* (pp. 129–185). Lincoln, NE: Buros Institute of Mental Measurements, University of Nebraska-Lincoln.

Marzano, R. J. (2006). *Classroom assessment and grading that work*. Alexandria, VA: Association for Supervision and Curriculum Development.

Marzano, R. J. (2007). *The art and science of teaching: A comprehensive framework for effective instruction*. Alexandra, VA: Association for Supervision and Curriculum Development.

Marzano, R. J. (2010). *Formative assessment and standards-based grading*. Bloomington, IN: Marzano Resources.

Marzano, R. J., & Pickering, D. J. (2007a). The case for and against homework. *Educational Leadership*, *64*(6), 74–79.

Marzano, R. J., & Pickering, D. J. (2007b). Errors and allegations: About research on homework. *Phi Delta Kappan*, *88*(7), 507–513.

Marzano, R. J., Pickering, D. J., & Pollock, J. E. (2001). *Classroom instruction that works: Research-based strategies for increasing student achievement*. Alexandria, VA: Association for Supervision and Curriculum Development.

McDonald, B., & Boud, D. (2003). The impact of self-assessment on achievement: The effects of self-assessment training on performance in external examinations. *Assessment in Education: Principles, Policy & Practice*, *10*(2), 209–220.

McMillan, J. H. (Ed.). (2013). *SAGE handbook of research on classroom assessment.* Thousand Oaks, CA: SAGE.

McMorris, R. F., & Boothroyd, R. A. (1993). Tests that teachers build: An analysis of classroom tests in science and mathematics. *Applied Measurement in Education, 6*(4), 321–342.

Mehrabian, A. (1981). *Silent messages: Implicit communication of emotions and attitudes.* Belmont, CA: Wadsworth.

Merton, R. K. (1968). The Matthew effect in science. Science, 159(3810), 56–63.

Moss, C. M. (2013). Research on classroom summative assessment. In J. H. McMillan (Ed.), *SAGE handbook of research on classroom assessment* (pp. 235–255). Thousand Oaks, CA: SAGE.

Moss, C. M., & Brookhart, S. M. (2012). *Learning targets: Helping students aim for understanding in today's lesson.* Alexandria, VA: Association for Supervision and Curriculum Development.

Moss, C. M., & Brookhart, S. M. (2019). *Advancing formative assessment in every classroom: A guide for instructional leaders* (2nd ed.). Alexandria, VA: Association for Supervision and Curriculum Development.

Munns, G., & Woodward, H. (2006). Student engagement and student self-assessment: The REAL framework. *Assessment in Education: Principles, Policy & Practice, 13*(2), 193–213.

National Center on Education and the Economy. (2007). *Tough choices or tough times: The report of the New Commission on the Skills of the American Workforce.* San Francisco: Wiley.

National Core Arts Standards. (n.d.). *National coalition for core arts standards writing teams.* Accessed at www.nationalartsstandards.org/credits#sthash.sEQv15aL.dpuf on September 19, 2016.

National Council for the Social Studies. (2013). *The college, career, and civic life (C3) framework for social studies state standards: Guidance for enhancing the rigor of K–12 civics, economics, geography, and history.* Silver Spring, MD: Author.

National Council of Teachers of Mathematics. (n.d.). *Executive summary: Principles and standards for school mathematics.* Accessed at www.nctm.org/uploadedFiles/Standards_and_Positions/PSSM_ExecutiveSummary.pdf on October 28, 2016.

National Education Association. (n.d.). *Preparing 21st century students for a global society: An educator's guide to the "Four Cs."* Accessed at www.nea.org/assets/docs/A-Guide-to-Four-Cs.pdf on May 13, 2016.

National Governors Association Center for Best Practices & Council of Chief State School Officers. (2010). *Common Core State Standards for English language arts and literacy in history/social studies, science, and technical subjects.* Washington, DC: Authors. Accessed at www.corestandards.org/assets/CCSSI_ELA%20Standards.pdf on May 13, 2016.

National Research Council. (2011). *Assessing 21st century skills: Summary of a workshop.* Washington, DC: National Academies Press.

National Research Council. (2012). *A framework for K–12 science education: Practices, crosscutting concepts, and core ideas.* Washington, DC: National Academies Press.

Natriello, G. (1987). The impact of evaluation processes on students. *Educational Psychologist, 22*(2), 155–175.

Neuman, S., & Celano, D. (2006). The knowledge gap: Implications of leveling the playing field for low-income and middle-income children. *Reading Research Quarterly, 41*(2), 176–201.

Newmann, F. M., Carmichael, D., & King, M. B. (2016). *Authentic intellectual work: Improving teaching for rigrorous learning.* Thousands Oaks, CA: Corwin Press.

Next Generation Science Standards. (n.d.). *Read the standards.* Accessed at www.nextgenscience.org/search-standards on October 7, 2016.

NGSS Lead States. (2013). *Next Generation Science Standards: For states, by states.* Washington, DC: The National Academies Press.

Nieto, S., & Bode, P. (2013). School reform and student learning: A multicultural perspective. In J. A. Banks & C. A. M. Banks (Eds.), *Multicultural education: Issues and perspectives* (8th ed.; pp. 395–415). Hoboken, NJ: Wiley.

No Child Left Behind (NCLB) Act of 2001, Pub. L. No. 107–110, § 115, Stat. 1425 (2002).

Nystrand, M., & Gamoran, A. (1991). Instructional discourse, student engagement, and literature achievement. *Research in the Teaching of English, 25*(3), 261–290.

O'Connor, K. (2009). *How to grade for learning, K–12* (3rd ed.). Thousand Oaks, CA: Corwin Press.

O'Connor, K. (2011). *A repair kit for grading: 15 fixes for broken grades* (2nd ed.). Boston: Pearson.

O'Neill, O. (2002). *A question of trust: The BBC Reith Lectures 2002.* Cambridge, UK: Cambridge University Press.

Organisation for Economic Cooperation and Development. (2012). *Education at a glance 2012: OECD indicators.* Accessed at http://dx.doi.org/10.1787/eag-2012-en on May 13, 2016.

Ornstein, P., Coffman, J., Grammer, J., San Souci, P., & McCall, L. (2010). Linking the classroom context and the development of children's memory skills. In J. L. Meece & J. S. Eccles (Eds.), *Handbook of research on schools, schooling, and human development* (pp. 42–59). New York: Routledge.

Parkes, J. (2013). Reliability in classroom assessment. In J. H. McMillan (Ed.), *SAGE handbook of research on classroom assessment* (pp. 107–123). Thousand Oaks, CA: SAGE.

Parsi, A., & Darling-Hammond, L. (2015). *Performance assessments: How state policy can advance assessments for 21st century learning.* Accessed at https://nasbe.nyc3.digitaloceanspaces.com/2020/02/Parsi-LDH-Performance-Assessment_Jan2015.pdf on January 24, 2022.

Pekrul, S., & Levin, B. (2007). Building student voice for school improvement. In D. Thiessen & A. Cook-Sather (Eds.), *International handbook of student experience in elementary and secondary school* (pp. 711–726). Dordrecht, Netherlands: Springer.

Pellegrino, J., & Goldman, S. (2008). Beyond rhetoric: Realities and complexities of integrating assessment into classroom teaching and learning. In C. A. Dwyer (Ed.), *The future of assessment: Shaping teaching and learning* (pp. 7–52). New York: Erlbaum.

Pink, D. H. (2009). *Drive: The surprising truth about what motivates us.* New York: Riverhead Books.

Pintrich, P. R. (2000). The role of goal orientation in self-regulated learning. In M. Boekaerts, P. R. Pintrich, & M. Zeidner (Eds.), *Handbook of self-regulation* (pp. 451–502). San Diego, CA: Academic Press.

Pintrich, P. R., & Zusho, A. (2002). The development of academic self-regulation: The role of cognitive and motivational factors. In A. Wigfield & J. S. Eccles (Eds.), *Development of achievement motivation* (pp. 249–284). San Diego, CA: Academic Press.

Popham, W. J. (2011). *Transformative assessment in action: An inside look at applying the process.* Alexandria, VA: Association for Supervision and Curriculum Development.

Popova, M. (n.d.). *Fixed vs. growth: The two basic mindsets that shape our lives.* Accessed at www.brainpickings.org/2014/01/29/carol-dweck-mindset on May 13, 2016.

Pushor, D. (2010). *Research for teachers: #1 parent engagement.* Accessed at www.etfo.ca/SupportingMembers/Resources/R4Tdocs/Research%20for%20Teachers%20-%20Number%201%20-%20Parent%20Engagement.pdf on August 18, 2021.

Rach, S., Ufer, S., & Heinze, A. (2012). Learning from errors: Effects of teachers training on students' attitudes towards and their individual use of errors. In Y. T. Tso (Ed.), *Proceedings of the 36th conference of the International Group for the Psychology of Mathematics Education* (Vol. 3, pp. 329–336). Taipei, Taiwan: The Psychology of Mathematics Education.

Ramdass, D., & Zimmerman, B. J. (2008). Effects of self-correction strategy training on middle school students' self-efficacy, self-evaluation, and mathematics division learning. *Journal of Advanced Academics, 20*(1), 18–41.

Rand, K. L., & Cheavens, J. S. (2009). Hope theory. In C. R. Snyder & S. J. Lopez (Eds.), *Oxford handbook of positive psychology* (2nd ed., pp. 323–333). Oxford, UK: Oxford University Press.

Reeves, D. (Ed.). (2007). *Ahead of the curve: The power of assessment to transform teaching and learning.* Bloomington, IN: Solution Tree Press.

Reeves, D. (2016a). *Elements of grading: A guide to effective practice* (2nd ed.). Bloomington, IN: Solution Tree Press.

Reeves, D. (2016b). *FAST grading: A guide to implementing best practices.* Bloomington, IN: Solution Tree Press.

Renner, R. (2018, December 11). *How to calculate difficulty index.* Accessed at www.theclassroom.com/calculate-difficulty-index-8247462.html on December 30, 2021.

Ritchhart, R. (2015). *Creating cultures of thinking: The 8 forces we must master to truly transform our schools.* San Francisco: Jossey-Bass.

Rodriguez, M. C., & Haladyna, T. M. (2013). Writing selected-response items for classroom assessment. In J. H. McMillan (Ed.), *SAGE handbook of research on classroom assessment* (pp. 293–311). Thousand Oaks, CA: SAGE.

Ross, J. A., Hogaboam-Gray, A., & Rolheiser, C. (2002). Student self-evaluation in grade 5–6 mathematics effects on problem-solving achievement. *Educational Assessment, 8*(1), 43–58.

Rubie-Davies, C. M., Weinstein, R. S., Huang, F. L., Gregory, A., Cowan, P. A., & Cowan, C. P. (2014). Successive teacher expectation effects across the early school years. *Journal of Applied Developmental Psychology, 35*(3), 181–191.

Ruiz-Primo, M. A., & Furtak, E. M. (2006). Informal formative assessment and scientific inquiry: Exploring teachers' practices and student learning. *Educational Assessment, 11*(3–4), 237–263.

Ruiz-Primo, M. A., & Furtak, E. M. (2007). Exploring teachers' informal formative assessment practices and students' understanding in the context of scientific inquiry. *Journal of Research in Science Teaching, 44*(1), 57–84.

Ruiz-Primo, M. A., & Li, M. (2011). *Looking into teachers' feedback practices: How teachers interpret students' work.* Paper presented at the annual meeting of the American Educational Research Association, New Orleans, LA.

Ruiz-Primo, M. A., & Li, M. (2013). Examining formative feedback in the classroom context: New research perspectives. In J. H. McMillan (Ed.), *SAGE handbook of research on classroom assessment* (pp. 215–232). Thousand Oaks, CA: SAGE.

Rumsey, C., & Langrall, C. (2016). Promoting mathematical argumentation. *Teaching Children Mathematics, 22*(7), 412–419.

Saavedra, R., & Kwun, S. K. (1993). Peer evaluation in self-managing work groups. *Journal of Applied Psychology, 78*(3), 450–462.

Sadler, D. R. (1989). Formative assessment and the design of instructional systems. *Instructional Science, 18*(2), 119–144.

Schafer, W. D. (1993). Assessment literacy for teachers. *Theory Into Practice, 32*(2), 118–126.

Scharber, C., Isaacson, K., Pyscher, T., & Lewis, C. (2016). Pathways for all: Teens, tech, and learning. In L. R. Miller, D. Becker, & K. Becker (Eds.), *Technology for transformation: Perspectives of hope in the digital age* (pp. 195–214). Charlotte, NC: Information Age.

Schimmel, B. J. (1983, April). *A meta-analysis of feedback to the learner in computerized and programmed instruction.* Paper presented at the annual meeting of the American Educational Research Association, Montreal, Canada.

Schimmer, T. (2014). *Ten things that matter from assessment to grading.* Boston: Pearson.

Schimmer, T. (2016). *Grading from the inside out: Bringing accuracy to student assessment through a standards-based mindset.* Bloomington, IN: Solution Tree Press.

Schimmer, T. (2019, November 19). Next generation assessment: Moving from counting to quality. *All Things Assessment.* Accessed at https://allthingsassessment.info/2019/11/19/next-generation-assessment-moving-from-counting-to-quality/ on January 21, 2022.

Schimmer, T., Hillman, G., & Stalets, M. (2018). *Standards-based learning in action: Moving from theory to practice.* Bloomington, IN: Solution Tree Press.

Schlechty, P. C. (2009). *Leading for learning: How to transform schools into learning organizations.* San Francisco: Jossey-Bass.

Schneider, M. C., Egan, K. L., & Julian, M. W. (2013). Classroom assessment in the context of high-stakes testing. In J. H. McMillan (Ed.), *SAGE handbook of research on classroom assessment* (pp. 55–70). Thousand Oaks, CA: SAGE.

Schumpeter, J. (2011). *Fail often, fail well.* Accessed at www.economist.com/business/2011/04/14/fail-often-fail-well on October 5, 2021.

Schunk, D. H. (2005). Self-regulated learning: The educational legacy of Paul R. Pintrich. *Educational Psychologist, 40*(2), 85–94.

Schunk, D. H., & Pajares, F. (2005). Competence perceptions and academic functioning. In A. J. Elliot & C. Dweck (Eds.), *Handbook of competence and motivation* (pp. 85–104). New York: Guilford Press.

Shavelson, R. (2007). *A brief history of student learning assessment: How we got where we are and a proposal for where to go next.* Washington, DC: Association of American Colleges and Universities.

Shavelson, R. J., Young, D. B., Ayala, C. C., Brandon, P. R., Furtak, E. M., Ruiz-Primo, M. A., et al. (2008). On the impact of curriculum-embedded formative assessment on learning: A collaboration between curriculum and assessment developers. *Applied Measurement in Education, 21*(4), 295–314.

Shepard, L. A. (2000a). The role of assessment in a learning culture. *Educational Researcher, 29*(7), 4–14.

Shepard, L. A. (2000b). *The role of classroom assessment in teaching and learning* (Technical Report No. 517). Los Angeles: University of California.

Shepard, L. A. (2013). Foreword. In J. H. McMillan (Ed.), *SAGE handbook of research on classroom assessment* (pp. xix–xxv). Thousand Oaks, CA: SAGE.

Shepard, L., Hammerness, K., Darling-Hammond, L., Rust, F., Snowden, J. B., Gordon, E., et al. (2005). Assessment. In L. Darling-Hammond & J. Bransford (Eds.), *Preparing teachers for a changing world: What teachers should learn and be able to do* (pp. 275—326). San Francisco: Jossey-Bass.

Shernoff, D. J. (2013). *Optimal learning environments to promote student engagement.* New York: Springer.

Shute, V. J. (2008). Focus on formative feedback. *Review of Educational Research, 78*(1), 153–189.

Skinner, E. A., & Pitzer, J. R. (2012). Developmental dynamics of student engagement, coping, and everyday resilience. In S. L. Christenson, A. L. Reschly, & C. Wiley (Eds.), *Handbook of research on student engagement* (pp. 21–44). New York: Springer.

Sladkey, D. (2016, September 30). *Ask me a question* [Blog post]. Accessed at http://teachhighschoolmath.blogspot.com/2016/09/ on October 5, 2016.

Slavin, R. E., Hurley, E. A., & Chamberlain, A. (2003). Cooperative learning and achievement: Theory and research. In W. M. Reynolds & G. E. Miller (Eds.), *Handbook of psychology* (Vol. 7, pp. 177–198). Hoboken, NJ: Wiley.

Solution Tree. (2018). *The handbook for embedded formative assessment.* Bloomington, IN: Solution Tree Press.

Spady, W. G. (1994). *Outcome-based education: Critical issues and answers.* Arlington, VA: American Association of School Administrators.

Starch, D., & Elliott, E. C. (1912). Reliability of the grading of high-school work in English. *The School Review, 20*(7), 442–457.

Stiggins, R. (2007). Assessment through the student's eyes. *Educational Leadership, 64*(8), 22–26.

Stiggins, R. (2008). Correcting "errors of measurement" that sabotage student learning. In C. A. Dwyer (Ed.), *The future of assessment: Shaping teaching and learning* (pp. 229–244). New York: Erlbaum.

Stiggins, R. J. (1991). Relevant classroom assessment training for teachers. *Educational Measurement: Issues and Practice, 10*(1), 7–12.

Stiggins, R. J. (2008). *An introduction to student-involved assessment for learning* (5th ed.). Upper Saddle River, NJ: Pearson/Merrill Prentice Hall.

Stiggins, R. J., & Conklin, N. F. (1992). *In teachers' hands: Investigating the practices of classroom assessment.* Albany, NY: State University of New York Press.

Tierney, R. D. (2013). Fairness in classroom assessment. In J. H. McMillan (Ed.), *SAGE handbook of research on classroom assessment* (pp. 125–144). Thousand Oaks, CA: SAGE.

Tomlinson, C. A., & Moon, T. R. (2013). Differentiation and classroom assessment. In J. H. McMillan (Ed.), *SAGE handbook of research on classroom assessment* (pp. 415–430). Thousand Oaks, CA: SAGE.

Topping, K. (2013). Peers as a source of formative and summative assessment. In J. H. McMillan (Ed.), *SAGE handbook of research on classroom assessment* (pp. 395–412). Thousand Oaks, CA: SAGE.

U.S. Department of Education. (2015). *Fact sheet: Testing action plan.* Accessed at https:// edtrust.org/wp-content/uploads/2014/09/Fact-Sheet-Testing-Action-Plan-Press-Release -from-Dept-of-Ed.pdf on August 6, 2016.

United States Medical Licensing Examination. (n.d.). *Eligibility for the USMLE steps.* Accessed at https://www.usmle.org/bulletin-information/eligibility on January 24, 2022.

Usher, E. L., & Pajares, F. (2008). Sources of self-efficacy in school: Critical review of the literature and future directions. *Review of Educational Research, 78*(4), 751–796.

Vallesi, L. (2020, June 5). *How do you calculate difficulty index?* Accessed at https:// findanyanswer.com/how-do-you-calculate-difficulty-index on December 30, 2021.

van Gennip, N. A. E., Segers, M. S. R., & Tillema, H. H. (2009). Peer assessment for learning from a social perspective: The influence of interpersonal variables and structural features. *Educational Research Review, 4*(1), 41–54.

van Zundert, M., Sluijsmans, D., & van Merriënboer, J. (2010). Effective peer assessment processes: Research findings and future directions. *Learning and Instruction, 20*(4), 270–279.

Vatterott, C. (2009). *Rethinking homework: Best practices that support diverse needs.* Alexandria, VA: Association for Supervision and Curriculum Development.

Vatterott, C. (2015). *Rethinking grading: Meaningful assessment for standards-based learning.* Alexandria, VA: Association for Supervision and Curriculum Development.

Wahlstrom, K. L., Seashore Louis, K., Leithwood, K., & Anderson, S. E. (2010). *Investigating the links to improved student learning: Executive summary of research findings.* Accessed at https://www.wallacefoundation.org/knowledge-center/Documents/Investigating-the-Links -to-Improved-Student-Learning-Executive-Summary.pdf on March 10, 2022.

Weaver, M. E. (1995). Using peer response in the classroom: Students' perspectives. *Research and Teaching in Developmental Education, 12*(1), 31–37.

Webb, N. L. (1997). Criteria for alignment of expectations and assessments on mathematics and science education [Research Monograph Number 6 ]. National Institute for Science Education: Madison, WI / Washington, DC: Council of Chief State School Officers . Accessed at https://files.eric.ed.gov/fulltext/ED414305.pdf on March 6, 2021.

Webb, N. L. (1999). Alignment of science and mathematics standards and assessment in four states [Research Monograph No. 18]. National Institute for Science Education, Madison, WI / Washington, DC: Council of Chief State School Officers. Accessed at https://files.eric.ed.gov/fulltext/ED440852.pdf on March 6, 2021.

Webb, N. L. (2002). *Depth-of-knowledge levels for four content areas.* Accessed at www.hed .state.nm.us/uploads/files/ABE/Policies/depth_of_knowledge_guide_for_all_subject_areas .pdf on May 16, 2016.

Webb, N. L., Alt, M., Ely, R., & Vesperman, B. (2005). *Web alignment tool (WAT) training manual.* Washington, DC: Council of Chief State School Officers.

Weiner, B. (1979). A theory of motivation for some classroom experiences. *Journal of Educational Psychology, 71*(1), 3–25.

Weinstein, R. S. (2002). Overcoming inequality in schooling: A call to action for community psychology. *American Journal of Community Psychology, 30*(1), 21–42.

Wessling, S. B. (n.d.). *Pinwheel discussions: Texts in conversation* [Video file]. Accessed at www .teachingchannel.org/videos/high-school-literature-lesson-plan on March 26, 2014.

White, K. (2017). *Softening the edges: Assessment practices that honor K–12 teachers and learners.* Bloomington, IN: Solution Tree Press.

White, K. (2019). *Unlocked: Assessment as the key to everyday creativity in the classroom.* Bloomington, IN: Solution Tree Press.

White, K. (2022). *Student self-assessment: Data notebooks, portfolios, and other tools to advance learning.* Bloomington, IN: Solution Tree Press.

Wiggins, G. (2013, February 12). Autonomy and the need to back off by design as teachers [Blog post]. *Granted, and....* Accessed at https://grantwiggins.wordpress.com/2013/02/12 /autonomy-and-the-need-to-back-off-by-design-as-teachers on November 27, 2016.

Wiggins, G. P. (1993). *Assessing student performance: Exploring the purpose and limits of testing.* San Francisco: Jossey-Bass.

Wiggins, G., & McTighe, J. (1998). *Understanding by design.* Alexandria, VA: Association for Supervision and Curriculum Development.

Wiggins, G., & McTighe, J. (2005). *Understanding by design* (Expanded 2nd ed.). Alexandria, VA: Association for Supervision and Curriculum Development.

Wilen, W. W. (1991). *Questioning skills, for teachers: What research says to the teacher* (3rd ed.). Washington, DC: National Education Association.

Wiliam, D. (2011). *Embedded formative assessment.* Bloomington, IN: Solution Tree Press.

Wiliam, D. (2013a). Feedback and instructional correctives. In J. H. McMillan (Ed.), *SAGE handbook of research on classroom assessment* (pp. 197–214). Thousand Oaks, CA: SAGE.

Wiliam, D. (2013b, June). *How do you prepare students for a world we cannot imagine?* [Keynote address]. Minnetonka Leadership Institute, Minnetonka, MN.

Wiliam, D. (2014, March). The right questions, the right way. *Educational Leadership, 71*(6), 16–19.

Wiliam, D. (2015, September). Designing great hinge questions. *Educational Leadership, 73*(1), 40–44.

Wiliam, D. (2018). *Embedded formative assessment* (2nd ed.). Bloomington, IN: Solution Tree Press.

Wiliam, D., Lee, C., Harrison, C., & Black, P. (2004). Teachers developing assessment for learning: Impact on student achievement. *Assessment in Education: Principles, Policy & Practice, 11*(1), 49–65.

Willis, J., & Adie, L. (2016, April). *Developing teacher formative assessment practices through professional dialogue: Case studies of practice from Queensland, Australia* [Conference presentation]. Annual meeting of the American Educational Research Association, Washington, DC.

Wilson, B., & Corbett, D. (2007). Students' perspectives on good teaching: Implications for adult reform behavior. In D. Thiessen & A. Cook-Sather (Eds.), *International handbook of student experience in elementary and secondary school* (pp. 283–314). Dordrecht, Netherlands: Springer.

Wininger, S. R. (2005). Using your tests to teach: Formative summative assessment. *Teaching of Psychology, 32*(3), 164–166.

Wolfe, P. (2010). *Brain matters: Translating research into classroom practice* (2nd ed.). Alexandra, VA: Association for Supervision and Curriculum Development.

Wolters, C. A. (2010). *Self-regulated learning and the 21st century competencies.* Accessed at https:// docplayer.net/22501778-Self-regulated-learning-and-the-21-st-century-competencies -christopher-a-wolters-ph-d-department-of-educational-psychology-university-of -houston.html on May 16, 2016.

Wormeli, R. (2006). *Fair isn't always equal: Assessing & grading in the differentiated classroom.* Portland, ME: Stenhouse.

Zimmerman, B. J. (2002). Becoming a self-regulated learner: An overview. *Theory Into Practice, 41*(2), 64–72.

Zimmerman, B. J. (2008). Investigating self-regulation and motivation: Historical background, methodological developments, and future prospects. *American Educational Research Journal, 45*(1), 166–183.

Zimmerman, B. J. (2011a). *Barry Zimmerman discusses self-regulated learning processes: Emerging research fronts commentary, December 2011.* Accessed at http://archive.sciencewatch.com /dr/erf/2011/11decerf/11decerfZimm on October 5, 2021.

Zimmerman, B. J. (2011b). Motivational sources and outcomes of self-regulated learning and performance. In B. J. Zimmerman & D. H. Schunk (Eds.), *Handbook of self-regulation of learning and performance* (pp. 49–64). New York: Routledge.

Zimmerman, B. J., & Schunk, D. H. (2011). Self-regulated learning and performance. In B. J. Zimmerman & D. H. Schunk (Eds.), *Handbook of self-regulation of learning and performance* (pp. 1–12). New York: Routledge.

# INDEX

### Essential Assessment
*Cassandra Erkens, Tom Schimmer, and Nicole Dimich*
Discover how to use the power of assessment to instill hope, efficacy, and achievement in your students. Explore six essential tenets of assessment that will help deepen your understanding of assessment to not only meet standards but also enhance students' academic success.
**BKF752**

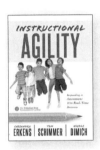

### Instructional Agility
*Cassandra Erkens, Tom Schimmer, and Nicole Dimich*
This highly practical resource empowers readers to become instructionally agile—moving seamlessly among instruction, formative assessment, and feedback—to enhance student engagement, proficiency, and ownership of learning. Each chapter concludes with reflection questions that assist readers in determining next steps.
**BKF764**

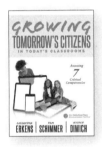

### Growing Tomorrow's Citizens in Today's Classrooms
*Cassandra Erkens, Tom Schimmer, and Nicole Dimich*
For students to succeed in today's ever-changing world, they must acquire unique knowledge and skills. Practical and research-based, this resource will help educators design assessment and instruction to ensure students master critical competencies, including collaboration, critical thinking, creative thinking, communication, digital citizenship, and more.
**BKF765**

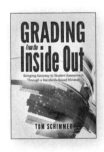

### Grading From the Inside Out
*Tom Schimmer*
The time for grading reform is now. While the transition to standards-based practices may be challenging, it is essential for effective instruction and assessment. Discover the steps your team can take to transform grading and reporting schoolwide.
**BKF646**

## Solution Tree | Press
a division of
Solution Tree

Visit SolutionTree.com or call 800.733.6786 to order.

# Wait! Your professional development journey doesn't have to end with the last pages of this book.

We realize improving student learning doesn't happen overnight. And your school or district shouldn't be left to puzzle out all the details of this process alone.

**No matter where you are on the journey, we're committed to helping you get to the next stage.**

Take advantage of everything from **custom workshops** to **keynote presentations** and **interactive web and video conferencing**. We can even help you develop an action plan tailored to fit your specific needs.

*Let's get the conversation started.*

Call 888.763.9045 today.

SolutionTree.com